IMAGES
of America

LINCOLN

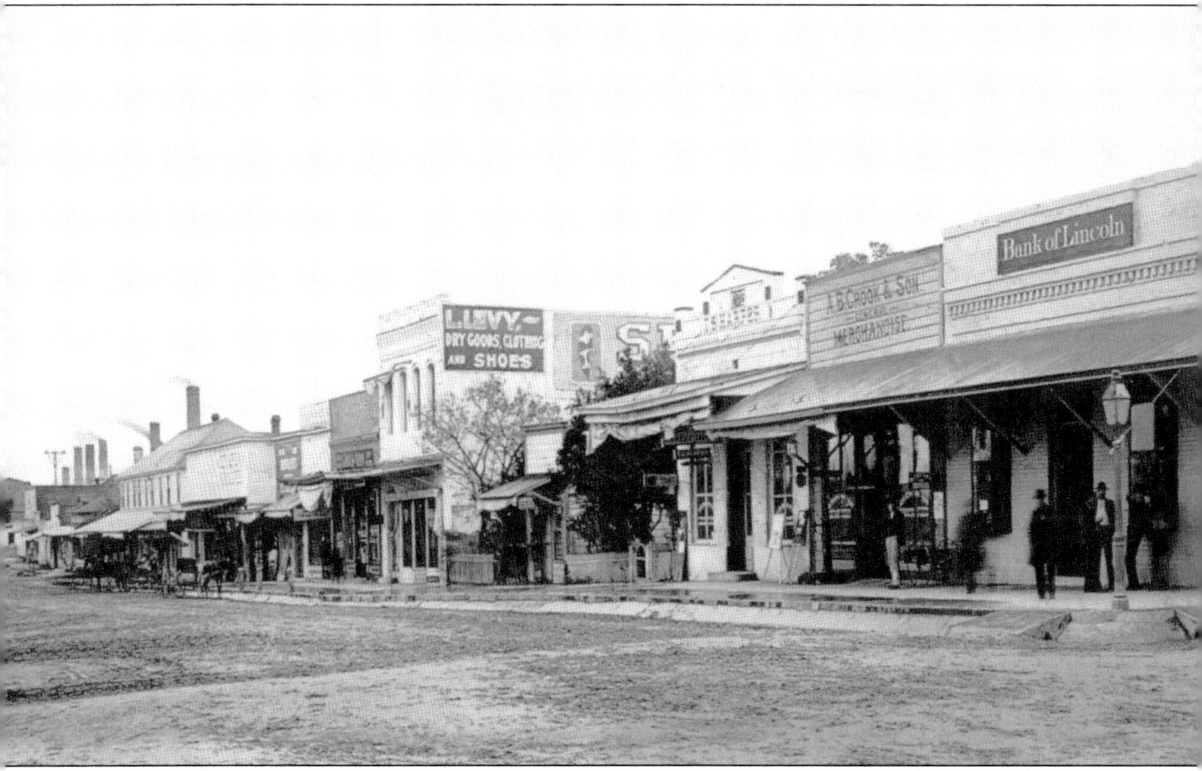

This 1902 photograph of G Street (now Lincoln Boulevard) shows Bank of Lincoln, A.B. Crook & Son General Store, and T.S. Harper Variety Store. A small food stand is in between L. Levy Dry Goods and Ingram's Drug Store. Continuing down the street are Ingram's Cash Bazaar, Vogt & Brown Grocery and Ice Cream Parlor, and the Lincoln Hotel. The Gladding, McBean & Company smoke stacks are visible in the background. At this time, the street was still dirt and was lit at night by gaslights. (Courtesy of the Lincoln Area Archives Museum.)

ON THE COVER: The two-story train depot on the northwest side of Fifth and G Streets is pictured here around 1905. The Fleming family's living quarters were on the second floor. Kathleen Fleming and one of her sons are looking out the second-story window. The stationmaster, Albert Charles Fleming, Kathleen's husband, is to the left of the man in the black suit holding papers. Albert was the son of Albert Carlyle Fleming and Elizabeth Higgins. (Courtesy of the Lincoln Area Archives Museum.)

IMAGES
of America

LINCOLN

Lincoln Area Archives Museum

ARCADIA
PUBLISHING

ISBN 978-1-4671-3205-3

Published by Arcadia Publishing
Charleston, South Carolina

Printed in the United States of America

Library of Congress Control Number: 2013957598

For all general information, please contact Arcadia Publishing:
Telephone 843-853-2070
Fax 843-853-0044
E-mail sales@arcadiapublishing.com
For customer service and orders:
Toll-Free 1-888-313-2665

Visit us on the Internet at www.arcadiapublishing.com

Contents

ACKNOWLEDGMENTS

If it were not for the pioneers and early settlers who found their way to Lincoln and the multigenerational families that call Lincoln home, there would not be a story to tell. We want to thank the founders of the Lincoln Area Archives—Jerry Logan, Don Logan, and Wes Freeman—for gathering the history of Lincoln and the surrounding area and preserving it for generations to come. Jerry Logan put ink to paper and has recorded thousands of pages of history in the form of his many books about Lincoln, Mt. Pleasant, Fruitvale, Gold Hill, Sheridan, and Coon Creek, to mention a few. The Lincoln Area Archives Museum is fortunate to have these writings and will continue to publish them so that anyone interested in the history of the town can read about life before television, cellphones, and lattes.

Shirley Farnsworth Kimbrough Russell picked up the baton when the archives became a museum and worked hard for many years to help shape it into what it is today. Of course, this was not accomplished alone. Without the volunteers who donate hundreds of hours, there would not be a museum to visit. Without the City of Lincoln allowing Lincoln Area Archives Museum to inhabit its current home in the old city hall building, we would not be able to display all the museum's wonderful artifacts. Without residents donating the artifacts, we would have nothing to display; without loyal memberships and donations, we would not have funds to keep the doors open; and without key members of this organization, this book would still be a dream.

All images are courtesy of the Lincoln Area Archives Museum unless otherwise noted.

INTRODUCTION

The rich history of Lincoln and the surrounding Western Placer County towns is preserved in the historical writings of Jerry Logan, a member of the Lincoln pioneer family. The allure of gold brought many miners to the Lincoln area when Claude Chana discovered the precious metal in Ophir in 1848. With the gold findings, many mining towns cropped up, including Coon Creek, Virginia(town), Gold Hill, Newtown, Whiskey Diggings, and Fox's Flat, to mention a few.

Charles Lincoln Wilson was the father of the town of Lincoln. His optimism resulted in the Sacramento Valley Railroad stretching from Folsom as far as the Auburn Ravine. The project's money ran out at that point, and the railroad ended just north of the ravine instead of continuing on to Marysville as planned. However, the citizens of Western Placer now had a rail terminal. This led to a new town full of residents eager to handle an expected influx of business and prosperity. The new town was given Wilson's middle name.

Wilson organized a new company, the California Central Railroad, in 1854 to continue the line on to Marysville. The officers of the railroad at the time were listed as Charles L. Wilson, president; William T. Sherman, vice president; C.A. McNulty, secretary; W.J. Pardee, treasurer; and Theodore D. Judah, chief engineer.

Judah owned the property on which Lincoln would later be built, and on October 18, 1859, he sold the property to Wilson. In November 1859, the townsite was surveyed by William J. Lewis and laid out in blocks and lots. The original land Wilson bought from Judah extended from Lincoln Avenue (now East Avenue) to O Street—although the mapped part stopped at K Street—and from First Street to Ninth Street, but it did not include the land now occupied by McBean Memorial Park. The land included 71 full blocks (a full block contained 16 lots) and 14 half blocks.

On November 23, 1859, at an auction in Sacramento at the St. George Hotel, 46 lots were sold; this event marks the official launch of Lincoln. The average price was about $90 (although prices ranged from as low as $20 to as high as $410). Capt. John Chapman soon began to build Lincoln's first two hotels—the Pioneer Hotel and the Phoenix. However, the railroad did not arrive for almost two more years, and although the hotels survived the delay, Captain Chapman went bankrupt.

After gold played out in some of the mines, copper was discovered, and the gold mines were developed into copper mines. Along with copper came the discovery of coal and, later, the discovery of clay. Wilson bored down on the coal bed with an eight-inch auger to test the mineral thoroughly. In analyzing the stone coal discovered in Lincoln, it was established that it was superior in quality and good for burning. On December 27, 1873, the Lincoln Coal Mine was in operation and shipping out coal. In addition to the coal, Wilson passed through two beds of very fine potter's clay. The first clay bed, which was 12 feet thick, was found three feet below the surface; the other bed was over the coal and about the same thickness.

The California Clay Manufacturing Company, owned by Charles Gladding, Peter McBean, and George I. Chambers, purchased Mr. Cook's ranch, which was located about a mile from

Lincoln on the Oregon & California Railroad. The clay beds promised better results for Lincoln than the coal mines, and extensive work began on manufacturing sewer and water pipes. The business started by Gladding, McBean, and Chambers came to be known as Gladding, McBean & Company.

The early pioneers are too numerous to mention in this short introduction, but two are especially noteworthy. John Ziegenbein was Lincoln's most successful early entrepreneur. He purchased a lot on G Street near the corner of Fifth Street, and eventually came to own 100 feet of frontage on G Street. His property stretched north from the corner of Fifth Street to directly across the street from the railroad depot. In 1862, Ziegenbein built Lincoln's first grocery store on the corner of Fifth and G Streets. At first he built a small wooden store, but he soon replaced it with a large brick building with unusually thick walls. The building still stands and is in use today. He also built a wooden warehouse, a stable, and other outbuildings on the corner lot to serve the store. A stationary scale stood out front. Ziegenbein controlled almost all of the gold exchange from the miners in the area. He eventually became the Wells Fargo agent in town. He also handled farm produce and sold groceries and other merchandise either for cash or in exchange for gold or farm products. (Ziegenbein later sold his Daneville store property to Henry Nader.) The Ziegenbein Building's one story housed a general store until 1890. By then, Albert Fleming owned the property, and it became known as the Fleming Building. Fleming divided the property internally into several small businesses. Through the years owners added annexes to the main building, but the original structure remains and still maintains its integrity.

James R. Nickerson, an early pioneer rancher famous for his gardens and orchards, owned a ranch about four miles out of town along Doty's Ravine, just east of McCourtney Road. In 1859, the editor of the *Placer Herald* visited the ranch and reported "3,000 peach trees of 200 kinds; 225 different varieties of apples; 125 different pears; 40 different plums; 3,000 bearing grape vines; 40,000 cuttings for sale." Nickerson began with a small vegetable garden while patiently clearing his land. He then sold the vegetables at high prices to miners in the area. Before long, he had one of the most celebrated fruit orchards in California. His vineyard and winery were legendary. Nickerson accumulated over 800 acres, with the orchard and vineyard covering 225 acres. The property passed through a number of hands, including those of H. Barrett, Mr. Hoitt, and George Warren. Today, Nickerson's former property is divided into many parcels.

Much of the evidence of the rich mining industry is gone, but some of the early farms, ranches, and buildings are still in the Lincoln area. Many roads and streets are named after area pioneers, and some families still live in homes built by their ancestors. Historical memorials are scattered throughout the area as a tribute to the early settlers and the proud heritage they left behind.

One

In the Beginning

For several thousand years, native Indians gathered food, hunted, and fished in Western Placer. Bear River (Nem Se'-u, or "Great River," in the Nishinam tongue) forms the northern border of Western Placer. The river also served as the dividing line for Indian nations. To the south of Bear River were the Nishinam, often referred to as the Nisenan, according to anthropologist and writer Stephan Powers, who lived in Sheridan in 1873. Pioneers in general classified all the Indians as Maidu, although the Nisenan were considered a subgroup of the southern Maidu.

Life was peaceful from the discovery of California in 1534 until around 300 years later. By the 1830s, fur trappers were penetrating the area, and by 1840, Sutter's Fort had been founded in Sacramento. Numerous trappers undertook expeditions to recruit Nishinam as laborers; many changes followed.

Lincoln's history begins in 1854, when the Sacramento Valley Railroad started planning a line from Sacramento to Folsom. By February 1856, the line was complete to Folsom and was to be extended to Marysville.

Chief engineer Theodore Judah claimed a parcel of land from the federal government where the railroad was to cross Auburn Ravine. This parcel held possibilities for development to turn it into a town with water, roads, agricultural land, mines, and the projected nearby railroads. When it became obvious that the railroad would not reach the site when expected, Judah sold the property to Charles Wilson for $600.

On October 31, 1861, the California Central Railroad arrived in town and began offering service between Lincoln and Sacramento. This brought the town to life. The first business to open its doors was the Logan Saloon, owned by Alexander Mills and operated by E.A. Gibson, both from Fox's Flat mining camp. Within a year, Lincoln was home to three hotels.

The railroad soon opened a large depot, Wells Fargo Express established an office, and a restaurant at the depot, stores, and a post office soon followed. Lincoln also had a justice of the peace and a constable. The town became a major connecting point as stagecoaches from the California Stage Company met trains in Lincoln—the end of the line to all points east, west, and north.

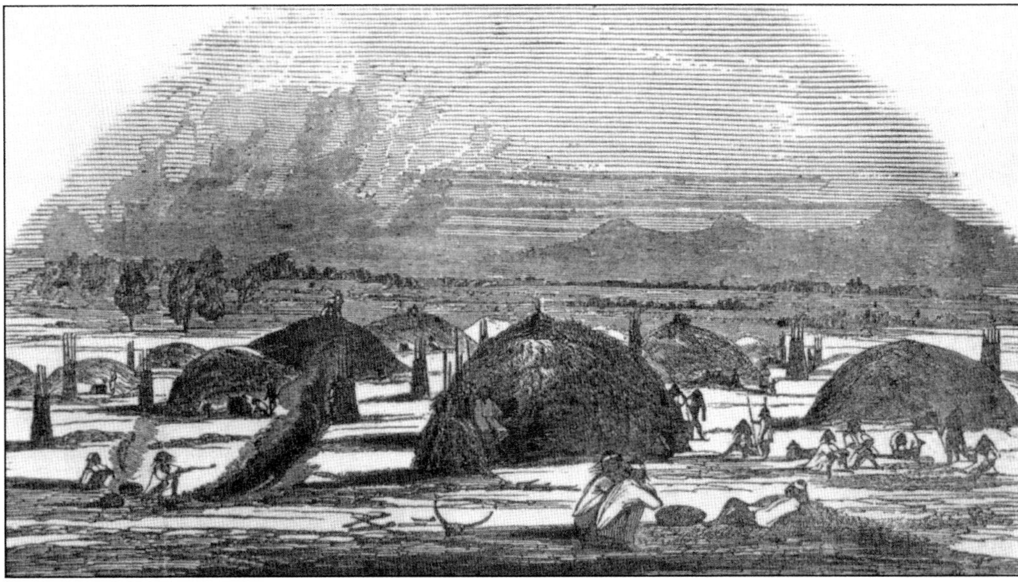

This 1852 drawing of the Nisenan village of Yupu, located near Lincoln, shows the Sutter Buttes in the background. The artist has depicted acorn granaries and large dome-shaped, earth-covered dwellings.

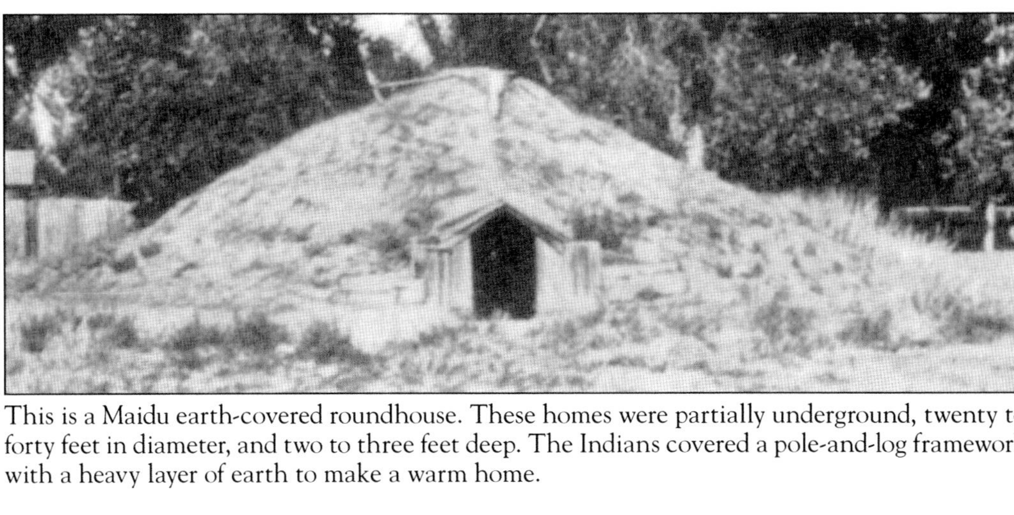

This is a Maidu earth-covered roundhouse. These homes were partially underground, twenty to forty feet in diameter, and two to three feet deep. The Indians covered a pole-and-log framework with a heavy layer of earth to make a warm home.

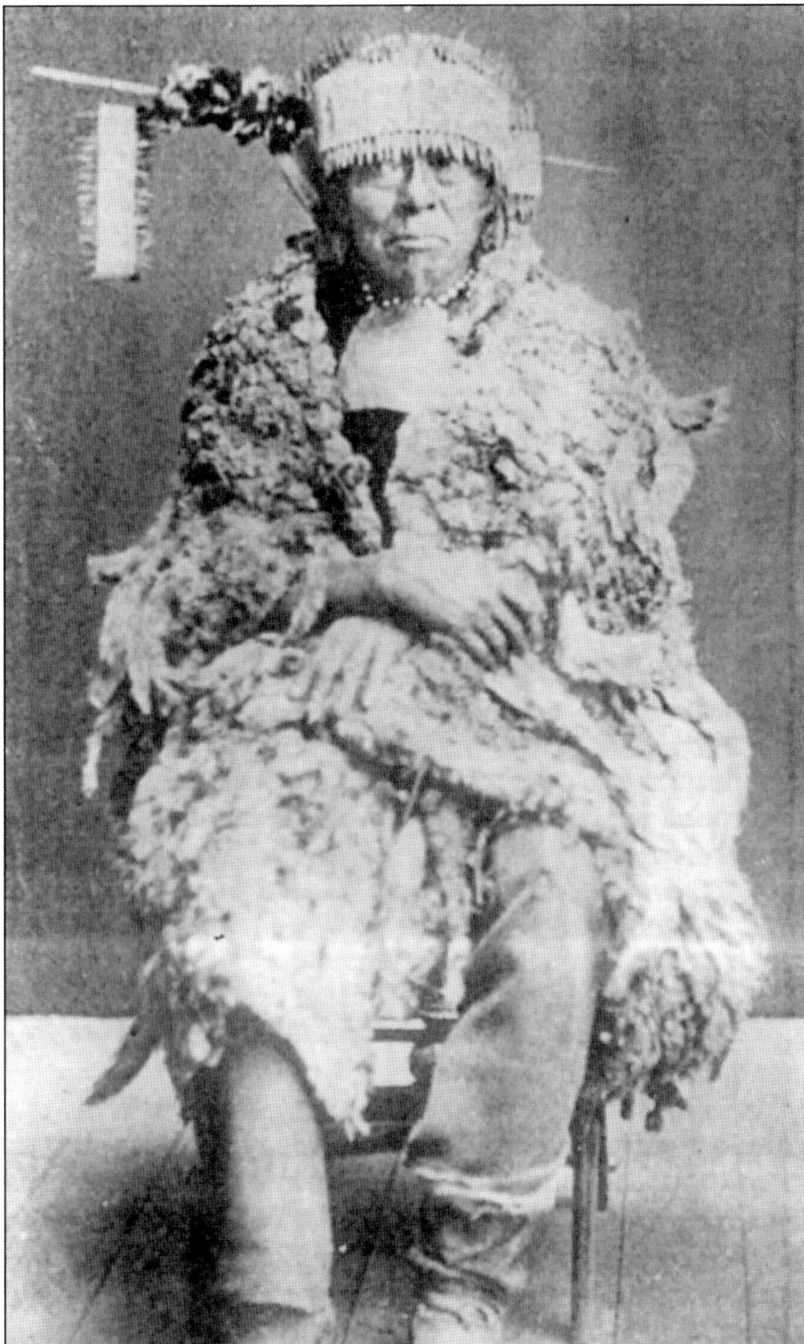

In this pre-1876 photograph, "Captain" Tom wears a woven rabbit-skin blanket, an abalone shell gorget, a flicker quill headband, and a hairpin with a flicker quill pendant. The white settlers used the term "captain" to identify headmen. Pieced together from dozens of skins, a blanket of rabbit and wildcat fur provided warmth in winter months as bedding or as a cloak. The chiefs or captains in most villages did not have broad powers but had a great deal of influence as moral exemplars and ceremonial leaders.

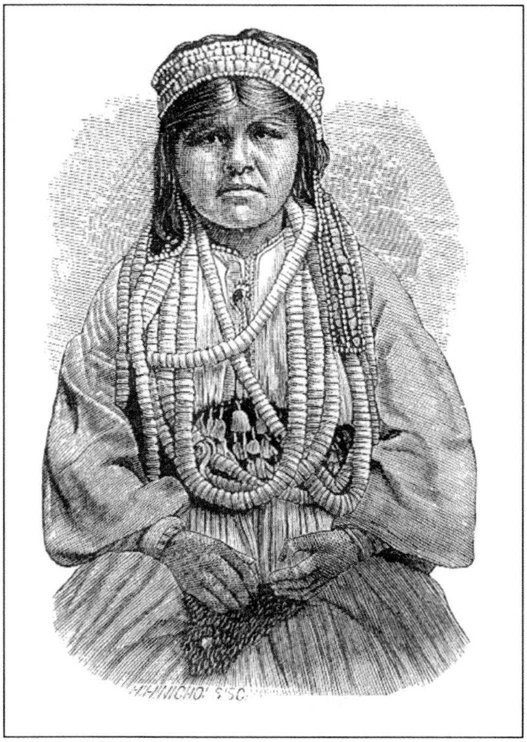

Reflecting her husband's elevated rank and high material worth, Captain Tom's wife wears a headband and belt studded with abalone shells. Her 11-yards-long string of shell bead money was estimated to be worth the impressive sum of $230 in 1874.

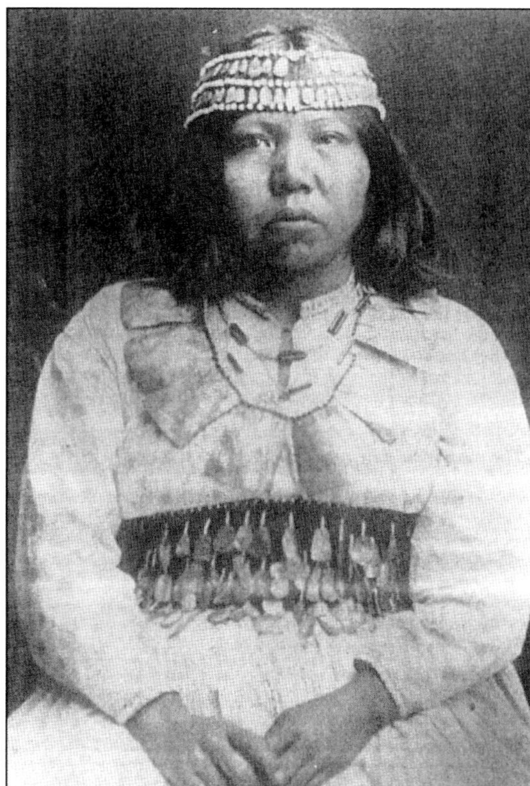

This woman, identified only as Captain Tom's daughter, wears a belt and headband of abalone shell pendants and necklace of large abalone pectorals over a pioneer-style cotton dress.

This Maidu Indian boy posed for a tintype photograph in 1853. For an image to be captured on a silvered plate, the subject had to hold still for 10 to 20 seconds. This proved difficult for many subjects, especially children, so it can be hard to find quality photographs of this type.

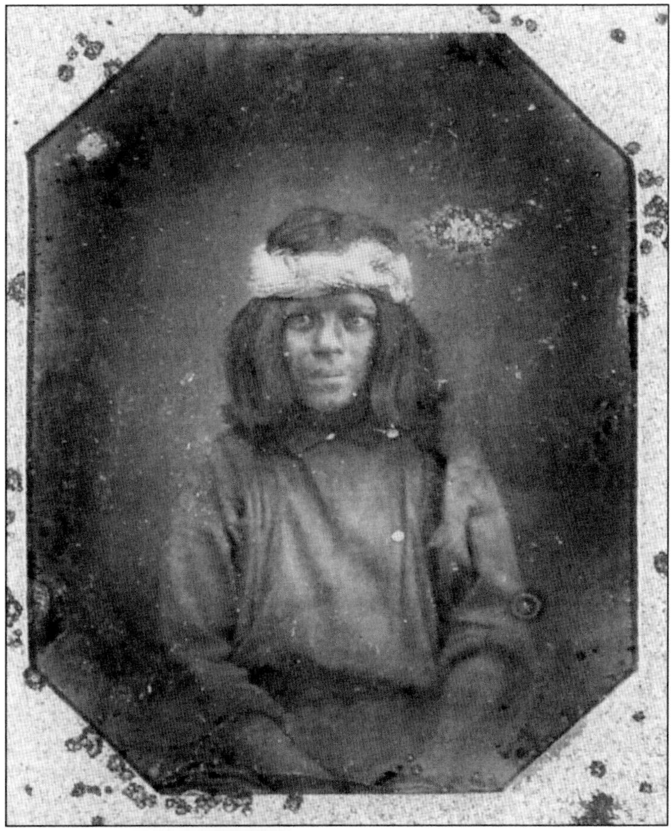

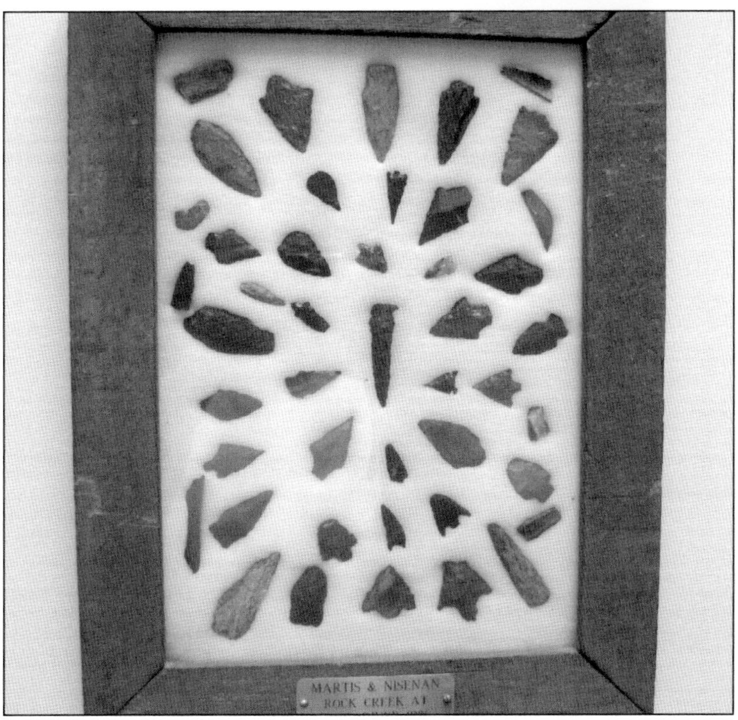

This display contains arrow points and artifacts found by Wes and Kathy Freeman during their many years of exploring historic rural Lincoln. The Freemans found several items along Bear River in Yuba County and Western Placer.

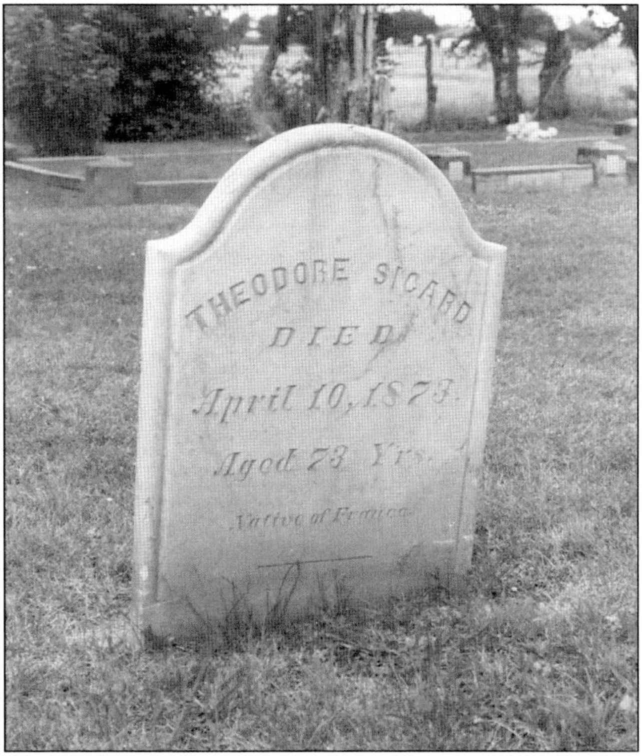

Theodore Sicard, a Frenchman, was the first European credited with settling in what is now Western Placer. In 1844, Sicard built an adobe house on the south side of Bear River directly across from what became Johnson's Ranch. The tract of land—a grant from the Mexican government—included approximately 18 square miles. Both William Johnson and Sicard planted and harvested crops in the area in 1845.

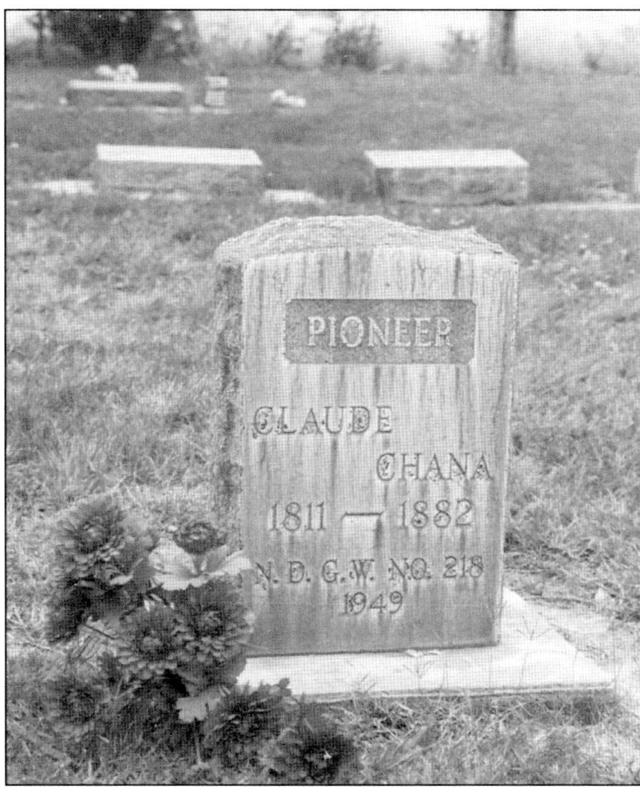

Two weeks before the Donner Party was trapped in the 1846 Sierra blizzards, Claude Chana's wagon train safely made it over the same mountains. Chana settled in the Johnson's Ranch area northwest of Lincoln. Chana is credited with discovering gold at Auburn Ravine, and a large statue of him in old-town Auburn honors his accomplishment.

Charles Lincoln Wilson was president of the California Central Railroad, which was building the railroad through Lincoln. The town was dubbed "Lincoln" in November 1859. His wife, Sara Jane Rood, reportedly suggested using his middle name for the town. Wilson had purchased the entire townsite one month earlier from Theodore Judah. The Wilsons built a large home on the southwest corner of Fifth and I Streets. Wilson, who was very active in the community, owned the Lincoln Coal Mine and numerous other businesses in town.

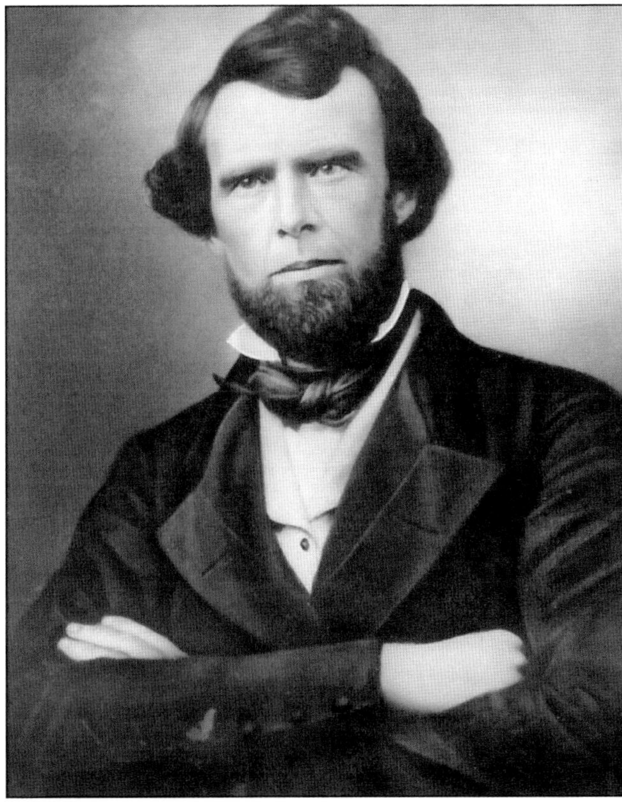

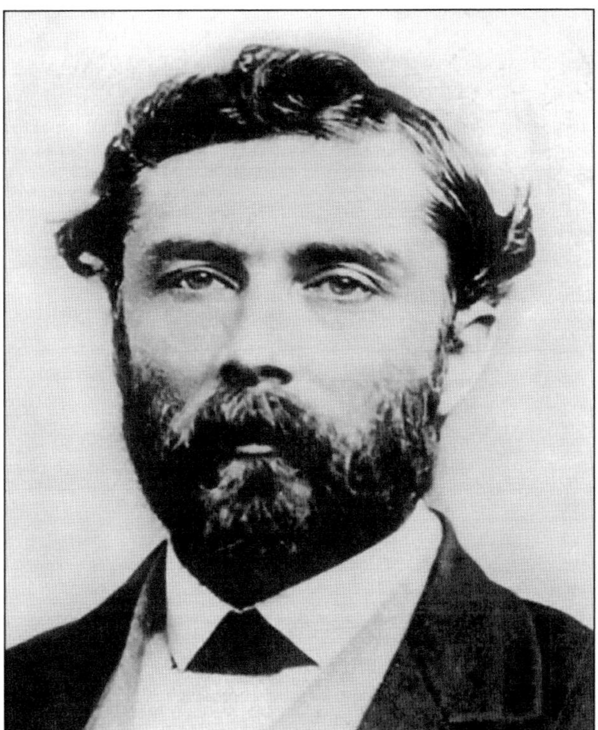

Theodore Judah was the chief engineer of the California Central Railroad project and had "patented" the government-owned land as soon as it was decided where the railroad would cross Auburn Ravine. Judah laid out the town of Lincoln just as he had done with Folsom. In 1861, the California Central Railroad arrived in Lincoln, and the town emerged as a bustling railroad terminal.

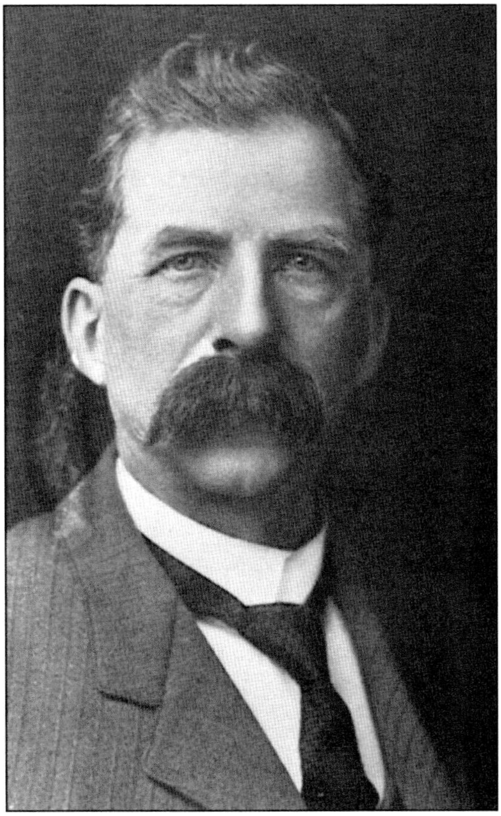

John Haenny served as Lincoln's first mayor. Before becoming mayor, he began blacksmithing for the California Central Railroad and continued working for the railroad until it reached Nevada. He farmed on Coon Creek and started a blacksmith shop at Ewing, between Lincoln and Sheridan. He relocated to Lincoln in 1871 and opened Haenny's Blacksmith and Carriage Shop on the corner of Fifth and F Streets. Haenny was also involved with city business and was one of the founders of the Bank of Lincoln.

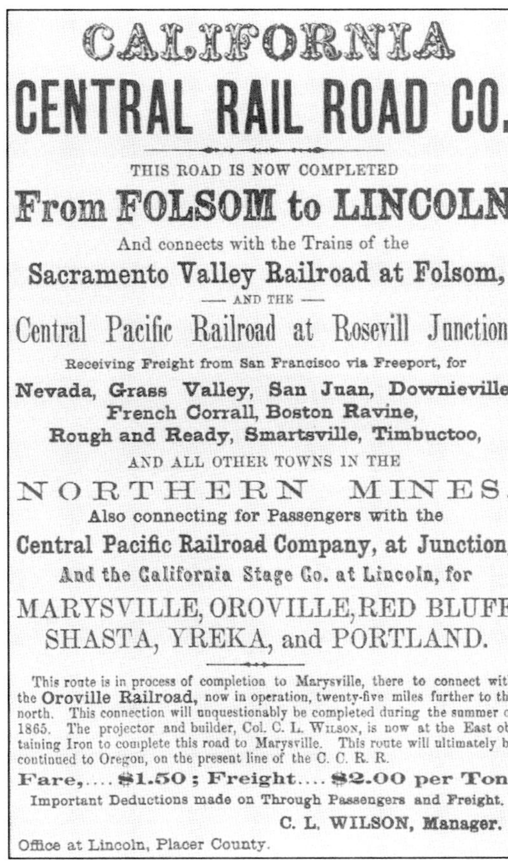

CALIFORNIA
CENTRAL RAIL ROAD CO.
THIS ROAD IS NOW COMPLETED
From FOLSOM to LINCOLN
And connects with the Trains of the
Sacramento Valley Railroad at Folsom,
— AND THE —
Central Pacific Railroad at Rosevill Junction,
Receiving Freight from San Francisco via Freeport, for
Nevada, Grass Valley, San Juan, Downieville,
French Corrall, Boston Ravine,
Rough and Ready, Smartsville, Timbuctoo,
AND ALL OTHER TOWNS IN THE
NORTHERN MINES.
Also connecting for Passengers with the
Central Pacific Railroad Company, at Junction,
And the California Stage Co. at Lincoln, for
MARYSVILLE, OROVILLE, RED BLUFF
SHASTA, YREKA, and PORTLAND.

This route is in process of completion to Marysville, there to connect with the Oroville Railroad, now in operation, twenty-five miles further to the north. This connection will unquestionably be completed during the summer of 1865. The projector and builder, Col. C. L. Wilson, is now at the East obtaining Iron to complete this road to Marysville. This route will ultimately be continued to Oregon, on the present line of the C. C. R. R.

Fare,.... $1.50 ; Freight.... $2.00 per Ton.
Important Deductions made on Through Passengers and Freight.
C. L. WILSON, Manager.
Office at Lincoln, Placer County.

This 1861 advertisement indicates the completion of the California Central Railroad from Folsom to Lincoln and its connection with Sacramento Valley Railroad at Folsom and the Central Pacific Railroad at Roseville Junction. The fare was $1.50, and freight was $2 per ton. This flyer also discusses the route that was in the process of completion to Marysville. The railroad would then connect with the Oroville Railroad and ultimately continue on to Oregon.

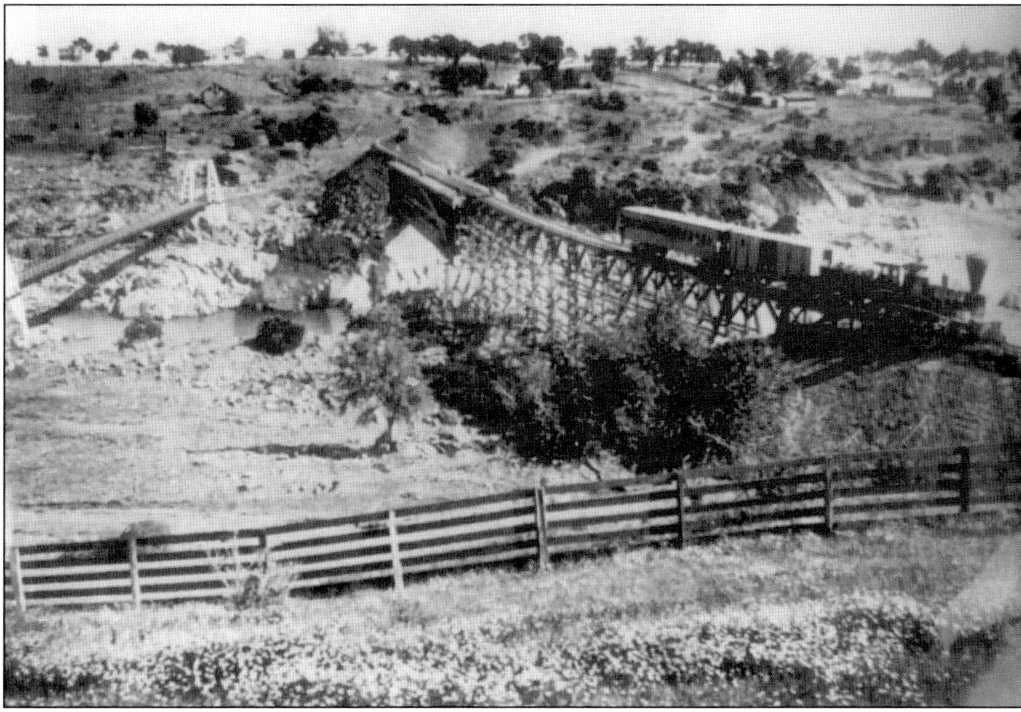

This photograph shows the California Central Railroad train leaving Folsom and traveling over the American River at Negro Bar on its way to Lincoln. It is probably in the general vicinity of the Rainbow Bridge at Greenback Lane. Passengers and freight were transported to and from Lincoln on this train.

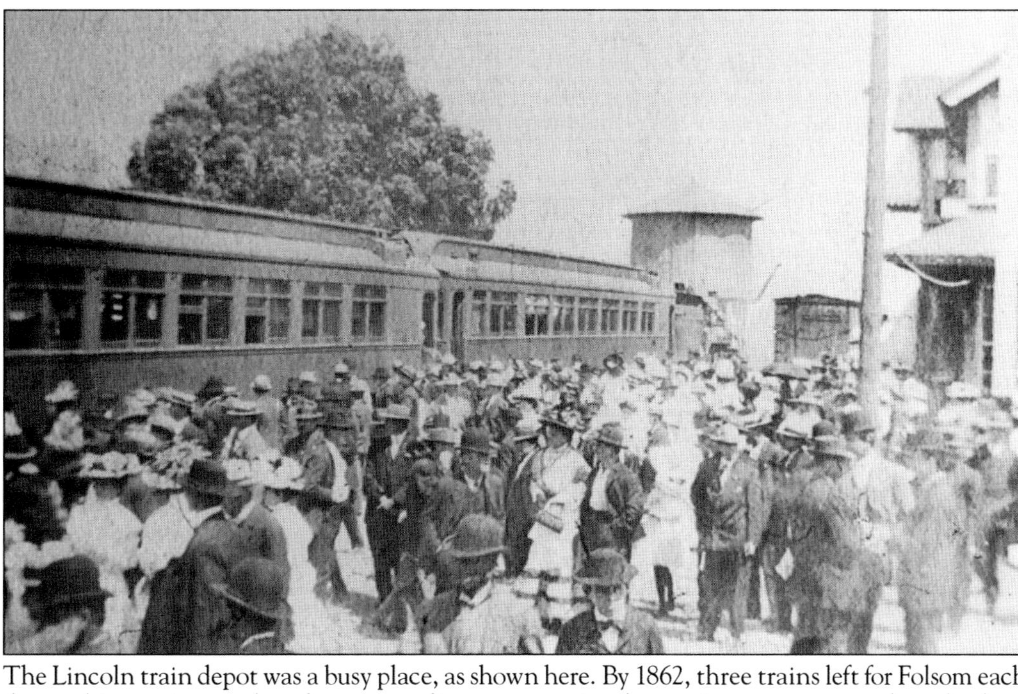

The Lincoln train depot was a busy place, as shown here. By 1862, three trains left for Folsom each day, making train travel to the surrounding towns easier than going on wagons or horseback.

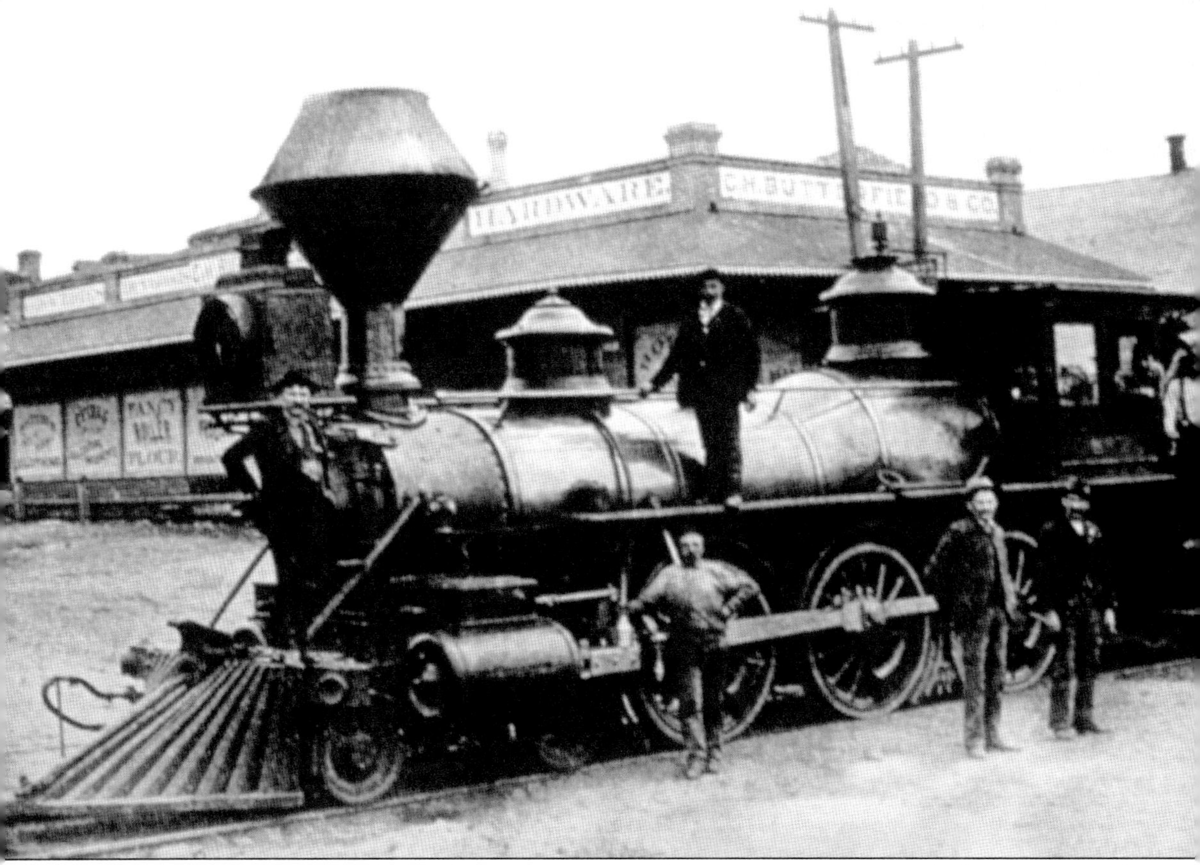

This California Central Railroad engine on the tracks in Lincoln is surrounded by unidentified men. The C.H. Butterfield and Company building is in the background. Local trees were being cut down to keep Gladding, McBean & Company in operation but also to run the trains.

Two

Gold, Coal, and Copper Mining

Claude Chana's eastern wagon train crossed the Bear River at Johnson's Crossing, where Chana met fellow Frenchman Theodore Sicard. Upon returning to Sicard's from a visit to Sutter's Fort, Chana heard about the Coloma gold discovery. Chana started back to Coloma with a party of men, including 25 Nishinam Indians. Chana's party stopped the first night in Coon Creek and the second night on Auburn Ravine, where they discovered gold on May 16, 1848.

In 1851, a group of Georgia miners left Ophir to prospect down Auburn Ravine. They followed a promising lead north out of the ravine to a conical hill and hit "pay dirt"—soon, they and other groups dug ditches to bring water from the Auburn Ravine to the hill to wash soil from the gold. They called this find Gold Hill.

In 1873, settlers around Lincoln found coal while digging wells. Newspaper reports induced Charles Wilson to do test borings at various sites on the north side of town, and he settled on a location at the north end of F Street. By May 1874, Lincoln was shipping 200 tons of coal per week by rail to Vallejo, Merced, Stockton, Marysville, and Sacramento. Lincoln coal was continuing to gain markets, as kitchen coal burned as clean as wood and created more heat per pound compared to other coal. The Sacramento Water Works used Lincoln coal to make steam, as it was found to be the cheapest, most effective fuel available.

In 1874, a coal mine was announced at J.D.B. Cook's ranch less than a mile northwest of Wilson's mine. That same year, a shaft was being sunk for coal on the land of O.P. Richardson on the banks of Bear River, about six miles from Sheridan. In 1902, a group of San Francisco investors heard about the discoveries and formed the Dairy Farm Mine northwest of Lincoln. Although they only found a small amount of gold in the beginning, they struck a rich vein of copper ore; copper was increasingly valuable at the time because of its use in the new electrical industries. From 1914 to 1918, the Dairy Farm Mine used a rail line to Sheridan to haul the large amounts of copper ore to Southern Pacific's main line.

For many years, interest in the mineral deposits the land might have to offer created a big industry in and around the Lincoln area.

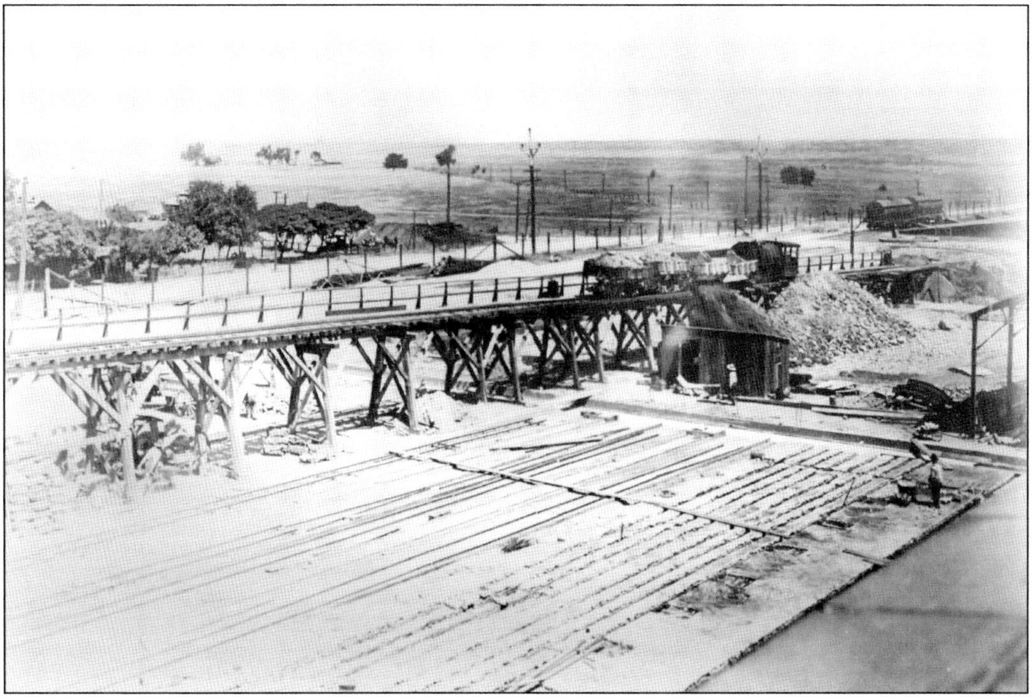

Some Sacramento capitalists purchased the Cook Ranch coal mine, visible behind the trees in the upper left, and referred to it as Cook and Spinks. In August 1877, they began sinking a shaft. In October, they were having problems trying to run a railroad switch and spur; the company was bringing up lots of coal but could not get it out of the area. By November 1877, the narrow gauge track that Gladding, McBean used for hauling clay was also shipping carloads of coal for the mine.

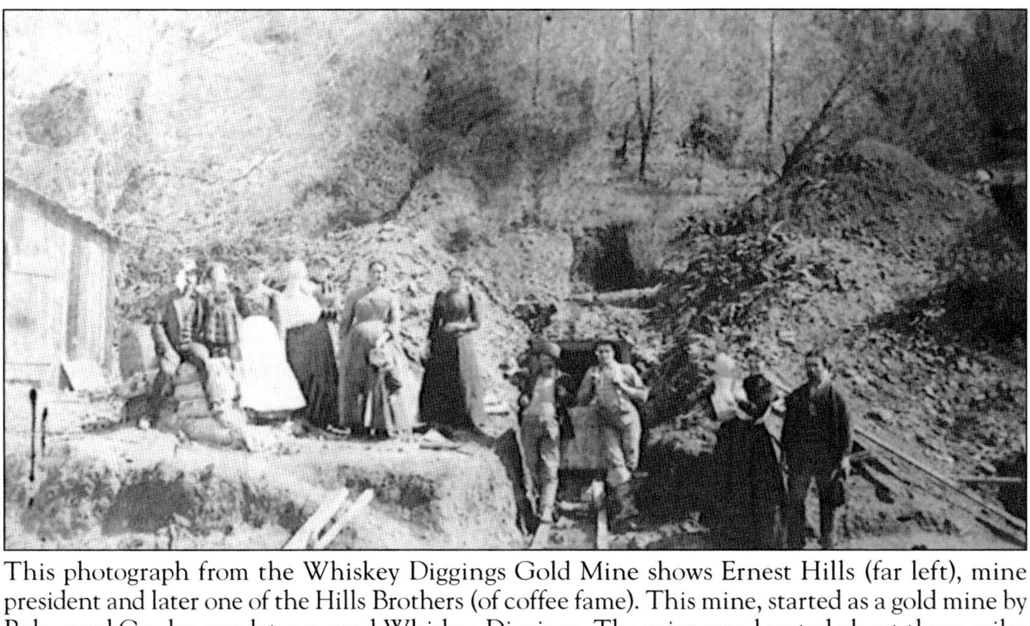

This photograph from the Whiskey Diggings Gold Mine shows Ernest Hills (far left), mine president and later one of the Hills Brothers (of coffee fame). This mine, started as a gold mine by Baker and Crosby, was later named Whiskey Diggings. The mine was located about three miles northwest of Mt. Pleasant, and the Whiskey Diggings ditch reached the town in 1855.

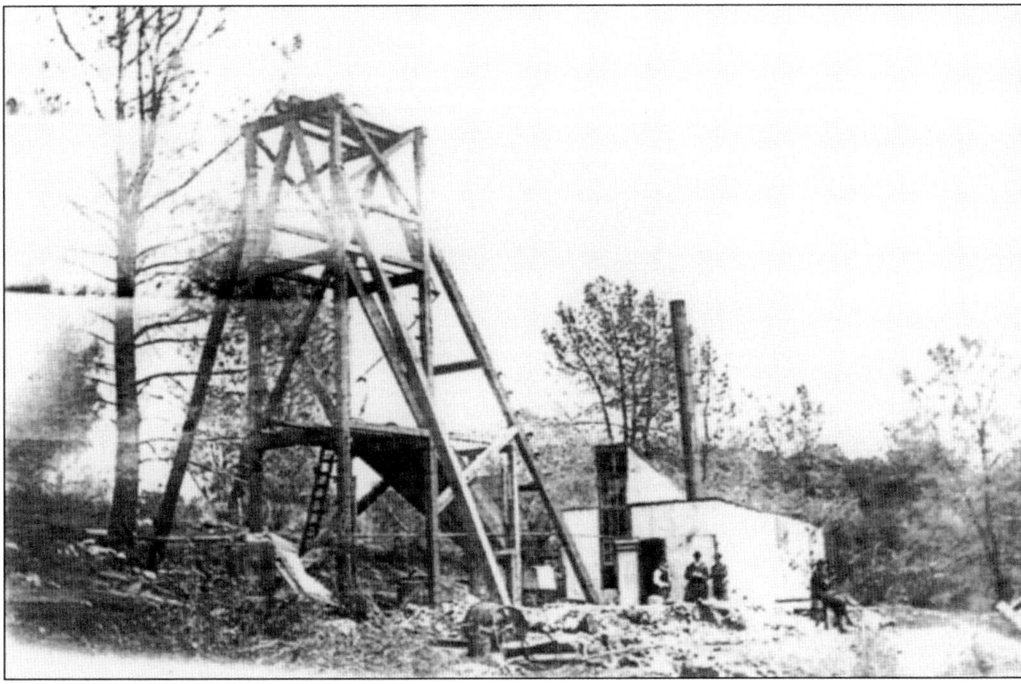

The Valley View Products Company established Kilaga Springs at the Whiskey Diggings mine site in 1923. The water was touted to have healing properties, and the company bottled and distributed water from the spring; later, a spa was established. The group behind the company consisted of E.M. Kimberlin of Oakland, Judge J.B. Landis of Auburn, and E.C. Gaylord of Lincoln. They created the name "Kilaga" by combining the first two letters of each of their last names.

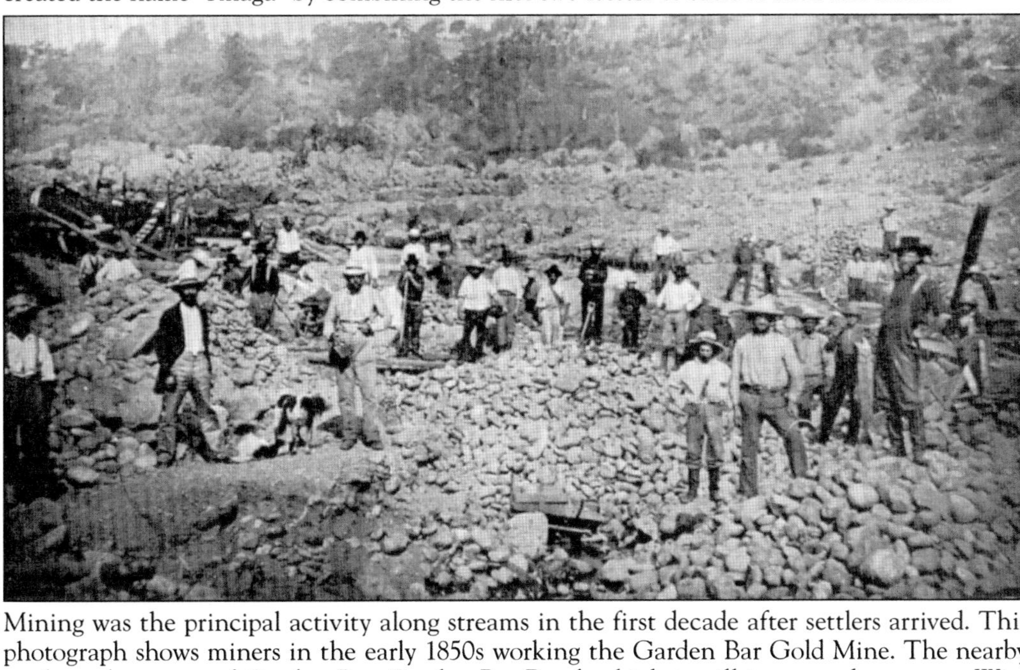

Mining was the principal activity along streams in the first decade after settlers arrived. This photograph shows miners in the early 1850s working the Garden Bar Gold Mine. The nearby road was later named Garden Bar. Garden Bar Road, which is still in use today, crosses Wise Road on the northeast side of Lincoln.

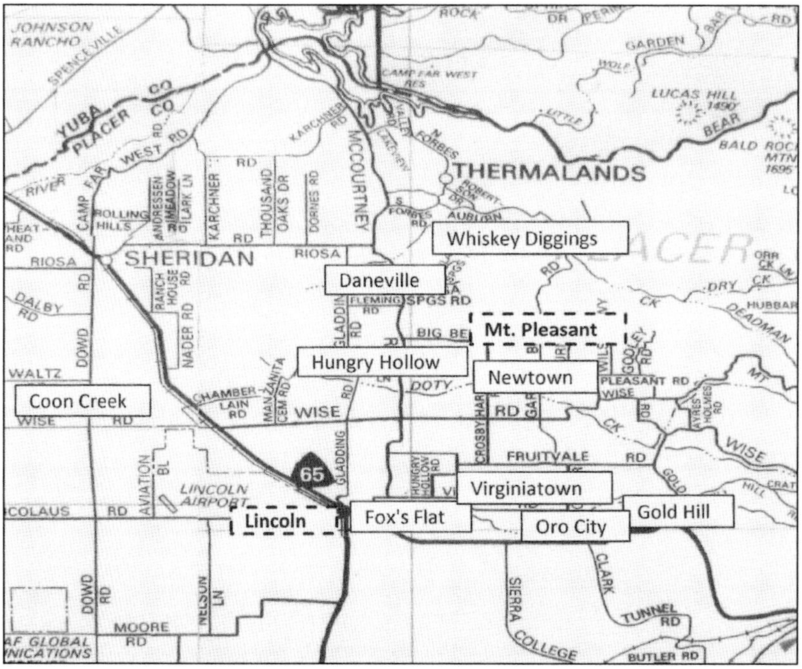

This map shows the general location of some of the mining towns that dotted the Lincoln area from about 1850 to the early 1900s. Miners set up camps all along creeks and ravines and in other areas to follow promising leads. In some instances, a camp turned into a town almost overnight; at other times, the miners moved on after a short while.

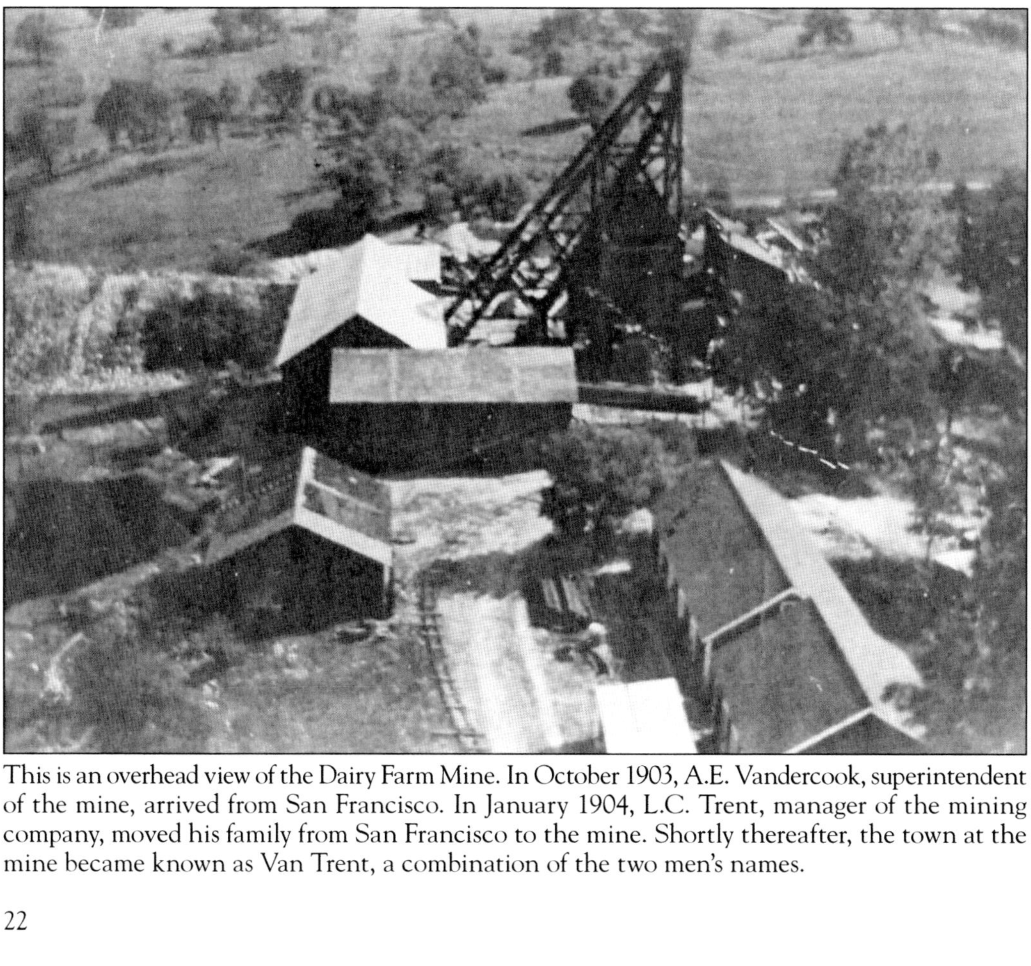

This is an overhead view of the Dairy Farm Mine. In October 1903, A.E. Vandercook, superintendent of the mine, arrived from San Francisco. In January 1904, L.C. Trent, manager of the mining company, moved his family from San Francisco to the mine. Shortly thereafter, the town at the mine became known as Van Trent, a combination of the two men's names.

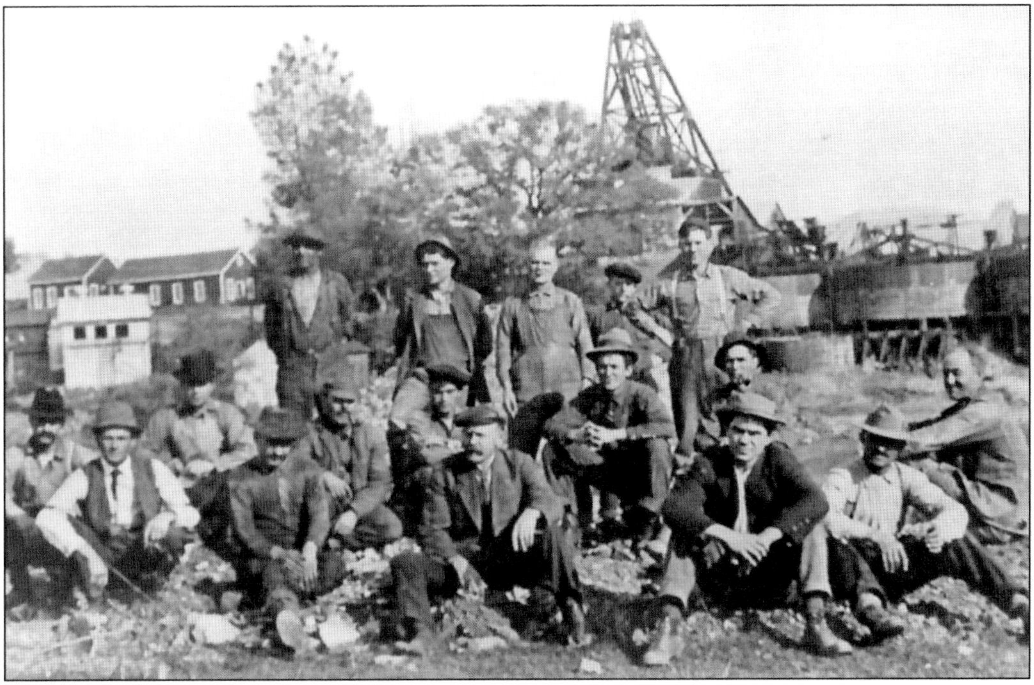

This photograph shows several Dairy Farm Mine workers with the mine complex in the background. The power plant is the white building at left, and the boardinghouse is visible behind it. The mine was located east of the town of Sheridan on McCourtney Road near the Bear River.

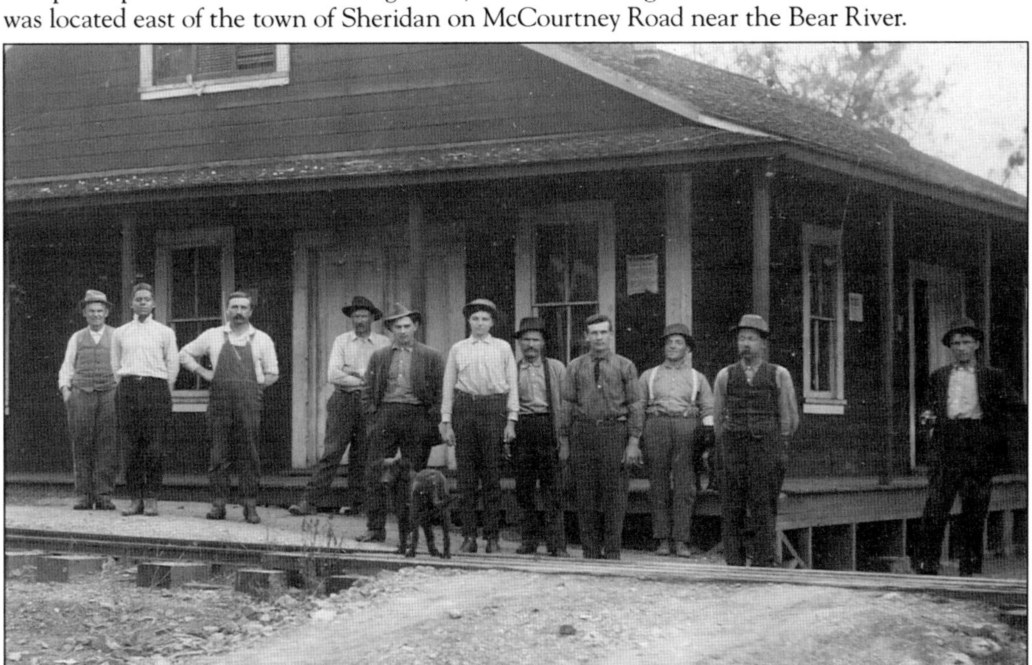

This is the store at Van Trent with narrow gauge railroad tracks visible in the foreground. The man at far left is probably Mr. Stull. Louis Ruiz is standing next to him in the white shirt. The other men are unidentified. Life at Van Trent slowed down when the mine closed in 1917 due to a shortage of cars that could ship ore during World War I.

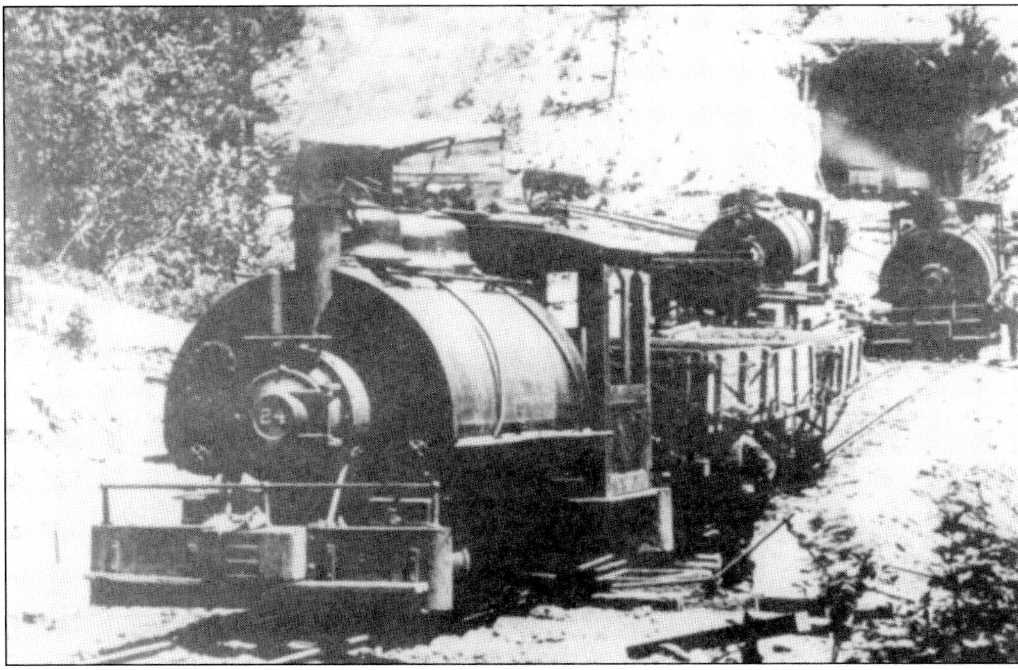

This narrow gauge railroad engine and cars are hauling ore from the Dairy Farm Mine to Sheridan. The first contract for building the railroad was dated July 25, 1914. It extended just north of Sheridan to Van Trent for eight and a half miles. The unloading site featured an inclined narrow gauge track that allowed ore cars to release their loads down chutes to waiting Southern Pacific Railroad cars.

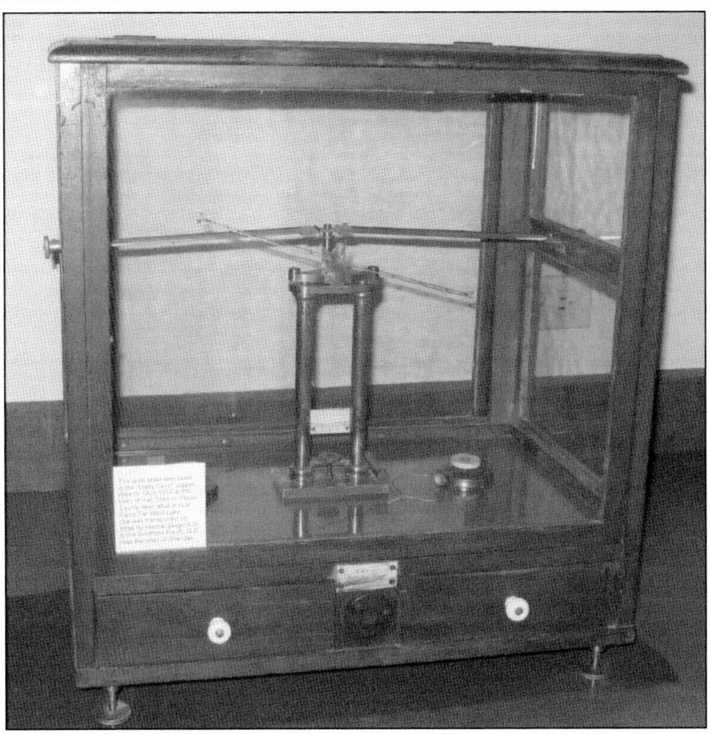

This gold scale was used at the Dairy Farm Mine town of Van Trent from 1903 to 1917. Many of the mines began as gold mines, but when the gold played out, other ore—such as copper—became the primary focus until prices dropped. The mining business adapted to whatever product the ground could produce.

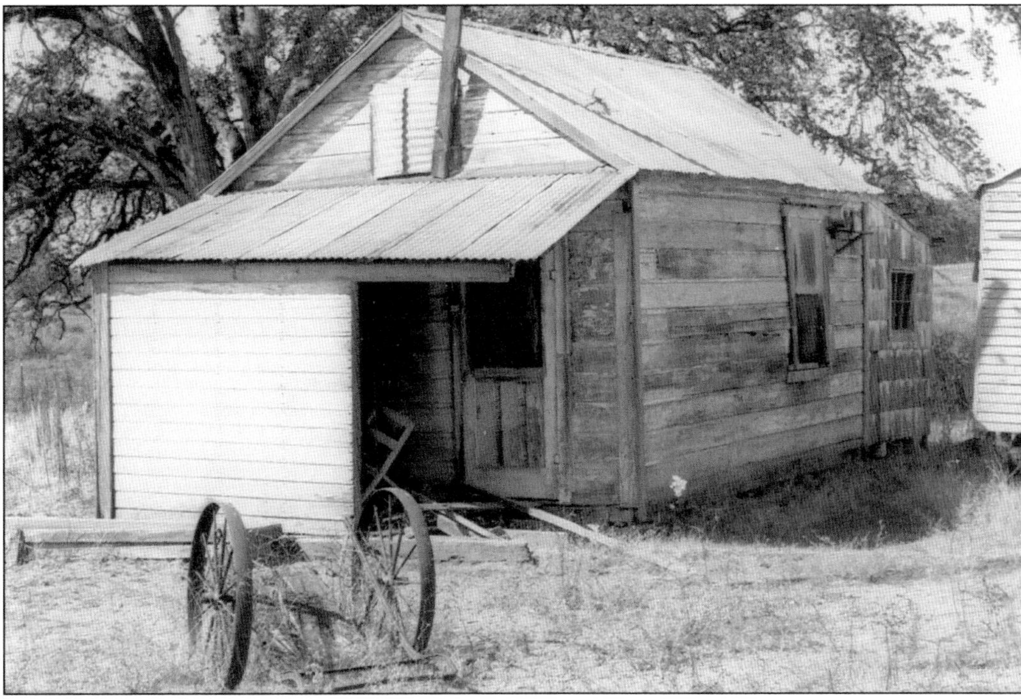

This building was used as a post office for the Dairy Farm Mine community of Van Trent from 1904 to 1918. Frank Peyton was the first postmaster. The building was moved to the Harley Hutchison property when the mine closed in the 1930s.

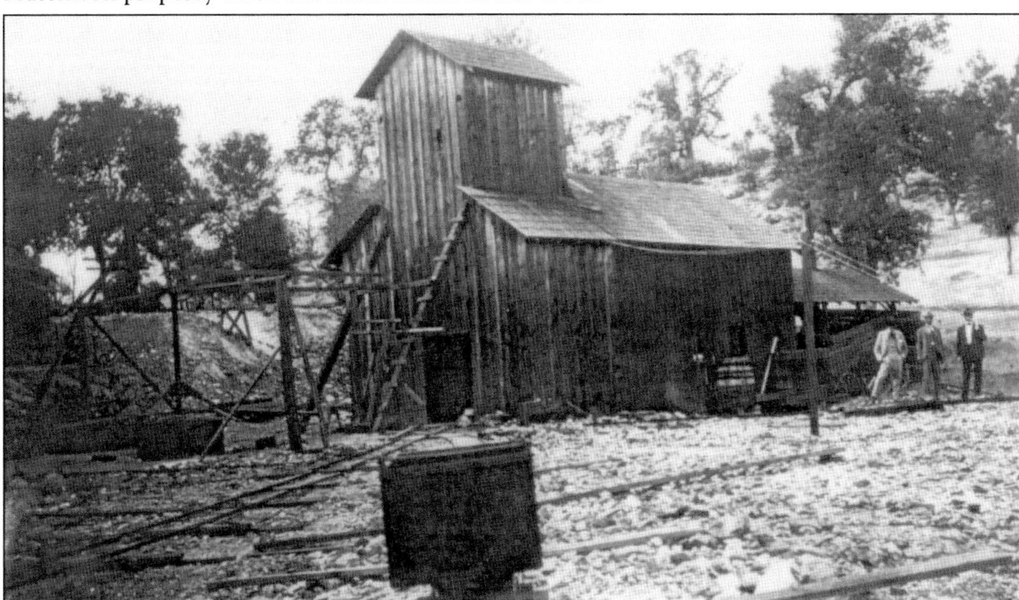

In 1864, articles in newspapers suggested that the copper rush was cooling down. In 1866, the Wilson Copper Mining Company, located in the town of Wilson, was put up for sale by the constable of Township Number 2 for nonpayment of debt ($96.75) to Oliver Linn. It reopened in 1906 as Algol Copper Mine. Wilson was located north of Mt. Pleasant on Garden Bar Road, between Coon Creek and Bear River.

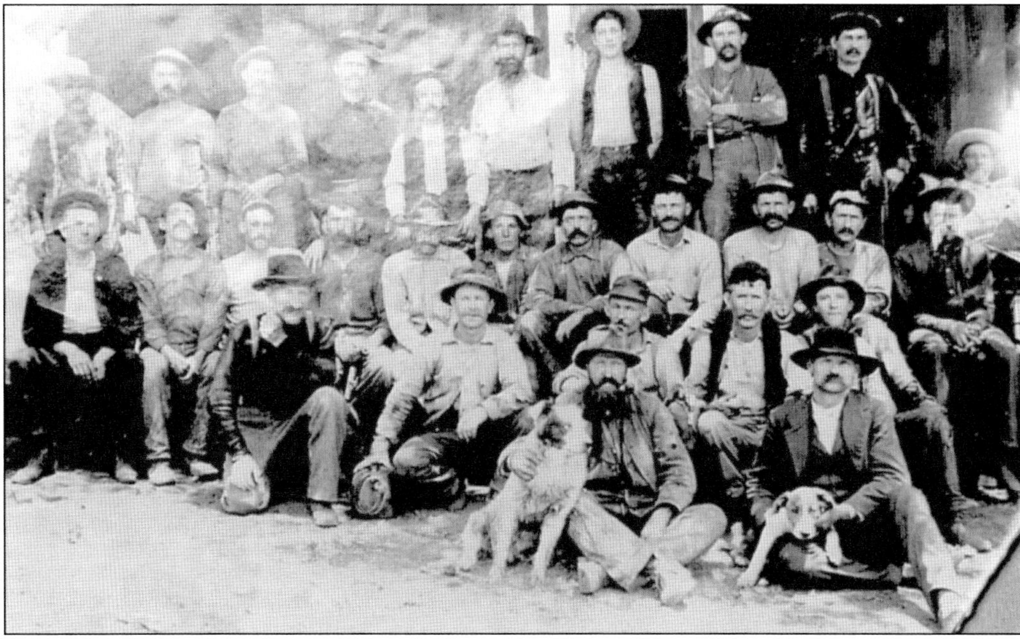

This 1906 photograph shows the Algol mine crew. Although the copper ore did not give out, the demand and prices for it did. When the Wilson mine reopened in 1906 as Algol Mine, it mainly produced gold. It even had a post office known as "Cain's." The mine superintendent was William Cain; the postmistress was his daughter, Edith Cain.

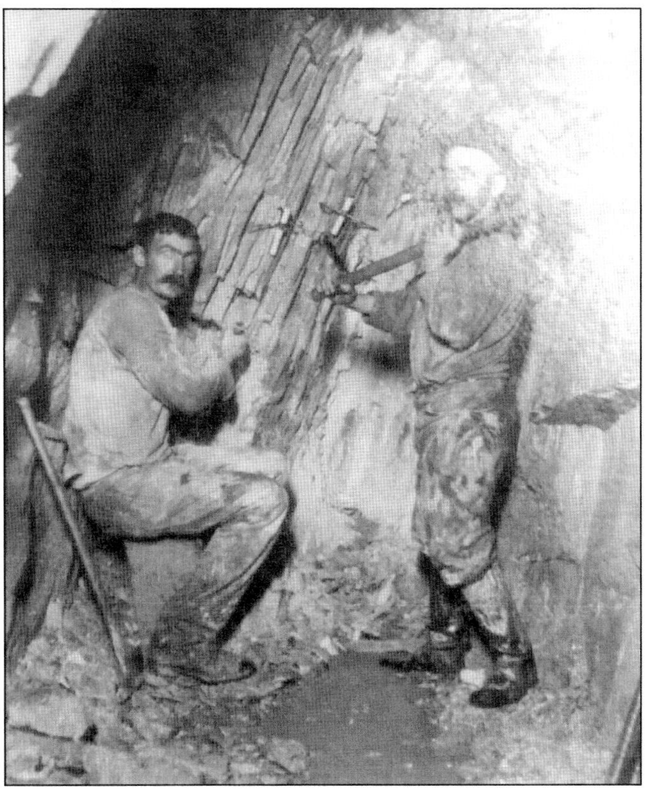

This photograph shows a couple of unidentified miners hard at work at the Algol Mine. Note the candles in metal holders that were held into place by spikes in the rock wall. Mining was hard, backbreaking work, but it appealed to many who had hopes of striking it rich.

Three

Gladding, McBean & Company

Following the discovery of coal beds in 1873, coal mining led to the uncovering of large deposits of high-quality clay at the main shaft near Seventh and F Streets. Charles Wilson owned the most productive coal/clay mine, located near the southeast corner of Seventh and G Streets. Cook's Ranch, north of Wilson's mine, also contained vast deposits of clay.

The California Clay Manufacturing Company, which consisted of Charles Gladding, Peter McBean, and George I. Chambers, heard about the superior quality of the clay and had two railroad carloads of Lincoln fire clay tested in San Francisco and Oakland potteries. The product was determined superior, and they purchased a portion of Cook's Ranch along the line of the Oregon & California Railroad, about a mile from Lincoln. An 1875 article in the *Record Union* notes that the clay beds promised better results for Lincoln than the coal mines. The building for the business, which would manufacture sewer and water pipe, was two stories high and 44 feet wide by 108 feet long. This business, which would come to be known as Gladding, McBean & Company (Gladding, McBean), was established in 1875 and is still in operation.

Almost hidden between aging mounds of clay one mile north of Lincoln, on the east side of Highway 65/G Street (now Lincoln Boulevard), are the dusty buildings of Lincoln Clay Products Inc. Many Lincolnites are not aware of the company's existence. This "new clay" business, which is not connected to Gladding, McBean to the south, opened in Lincoln in 1907 as the Pyrmont Brick Company. Plans called for the building of a brick factory at the Lincoln site, but only clay mining took place there. The company mining the clay was incorporated in 1911 as the Lincoln Clay Products Company with Michael J. Dillman as president. Dillman continued in that position until 1939. Michael J. Dillman Jr. was elected president and worked for the company well beyond 1950. The company served as a supplier of clay rather than as a manufacturer. It shipped fire clay, terra cotta clay, and pulverized and powdered clay throughout the United States and abroad.

With these two businesses in town, Lincoln truly was "Clay City."

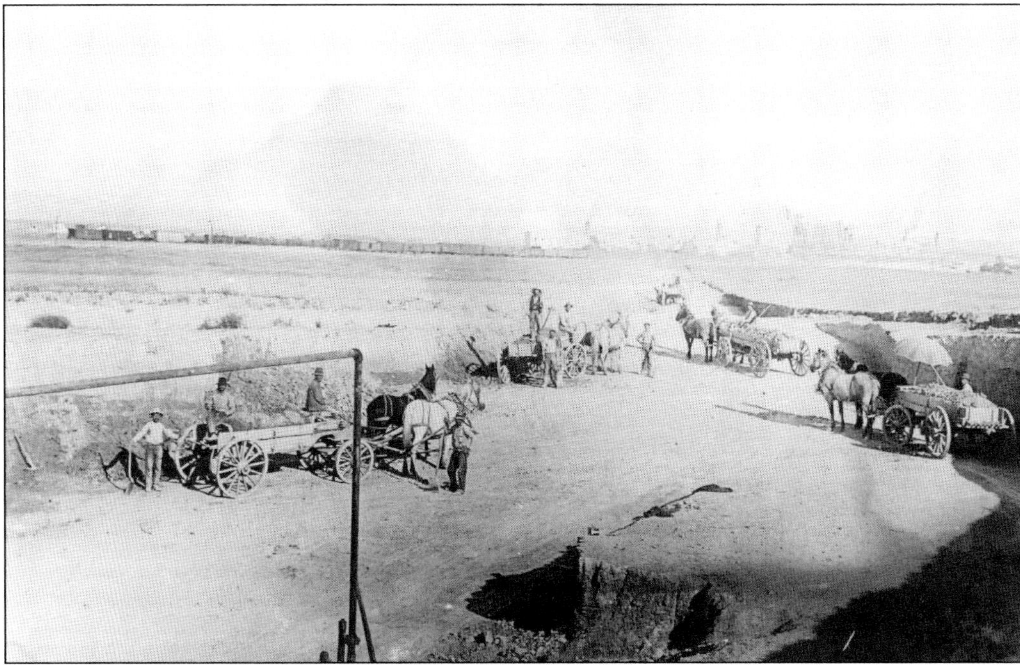

This 1915 photograph shows the Gladding, McBean clay pits on Nicolaus Road. The horses with wagons loaded with clay have just climbed out of the pits and are headed for the pottery in the background.

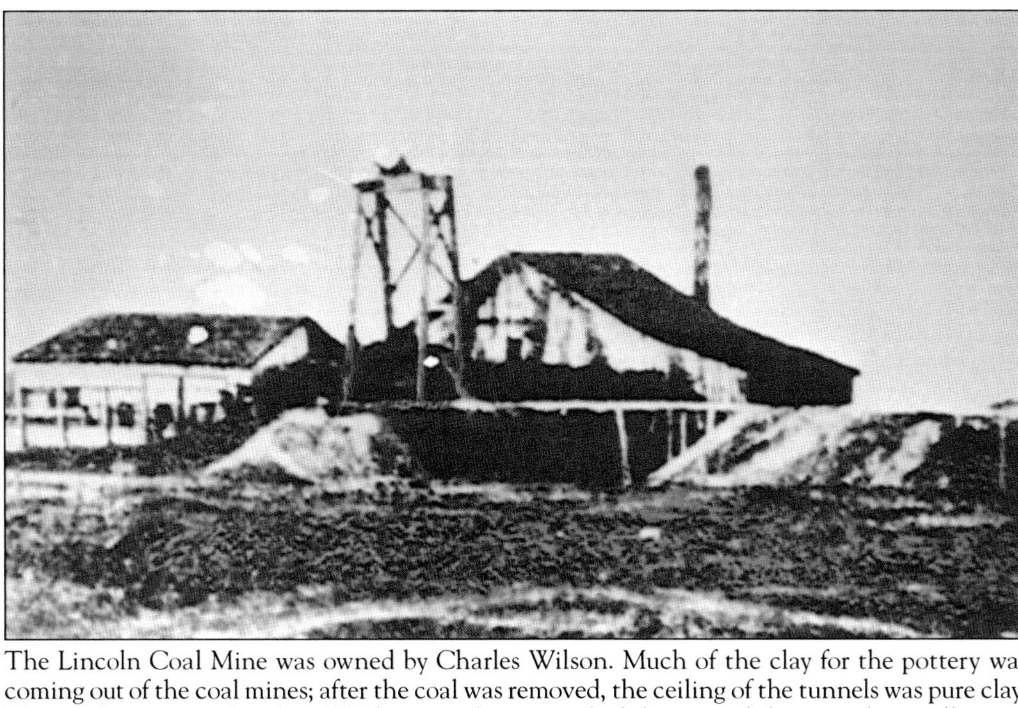

The Lincoln Coal Mine was owned by Charles Wilson. Much of the clay for the pottery was coming out of the coal mines; after the coal was removed, the ceiling of the tunnels was pure clay. This coal mine was closed in 1876 because the removal of clay caused the tunnels to collapse.

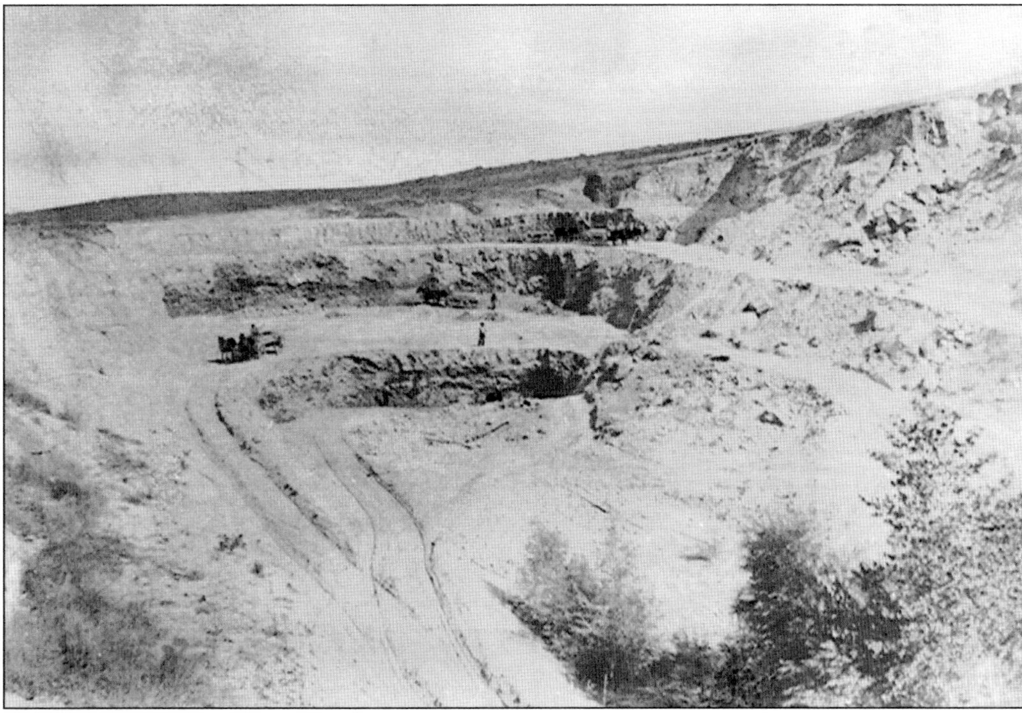

This horse-drawn wagon climbing out of the coal/clay mine will deliver clay to Gladding, McBean. C.C. Sanders had the contract in 1888 to haul clay to the pottery, but his four teams of horses could not keep up with the demand of over 30 loads per day.

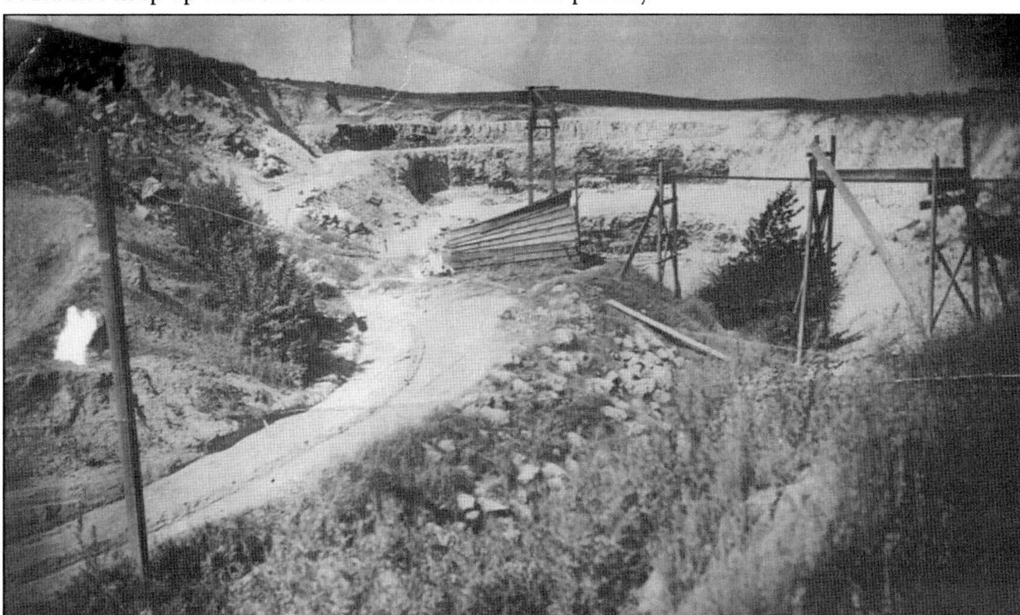

This photograph shows another horse-drawn wagon traveling to get a load of clay. Gladding, McBean had its own teams of horses to haul out the clay, and also contracted out for some of the work. The company's six horse-and-wagon teams were kept busy hauling clay all day. This image shows the various elevations that have already been mined.

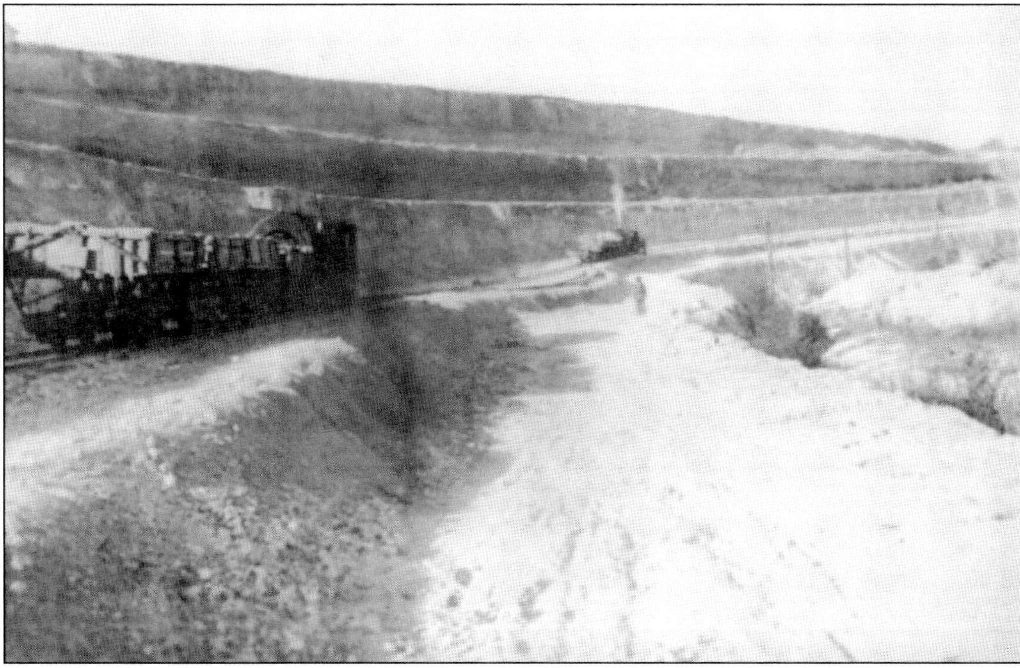

One of two steam locomotives used in clay mining in 1908 is pictured here. A narrow gauge railroad ran from the clay pit to the pottery. To this day, clay is removed from the pit and transported to Gladding, McBean.

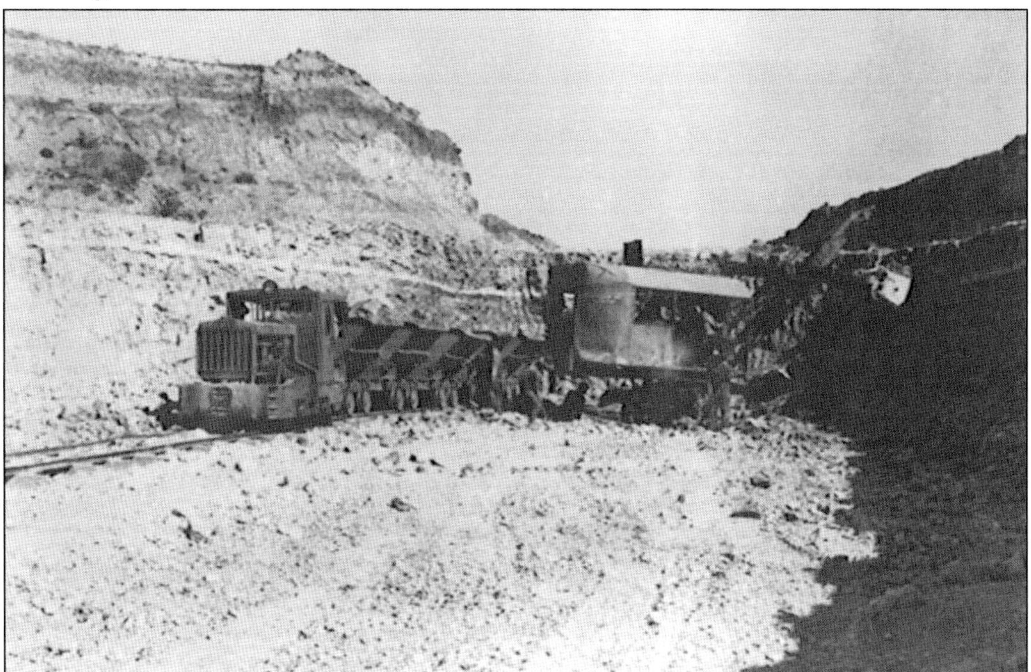

After the clay was brought out of the clay pits, a steam shovel was used to load it into small railroad cars. The cars were attached to a narrow gauge train that hauled the clay a short distance to Gladding, McBean, where it was then processed. Clay was also obtained from coal-mining excavations.

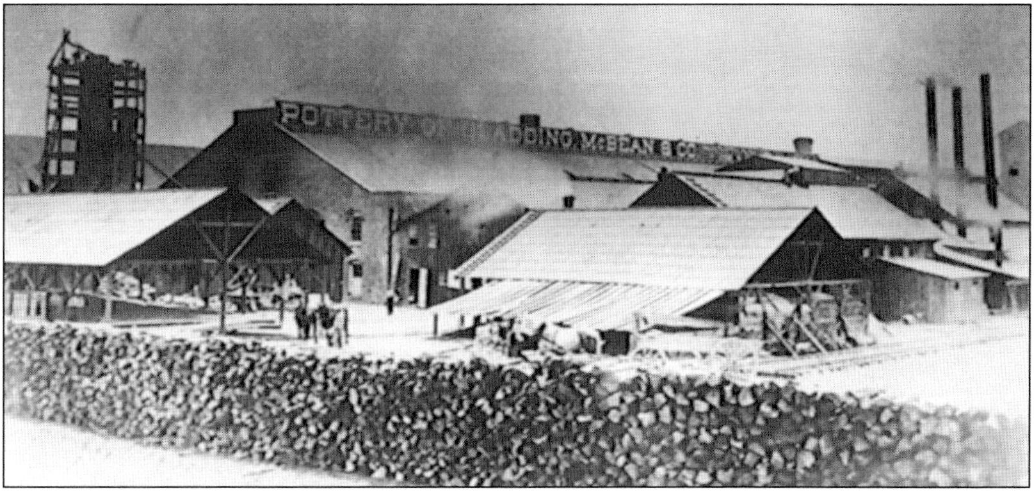

By 1883, the enclosed floor space at Gladding, McBean totaled two acres. The company made a special press for molding and shaping clay pipe. Wood was used to fuel the drying kilns. Kiln No. 1 required eight and a half cords of pine and two and three-quarter cords of oak. Kiln No. 2 required eleven cords of pine and three and a half cords of oak.

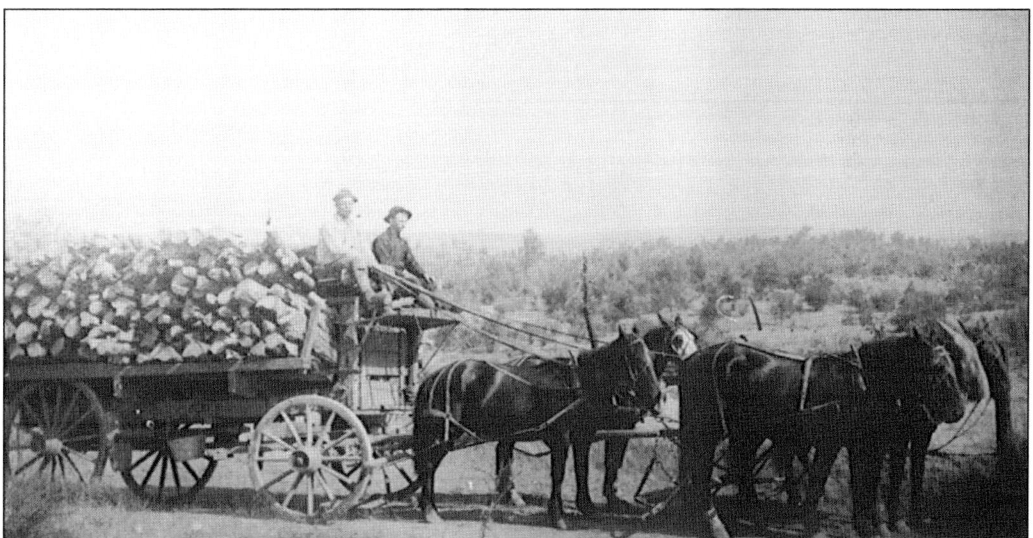

Many farmers in the Lincoln area cut and delivered wood to Gladding, McBean. The farmers were able to use the cut wood to pay off the mortgage on their property as well as having the land cleared for farming. Between the trains and Gladding, McBean, demand for wood was ever-present and very profitable for farmers. Gladding, McBean alone burned about 10,000 cords of wood each year.

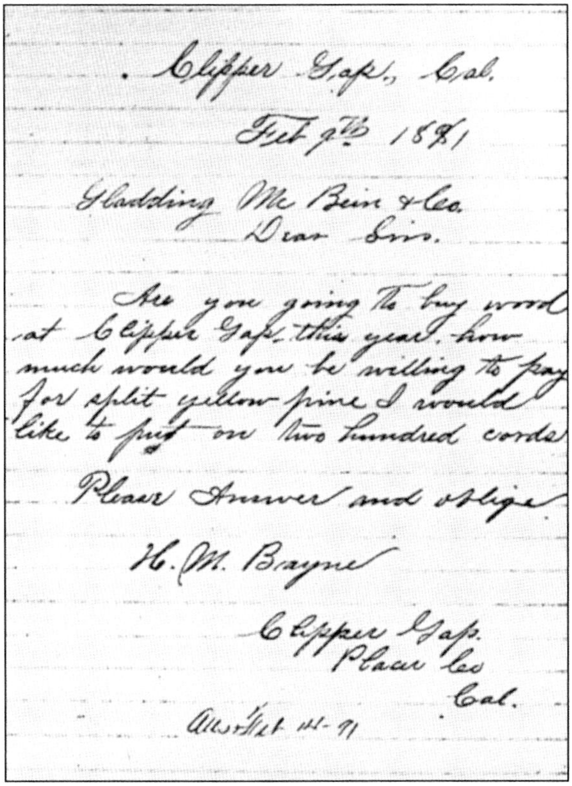

Clipper Gap., Cal.

Feb 7th 1891

Gladding McBein & Co.

Dear Sirs.

Are you going to buy wood at Clipper Gap. this year. how much would you be willing to pay for split yellow pine I would like to put on two hundred cords

Please Answer and oblige

H. M. Brayne

Clipper Gap. Placer Co Cal.

Ans Feb 11-91

This 1891 letter, written by H.M. Brayne from Clipper Gap, is inquiring about how much wood Gladding, McBean needed and how much they were willing to pay for it in order to fire their kilns. By 1877, all the area within 10 miles of Lincoln had been stripped of wood, and woodcutters were already within seven miles of Auburn.

The clay pipes produced at Gladding, McBean were fired in an 18-foot-diameter kiln for 45 to 50 hours after seasoning. The superior clay allowed for the extreme heat required for firing. The pottery eventually completed a larger kiln, and by 1882, it was producing ironstone sewer pipe, chimney tops, fire brick, terra cotta ware, vases, urns, flowerpots, and other decorative vessels. By 1896, the kilns were fired using oil instead of wood.

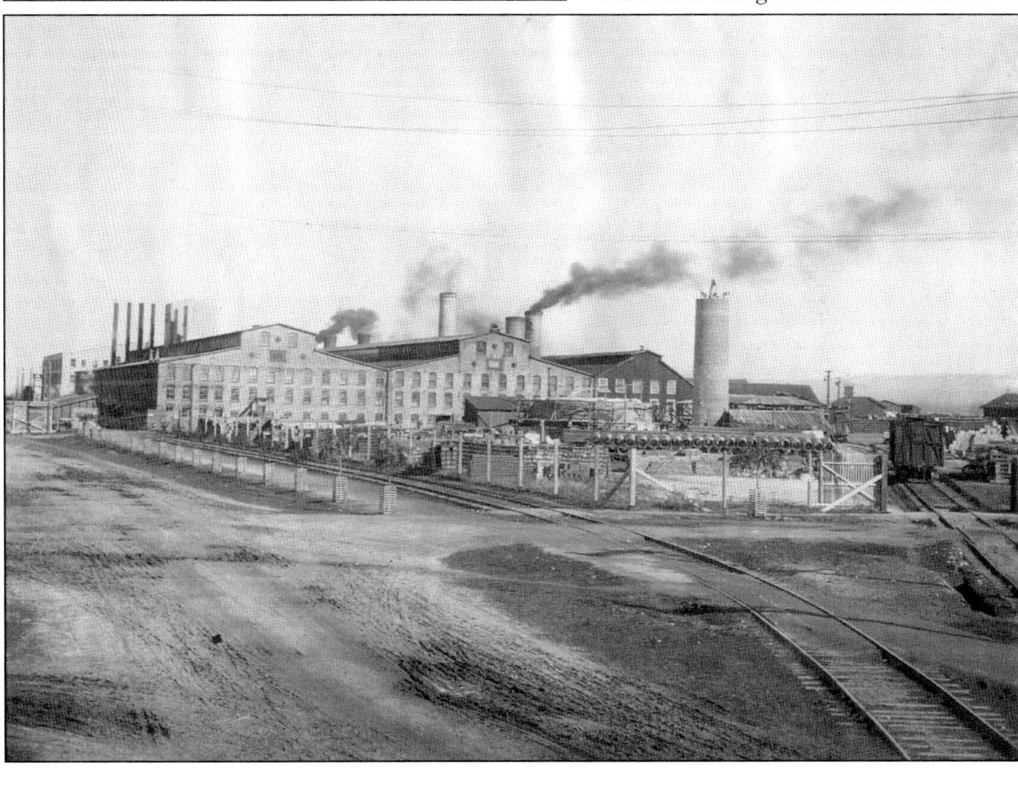

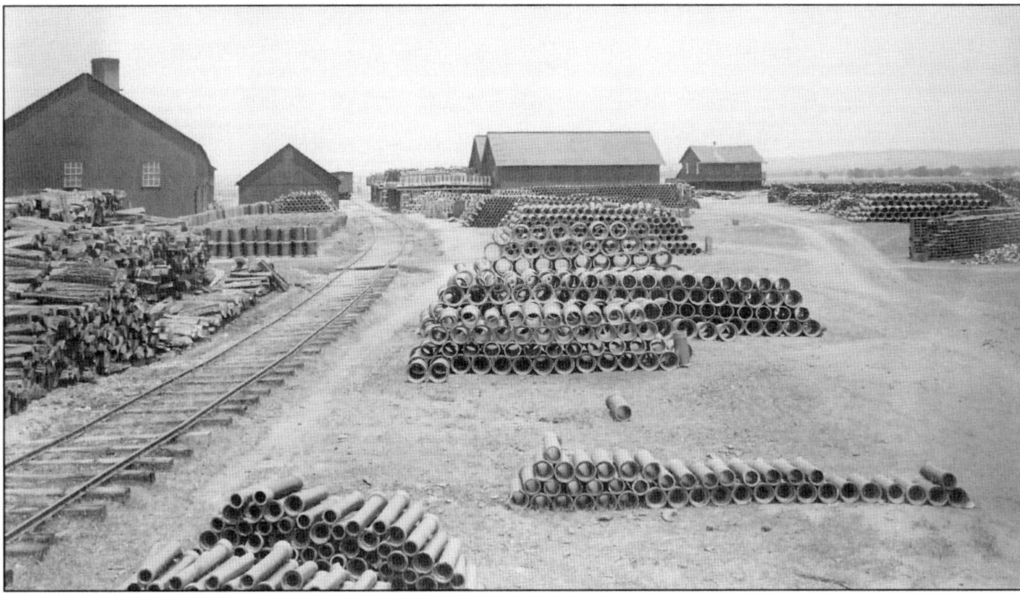

This 1890 photograph of Gladding, McBean shows the rail line into the pottery and stacked, finished pipe ready for shipment. Pipe and other Gladding, McBean products were shipped all over the United States. The stacks of wood on the left side of the tracks were used to fuel the trains coming in and out of the pottery and to fire the kilns.

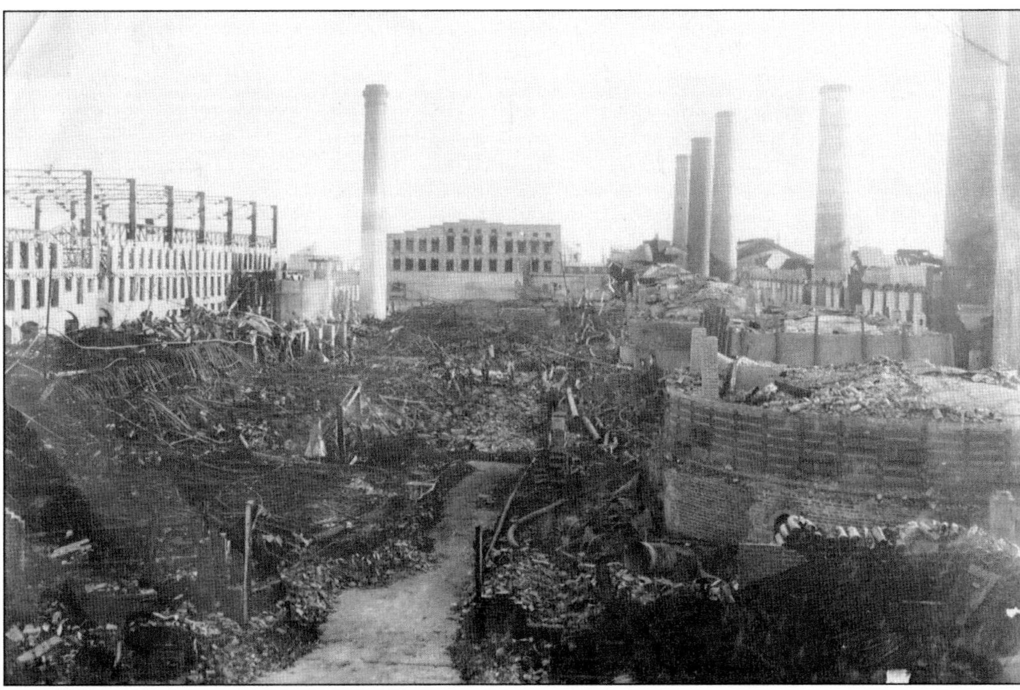

In 1918, fire struck Gladding, McBean and destroyed much of the pottery. Here, workers are using horse-drawn wagons to go through the wreckage and salvage what could be reused. The company immediately rebuilt using fireproof materials, including concrete and clay building blocks that it manufactured.

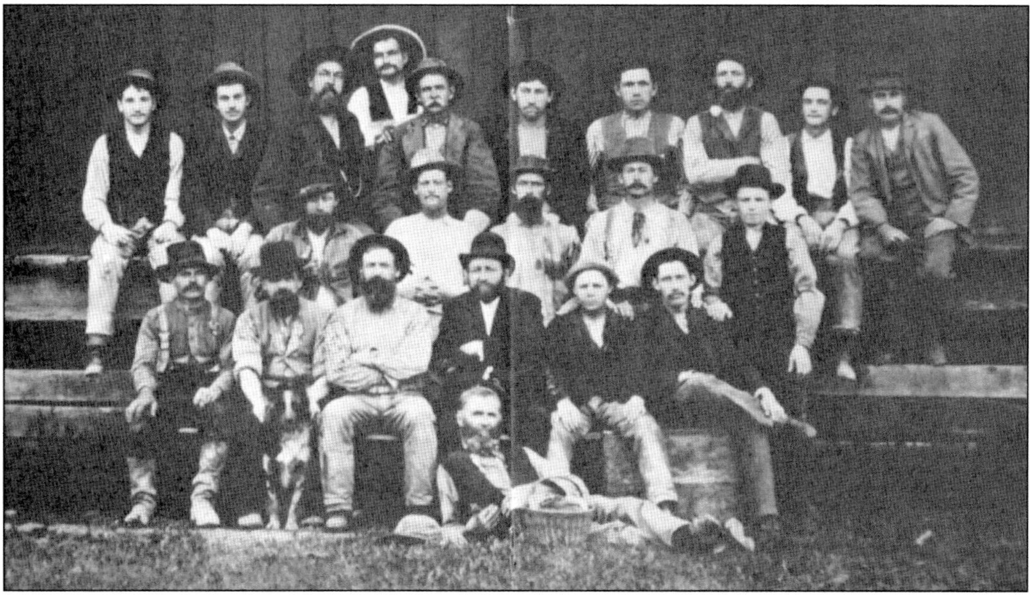

When Gladding, McBean started in 1875, the company had 22 employees, pictured here. The men are, from left to right, (first row) three unidentified, E.O. Matthews, unidentified, and ? Hotchkiss; (second row) John Goy, ? Walker, unidentified, H.P. Sartain, and unidentified; (third row) three unidentified, Will Allen, C.C. Sanders, Will Elder, Frank Cook, unidentified, Grant Allen, and Albert Gladding. The man reclining on the grass is unidentified.

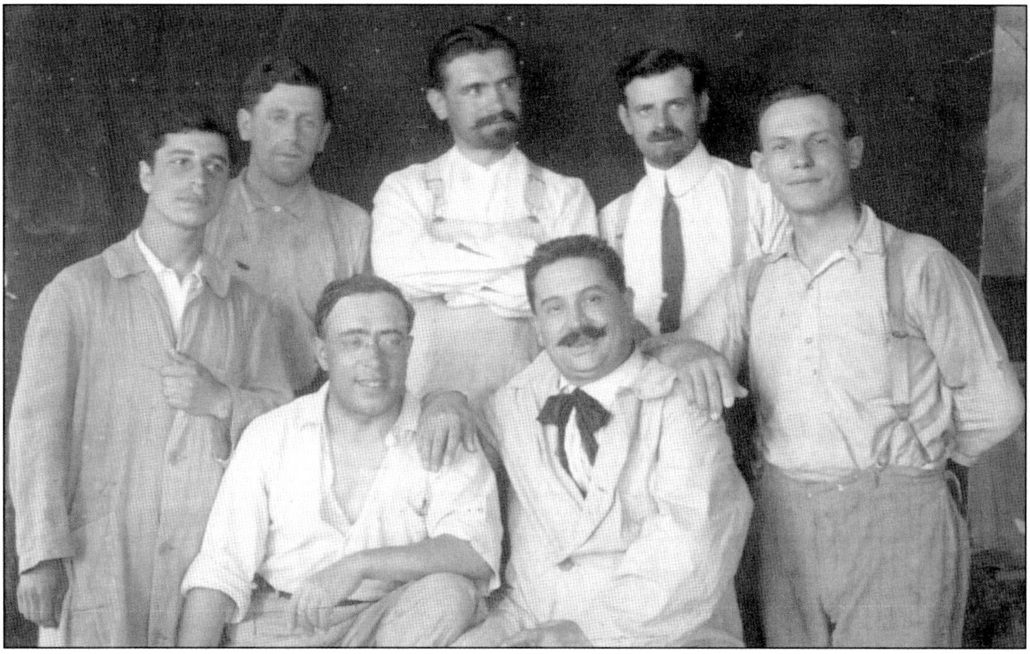

These artists and sculptors are pictured at Gladding, McBean. The man on the left in the front row is Pio Tognelli, and Ernest Kadel is standing at far right with his arm on the shoulder of the sitting man with the mustache; the others are unidentified. Tognelli was a renowned sculptor and modeler from Florence, Italy. He joined Gladding, McBean in 1909 and was appointed chief modeler in 1912.

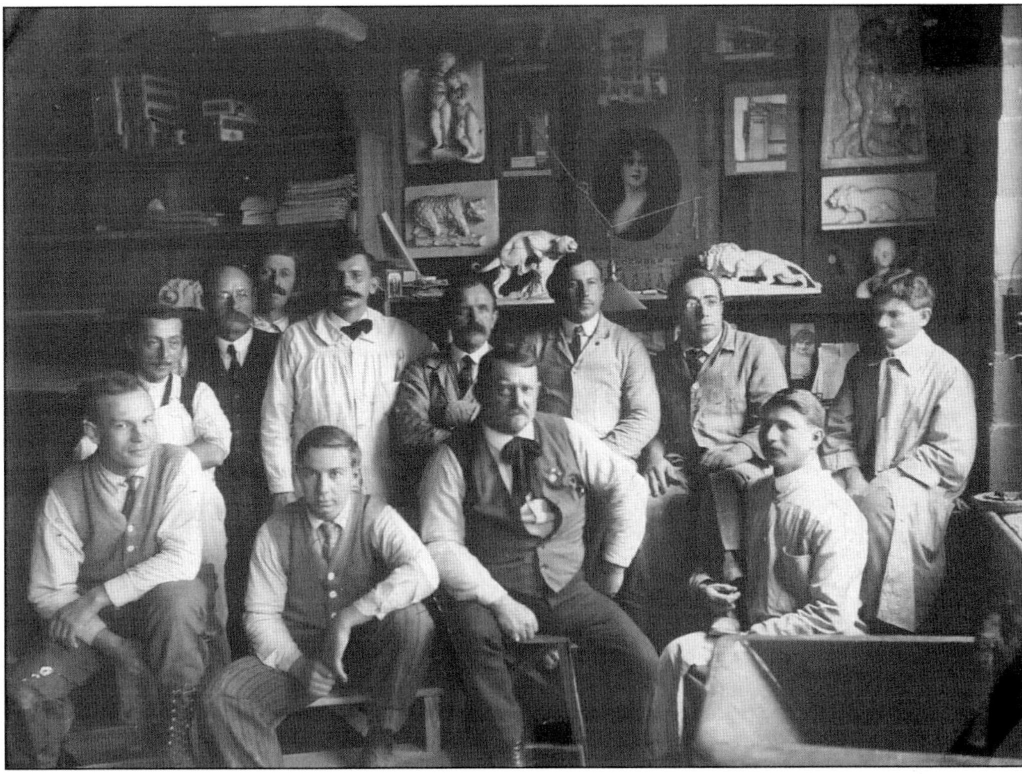

After Pio Tognelli moved his family to San Francisco in 1923 to open a private studio, he continued to direct the sculptural and architectural work of Gladding, McBean for several years. His successor was Ernest Kadel, from Germany, who also became a legend at the pottery and served until his death in 1959. This group of artists and sculptors are pictured in Kadel's office.

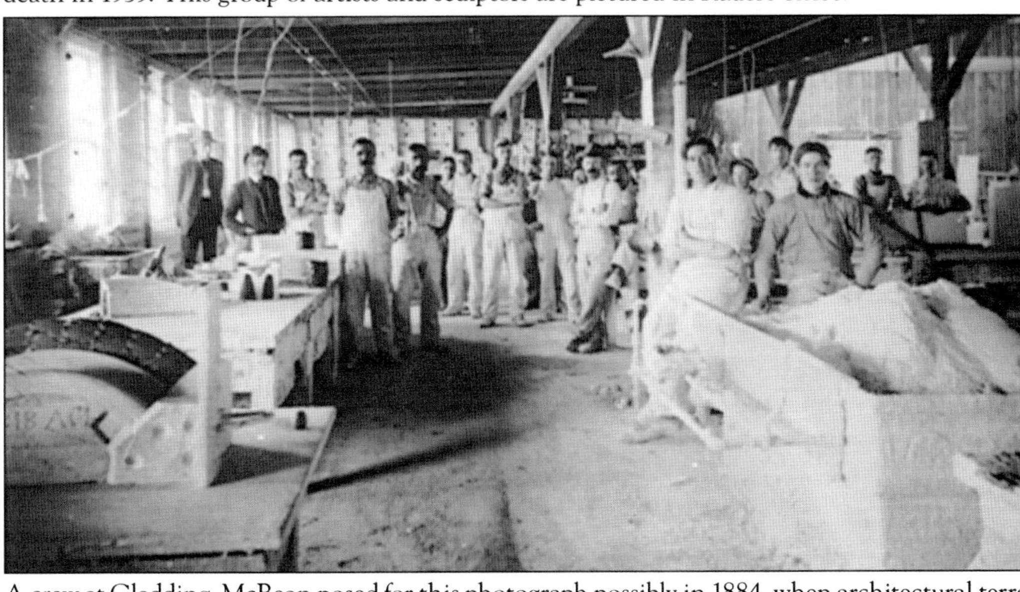

A crew at Gladding, McBean posed for this photograph possibly in 1884, when architectural terra cotta was added to the company's product line. Architectural terra cotta was requested from all over the United States and can still be seen on many buildings today.

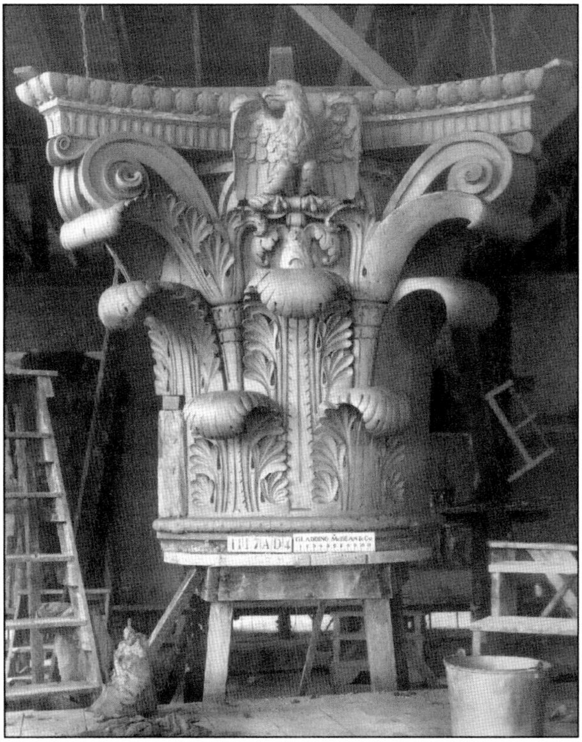

This piece of architectural terra cotta is the top portion of a column that was created in 1914 for the Fireman's Fund Building in San Francisco. Gladding, McBean not only made new designs based on drawings provided by clients, they also offered replacement pieces for buildings that had been damaged.

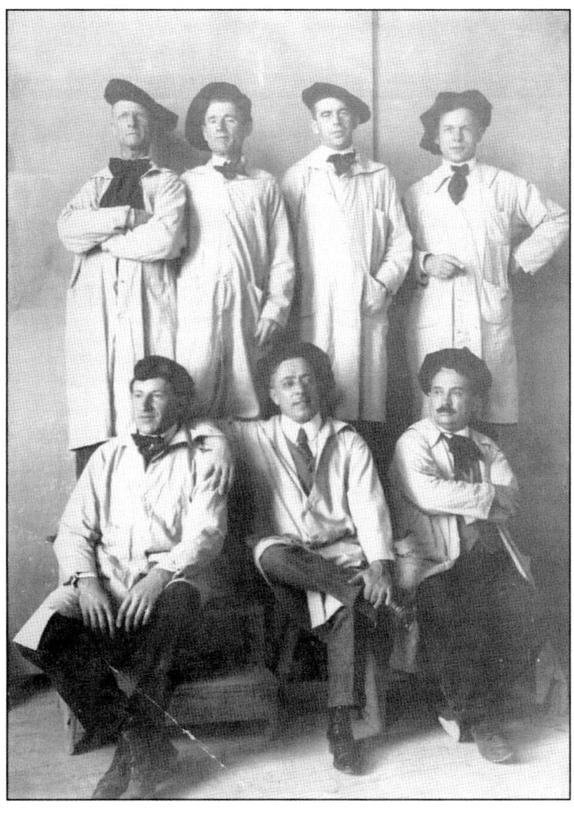

The skilled labor in the Gladding, McBean modeling department had to be of the highest quality. As a result, most of the sculptors that first worked at Gladding, McBean came from Italy. The head of the department was frequently a true sculptor who was familiar with every style of architectural ornament.

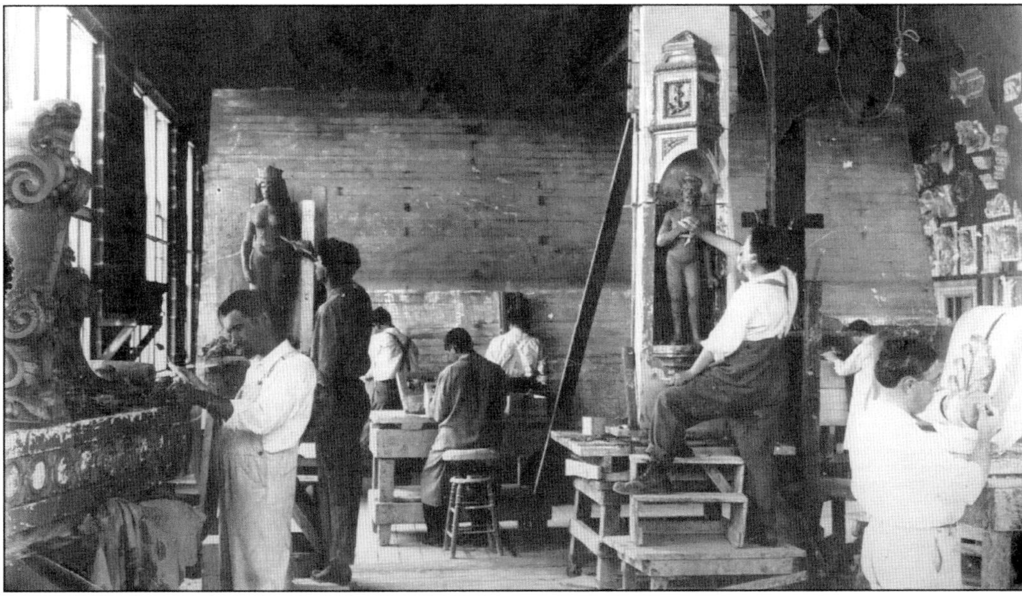

A group of Italian sculptors at Gladding, McBean are shown working in clay on various types of models and architectural pieces. This work was all done by hand by the talented sculptors. After a sculptor completed a model, the company then made a plaster mold of it in order to create reproductions.

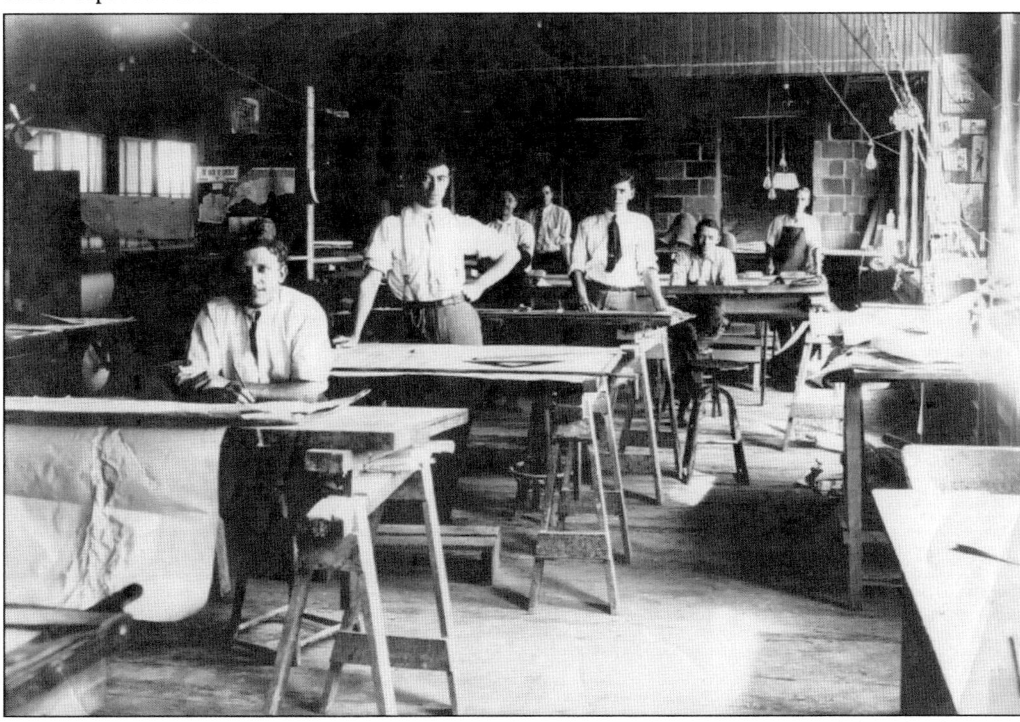

The drafting department was an integral part of developing the terra cotta models. The drawings had to show the size of every anchor, its attachment to the piece with the necessary aperture, and the attachment to the frame. After scale drawings were sent to the architect for approval, the drafting department created full-size drawings to be used by the modelers and molders.

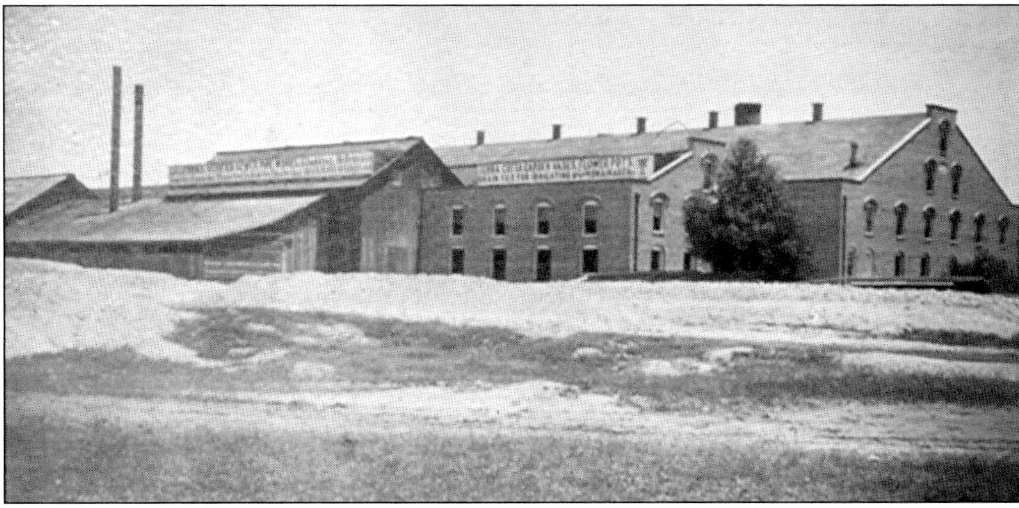

The home office in San Francisco, which includes a warehouse, is advertised on a sign on the side of a Gladding, McBean building in Lincoln. The sign reads "California Vitrified Sewer Pipe Works at Gladding, McBean & Company off Market Street in San Francisco." The back building advertises terra cotta garden vases, flowerpots, and drain tile for irrigation and land drainage.

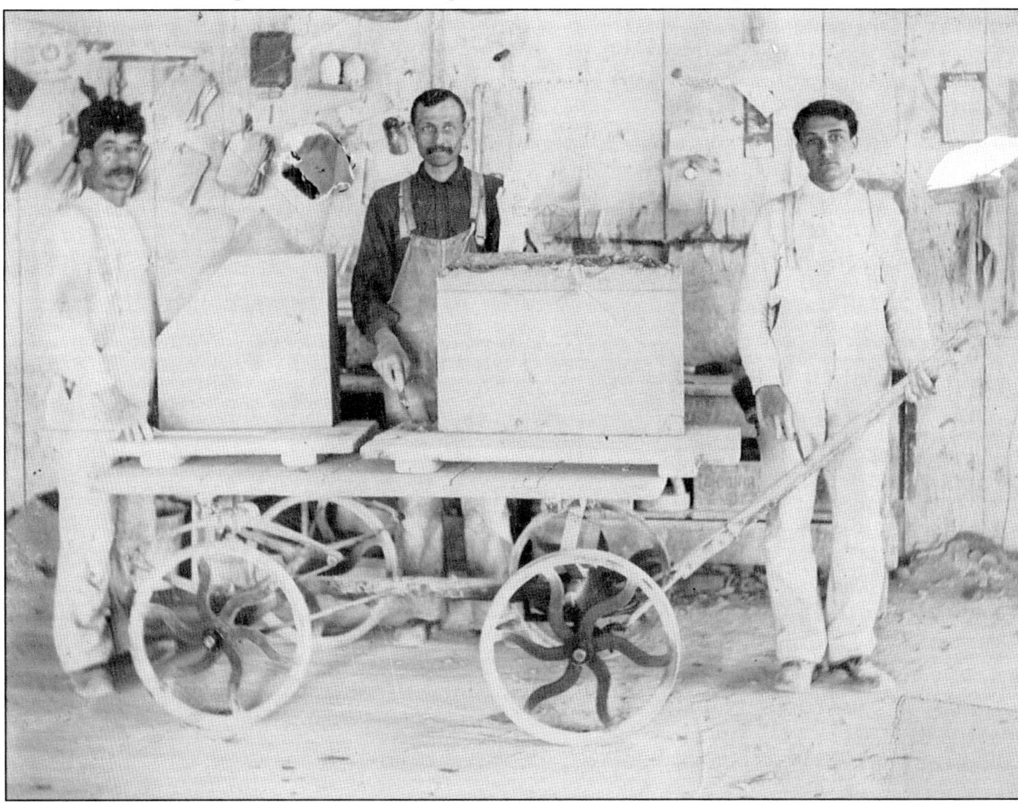

Three unidentified workers at Gladding, McBean use a wooden cart to move heavy molded sculptures to the next step in the curing process. Sculptures were unmolded, put in a drying room and dried, then fired in kilns. Workers then applied various paint for finishes before the pieces were fired again.

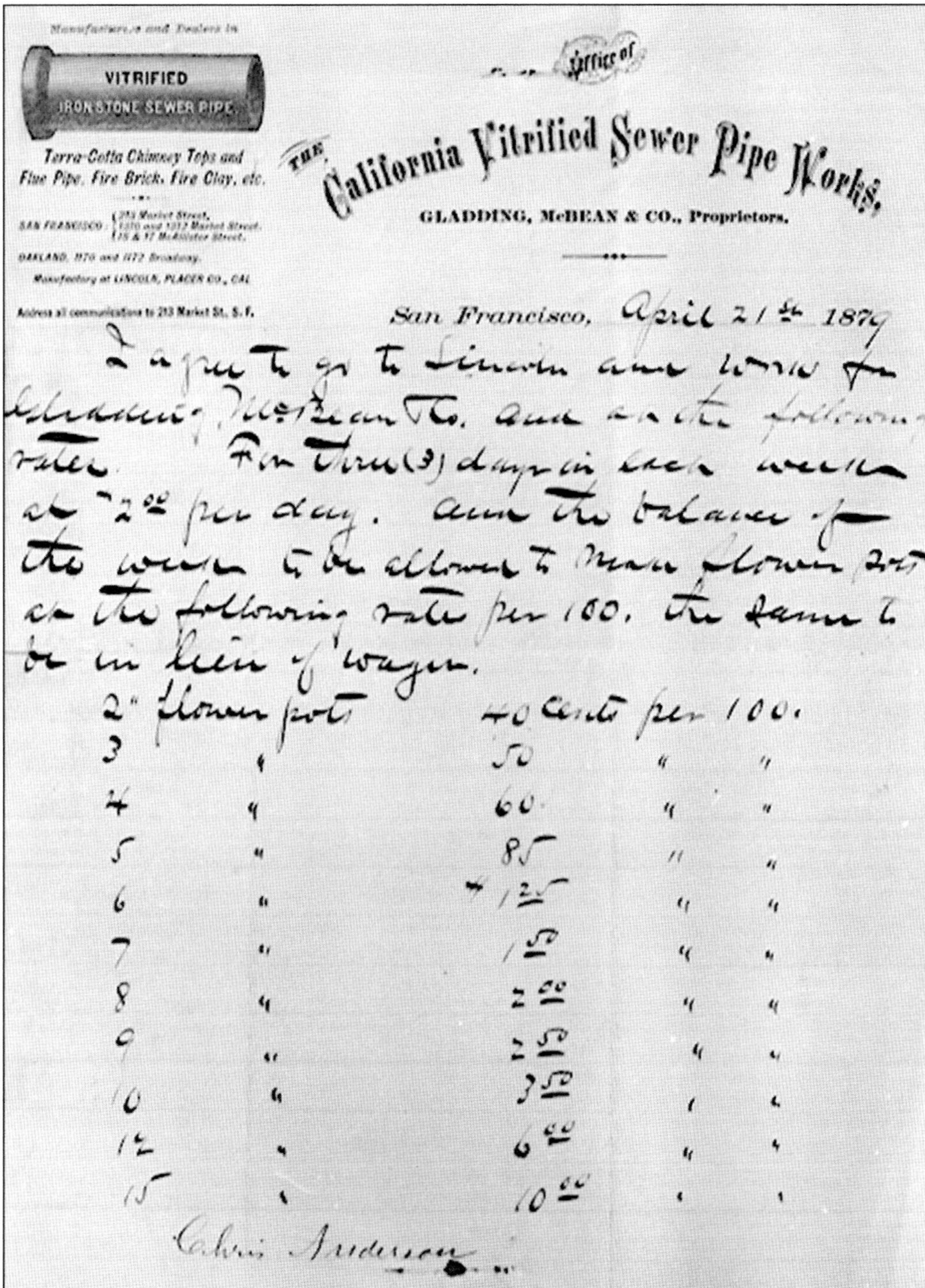

Manufacturers and Dealers in

VITRIFIED IRONSTONE SEWER PIPE.

Terra Cotta Chimney Tops and Flue Pipe, Fire Brick, Fire Clay, etc.

San Francisco: 213 Market Street, 1310 and 1312 Market Street, 15 & 17 McAllister Street.

Oakland, 1170 and 1172 Broadway.

Manufactory at Lincoln, Placer Co., Cal.

Address all communications to 213 Market St., S.F.

Office of

The California Vitrified Sewer Pipe Works,

GLADDING, McBEAN & CO., Proprietors.

San Francisco, April 21st 1879

I agree to go to Lincoln and work for Gladding McBean & Co. and at the following rates. For three (3) days in each week at $2.00 per day. and the balance of the week to be allowed to make flower pots at the following rate per 100. the same to be in lieu of wages.

2" flower pots	40 cents	per	100.
3 "	50	"	"
4 "	60	"	"
5 "	85	"	"
6 "	1.25	"	"
7 "	1.50	"	"
8 "	2.00	"	"
9 "	2.50	"	"
10 "	3.50	"	"
12 "	6.00	"	"
15 "	10.00	"	"

Chris Anderson

This is a Gladding, McBean work contract signed by Chris Anderson on April 21, 1879. This gentleman was listed as a potter from Denmark. The contract says: "I agree to go to Lincoln and work for Gladding, McBean for the following rates. For three (3) days in each week at $2 dollars per day. And the balance of the week to be allowed to make flower pots at the following rate per 100. The same to be in lieu of wages: 2 flower pots 40¢ per 100, 3 flower pots 50¢ per 100, 4 flower pots 60¢ per 100, 5 flower pots 85¢ per 100, 6 flower pots $1.25 per 100, 7 flower pots $1.50 per 100, 8 flower pots $2 per 100, 9 flower pots $2.50 per 100, 10 flower pots $3 per 100, 12 flower pots $6 per 100, 15 flower pots $10 per 100."

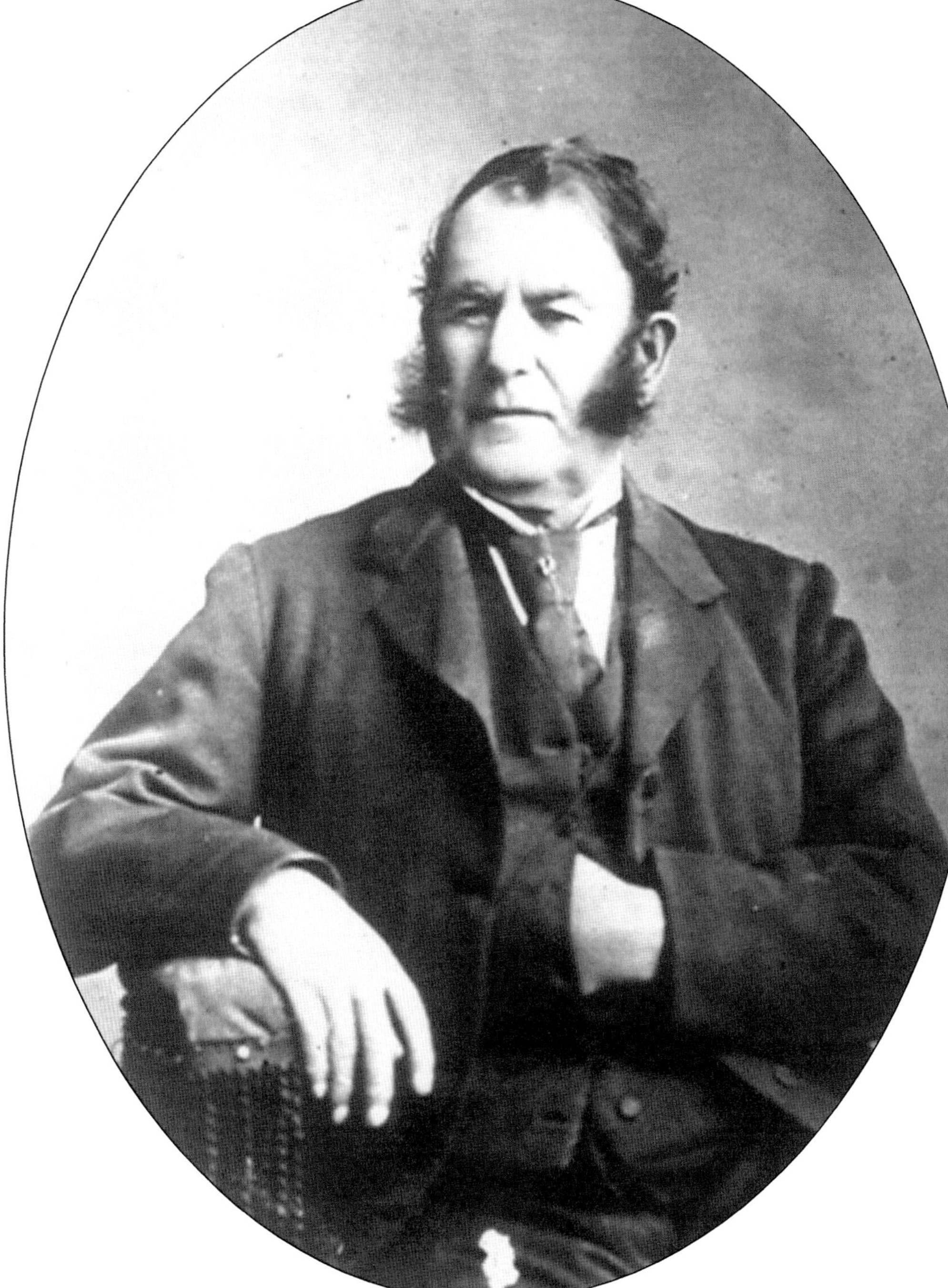

Charles Gladding, the principal founder and president of Gladding, McBean, was in the clay business in San Francisco for 25 years prior to the discovery of clay in Lincoln. He invented and received a patent for a new and improved stoneware kiln while in Lincoln. Gladding died in Rome, Italy, in January 1894. Upon Gladding's death, Peter McBean became president, and Albert J. Gladding, Charles Gladding's son, became vice president.

Albert Gladding came to Lincoln with his father, Charles, in 1875 and took an active role in creating the nucleus of the Gladding, McBean business. Albert started from the bottom and worked his way up, spending time in the different departments and learning all about the manufacturing of architectural terra cotta, tile, and brick. This work allowed him to gradually assume management of the pottery.

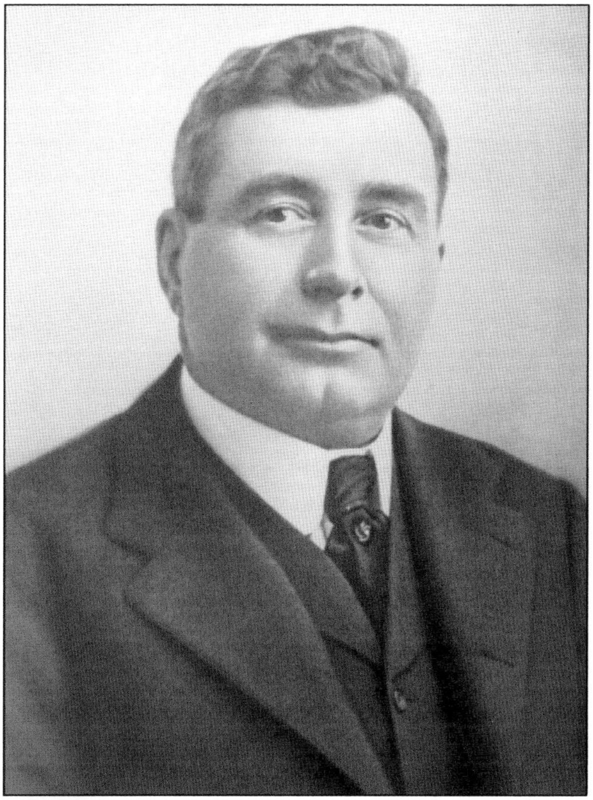

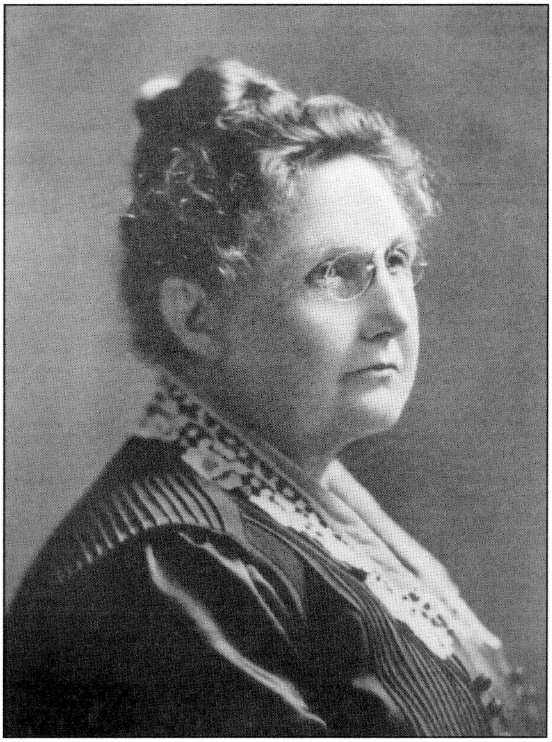

Carrie Chandler and Albert Gladding married in 1883 and had 10 children who were born and raised in Lincoln. The children attended Lincoln schools, and all attended college. The boys served in various capacities at Gladding, McBean, including as superintendent and working in the office. Carrie was very interested in education and served as a member and clerk of the board of trustees for Lincoln grammar schools. She was active in the great Frances Willard movement for temperance and served as president of the Woman's Christian Temperance Union for Western Placer.

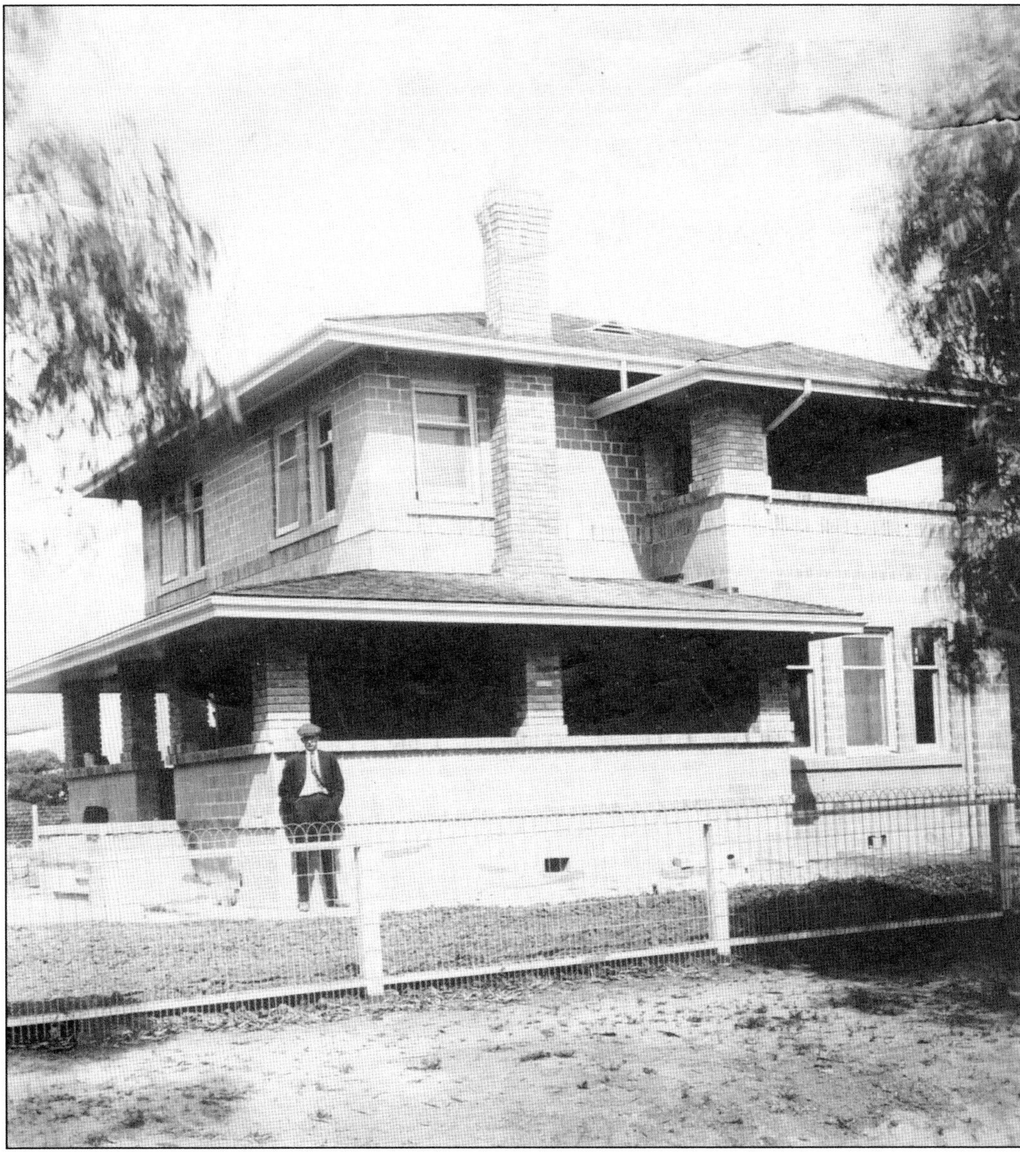

Two homes on Seventh Street in Lincoln were built for Gladding family members. Charles Gladding built this house for his wife, Sarah, and their daughter, Flora, in 1878. The Gladdings were originally from Chicago and were quite the "city girls"—they even considered Oakland a "hick town." Both women despised Lincoln and its then-unpaved streets, lack of high society and entertainment, and the dusty, smoky wood-burning kilns at the pottery just across the street. Charles soon bought a home in San Francisco and worked out of the San Francisco office, leaving the Lincoln pottery almost completely in his son Albert's hands. This house still stands.

Four

Ranches and Farms

Gold, copper, and coal dwindled in importance as Lincoln settlers began to realize that the area's real mother lode was agriculture. In 1845, Theodore Sicard planted and harvested wheat south of Bear River. Claude Chana noticed that pits of dried fruits brought from the East were being discarded. After gathering what they could, Chana and Sicard planted the pits, along with almonds Chana had been saving. In 1848, the men planted apple and pear seeds, plum pits, and 200 grape cuttings from Mission San Jose. Everything grew well, and the men realized that high profits could be gained from selling fruit, vegetables, and wine to miners and early settlers.

Coon Creek attracted the earliest farmers in the Lincoln area. Christian Kier settled near there in 1846, and Cornelius Quinn arrived in 1849. Stock raising and farming soon became more important in the area than mining. Quinn, the first to sow and harvest grain in the Coon Creek area, soon became a wealthy rancher with herds ranging as far as the site on which Lincoln was built. Quinn later formed a partnership with Paul Cox (Cox and Quinn) to operate ranches east of McCourtney Road along Coon Creek.

Many other settlers who arrived in the 1850s and 1860s started ranches and farms. An advertisement in 1864 announced the sale of J.P. Dameron's ranch: "140 acres under cultivation, 25 acres of hay, 150 head of fat cattle, horses, 2,000 bushels of barley, 1,500 bushels of wheat, 40 tons of hay." The settlers built large homes on these properties, and the ranches and farms were often passed down through generations.

James R. Nickerson's ranch on Doty Ravine was a showplace of early agriculture. Nickerson cultivated hundreds of varieties of fruits and grapes there. In 1863, area ranches with the largest assessed value included those of Joseph Walkup (Auburn Ravine), Titus Ewing (Coon Creek), Thomas Chamberlain (Coon Creek near Manzanita Cemetery), and Jonathan Mariner (Coon Creek and Dowd Road). By 1892, Western Placer's largest ranches were owned by J. Parker Whitney, William Kaseberg, Elizabeth Jane Atkinson, Peter Ahart, J.S. Mariner, James French, and Christian Kier.

Lincoln area ranch and farm products were very familiar to early California State Fair patrons. In 1869, the Chamberlains won a medal for the best 500-acre grain farm in California. Nickerson won wine and fruit awards in 1871. In 1872, fair honors went to E.J. Sparks for wheat and Joshua Reeves for livestock.

These early beginnings of Lincoln area agriculture created a foundation for an industry that still thrives today.

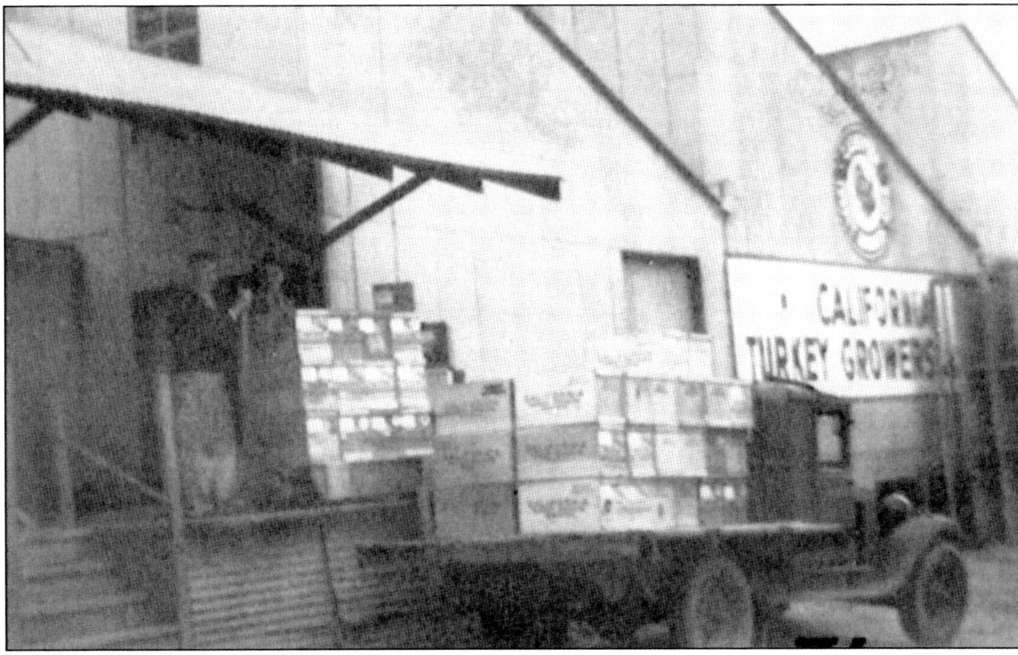

Turkeys were plentiful in the area in the 1860s. Ralph B. Aitken was one of the first in the area to gather turkeys off the range and raise them in brooder pens. Several ranches arose near Lincoln and east of Sheridan. In 1871, turkeys sold for $1 or $2 each. In 1874, a turkey plague wiped out flocks on the ranches east of Sheridan, but many were spared, and turkey ranching became big business in Lincoln.

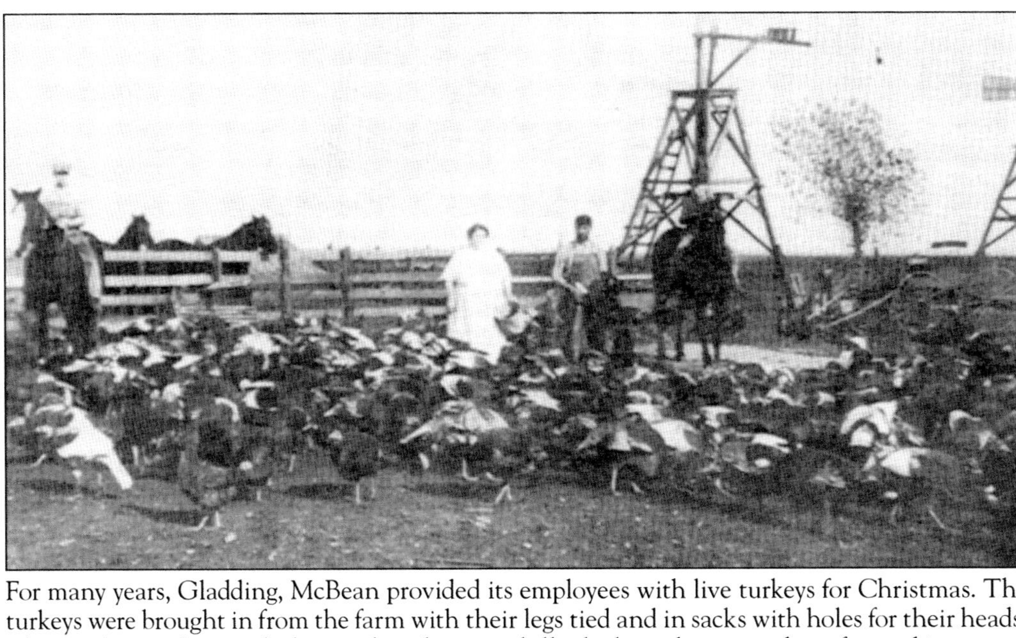

For many years, Gladding, McBean provided its employees with live turkeys for Christmas. The turkeys were brought in from the farm with their legs tied and in sacks with holes for their heads. The employees then took their turkeys home to kill, pluck, and prepare them for cooking.

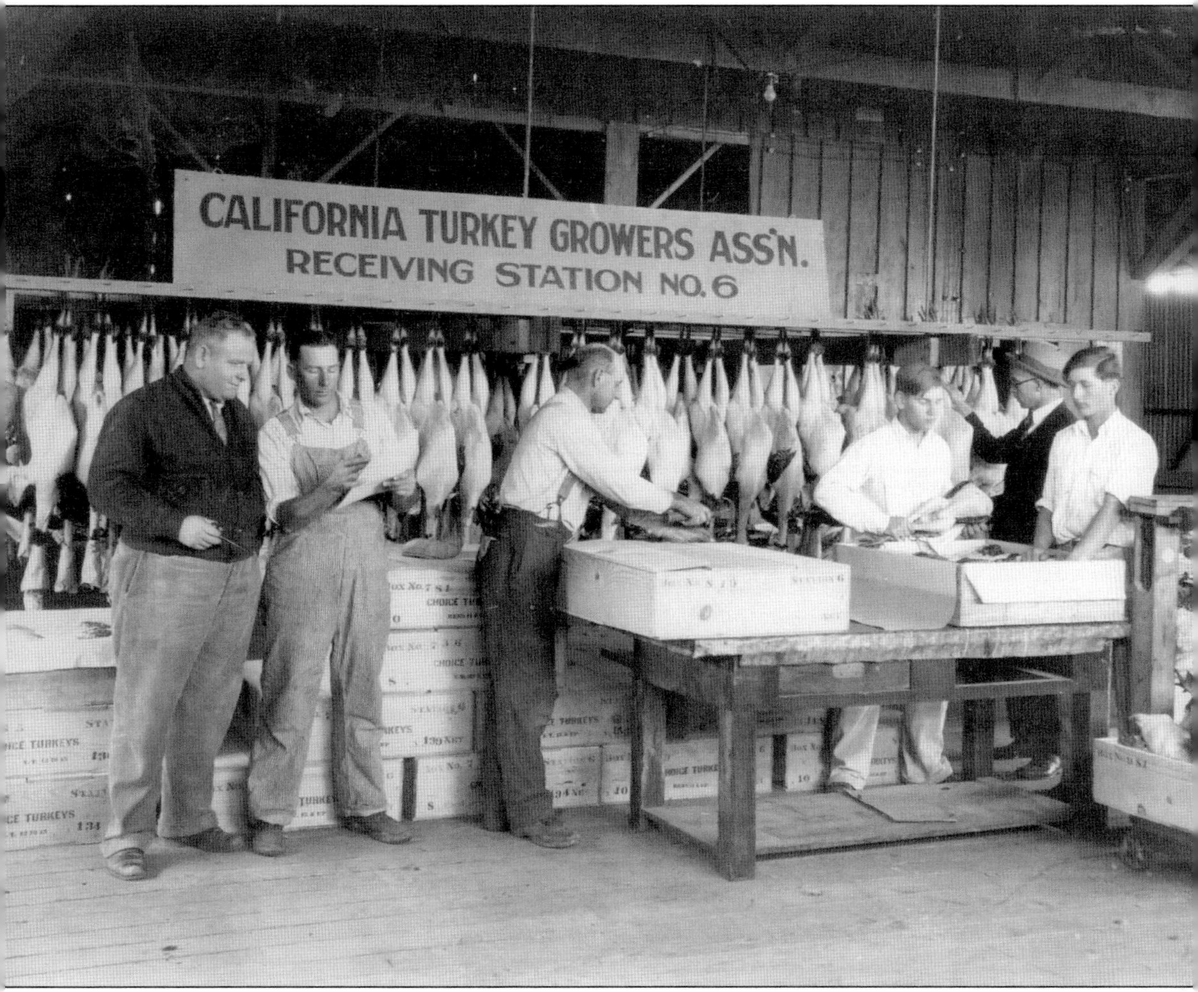

In 1929, a turkey-packing house was established in the old Stuart Fruit Company building just south of the southeast corner of Seventh and H Streets, near the grain elevator. Two railroad carloads of processed turkeys were shipped for Christmas that year. In later years, the California Turkey Growers Association took over Lincoln's turkey-packing business.

BOYDEN'S DAIRY

ED. BOYDEN, Proprietor

Quarts, $2 per month. Pints, $1 per month

First Consideration: Cleanliness, Phone Farmer's 21x4

Lincoln has been home to many retail dairies and creameries over the years. Some were located within the city limits, and others were nearby, but all did business in Lincoln. In August 1915, Ed Boyden established a dairy at his farm on Moore Road (currently the Scheiber Ranch). Ed's father was Lincoln pioneer Allen G. Boyden, and his sister "Pet" Boyden married Charles Lincoln Wilson Jr., son of Lincoln's founder. Ed Boyden's milk house was constructed of modern tile and publicized as perfectly sanitary. The 1916 Boyden's Dairy advertisement above lists his monthly prices. Another business, the Lincoln Dairy, operated from 1913 through at least 1931 with many different owners. The below photograph shows Murle Parscale (left) and Noble Ballou on one of the dairy's delivery trucks. Some other local dairymen included M. Costa, the Culbertson brothers, Paul Ferrari, J.D. Logan, the Scheiber brothers, and Frank Schuler.

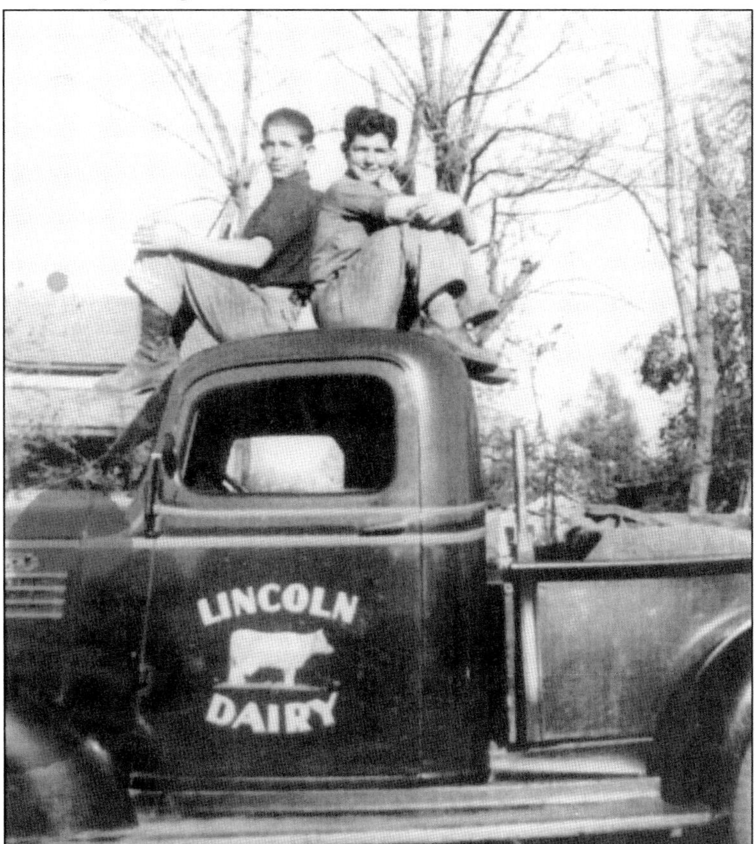

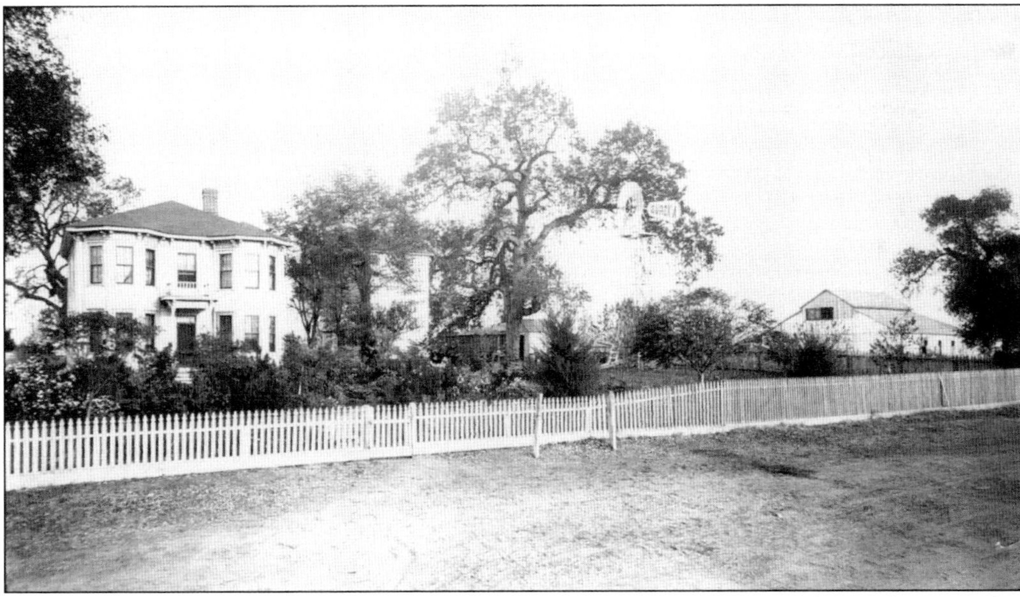

After leaving Wales in 1852 as a child, Catherine Reese and her family crossed the Atlantic, sailing up the Mississippi River before setting out in covered wagons toward California. Her youngest brother died during the trip and was buried along the trail. In California, Catherine married J.B. Brown, from Virginia, and they built a two-story home on Pioneer Lane (now Leavell Lane) along Auburn Ravine in Lincoln. They raised a family of six children on this family farm.

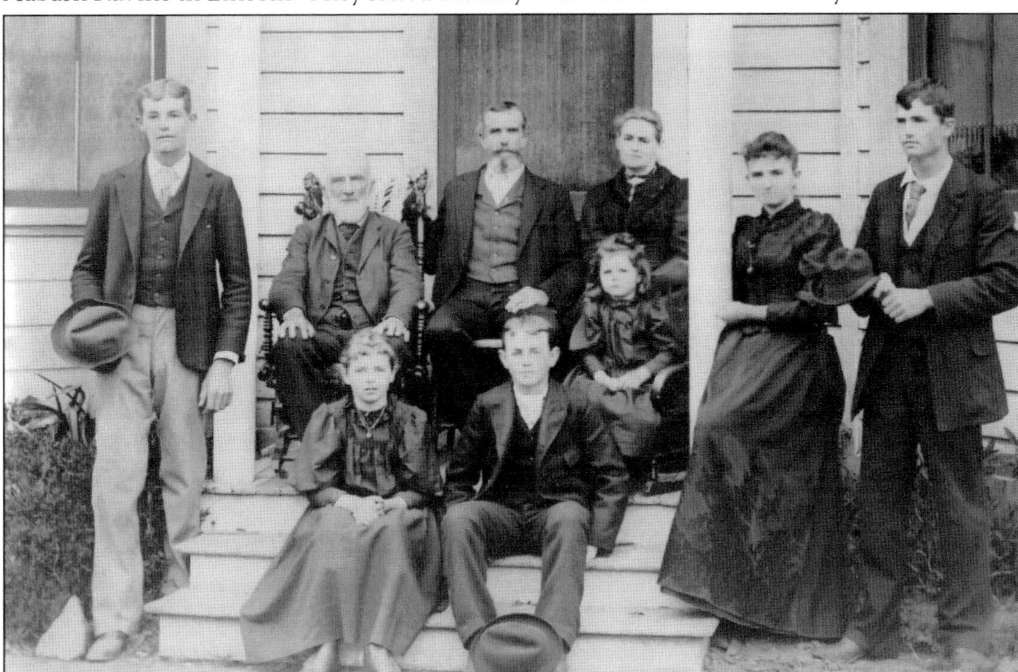

The J.B. Brown family gathers for a photograph in front of their farmhouse east of Lincoln on present-day Leavell Lane and Highway 193. Pictured are, from left to right, (first row, seated on the steps) Jessie Jane and Fred; (second row) George Brown, Fleming Trig Brown, J.B. Brown, Catherine (little Ora is in the chair in front of her), Mame, and Lloyd.

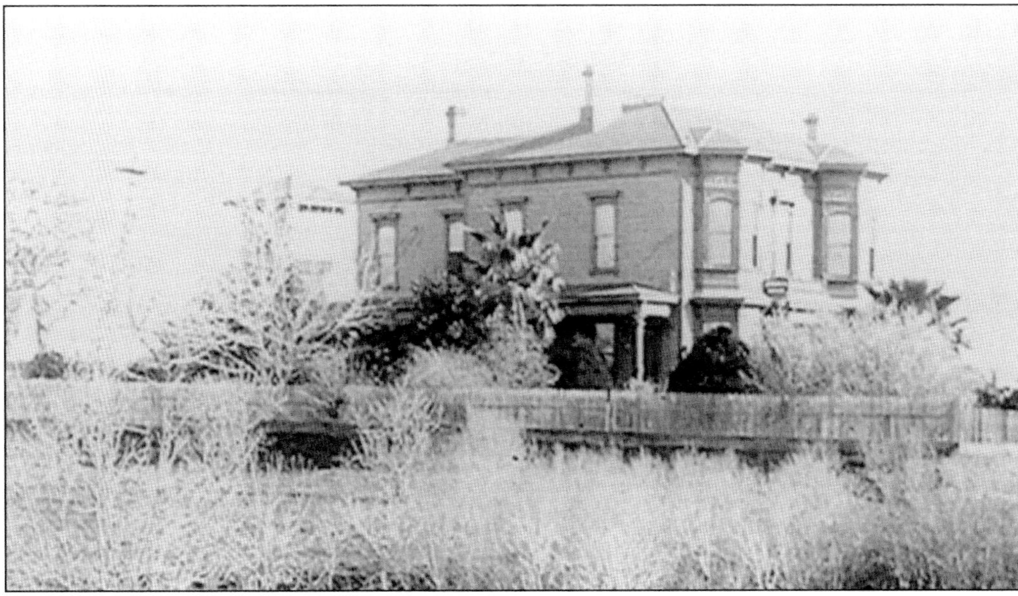

Christian Kier came to California in 1846 and was one of the earliest settlers in the Lincoln area. The Kier home was located at the present-day intersection of McCourtney and Fleming Roads. By the late 1850s, a small town that developed in the area was called Daneville, since many of the farmers in the area were Danes.

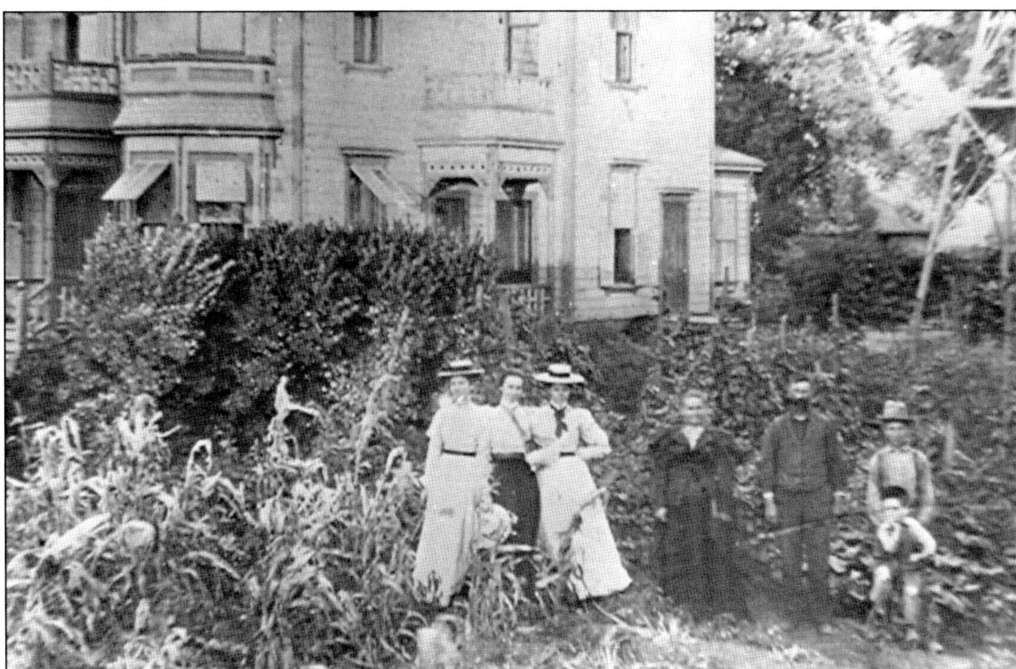

Just after 1900, Melville Lawrence and Harry Comstock purchased the old Kier ranch. Locals soon referred to it as the Comstock Ranch, although its official name was the Oakwood Stock Ranch. It was most famous for the thoroughbred racing horses raised and trained there, then shipped all over the United States. In 1942, Harley and Foryst Hutchinson bought the 1,274-acre site, and their family still owns the property.

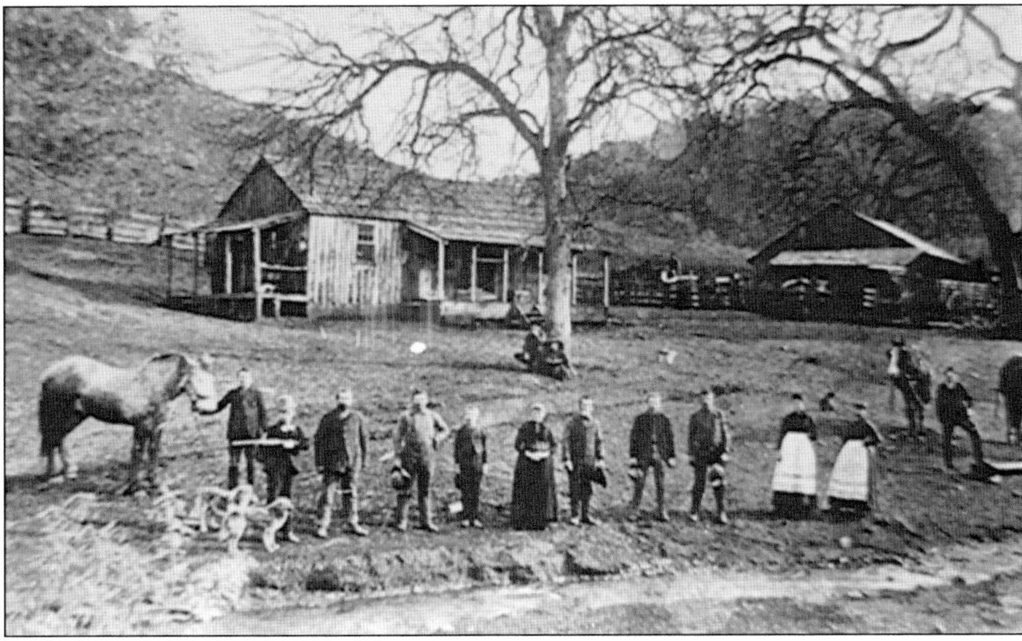

This is the Robert Tofft Sr. family home. As a sailor, Tofft emigrated from Denmark to San Francisco in 1850. He found his way to Sacramento and eventually landed in Daneville. He helped John Ziegenbein build a store at the corner of Fifth and G Streets in Lincoln and also worked for Christian Kier as a foreman. Tofft went back to Denmark for his wife and son and, in 1865, settled on this 120-acre ranch near the Whiskey Diggings mine.

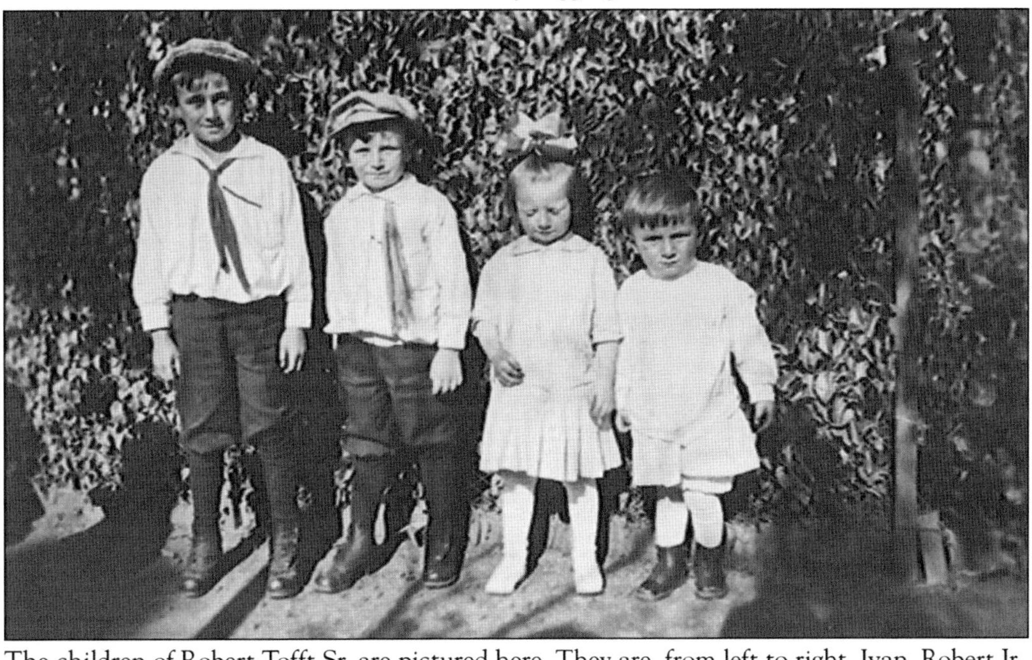

The children of Robert Tofft Sr. are pictured here. They are, from left to right, Ivan, Robert Jr., Jean, and Jack. Robert Jr. married Anna Maria Kier in 1881. Anna Maria's parents were early Daneville settlers Christian and Johanna Kier. Johanna was the daughter of William and Maria Ziegenbein and the sister of John Ziegenbein, Lincoln's first entrepreneur.

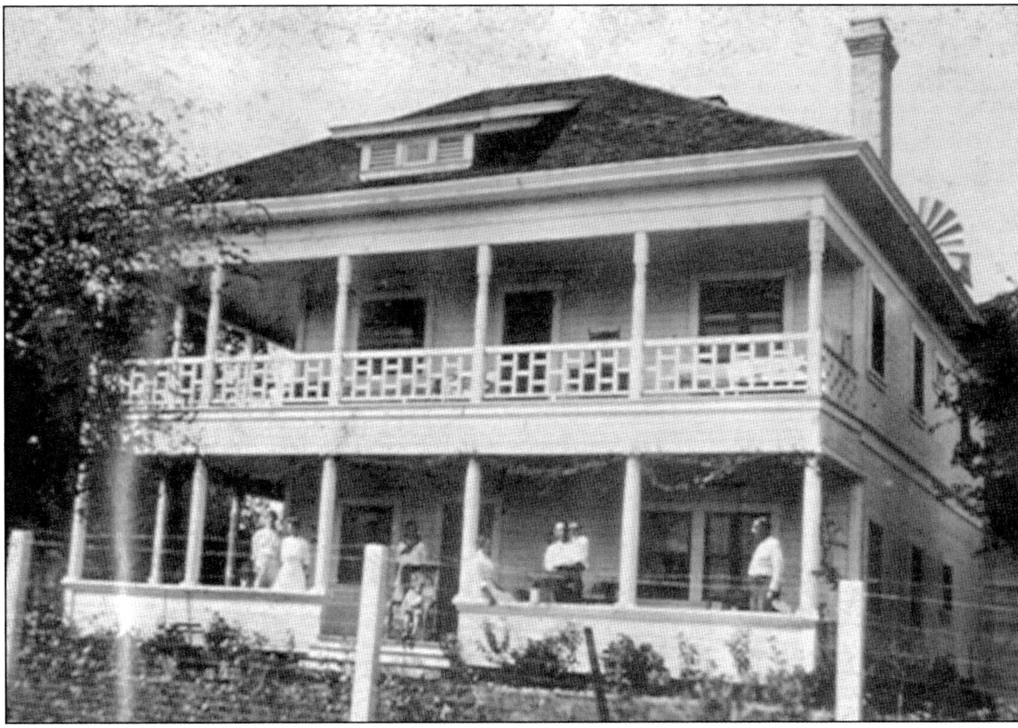

This August 22, 1915, photograph shows the Joel Fowler home on Fruitvale Road. The home was near the Fruitvale School and was set back from the road. Joel's wife was named Vera, and the Fowler family were the benefactors of the land for the Fruitvale School.

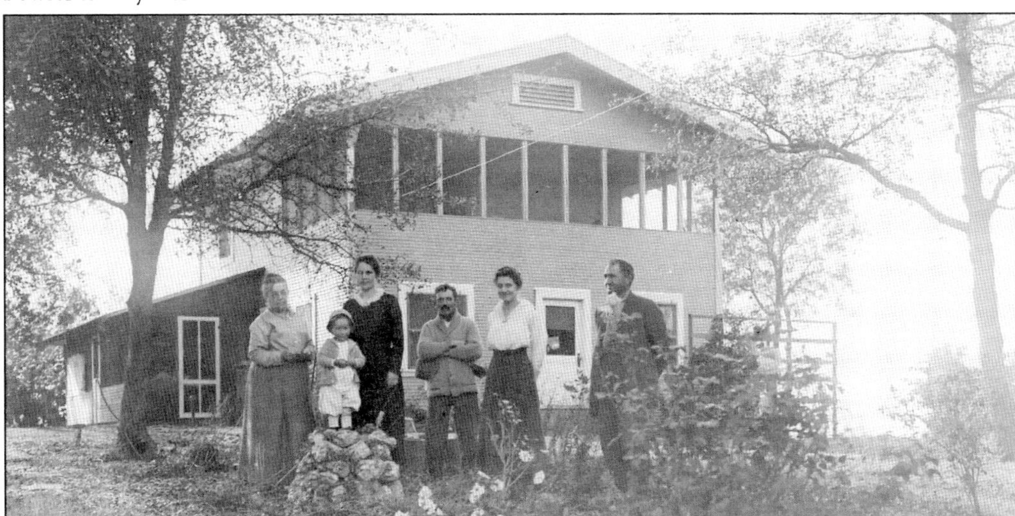

Jeremiah and Elizabeth Fowler came around Cape Horn in 1849. Robert Eugene Fowler, of Fowler's Nursery on Fowler Road, and Herbert Fowler, on Godley Road, are descendants of Jeremiah. Frank Herbert, Jeremiah and Elizabeth's son, married Isabella (Belle) Fagg in Lincoln in 1884. She was the daughter of George Fagg, a pioneer settler in the Fruitvale/Gold Hill area. This is a photograph of the Fowler home on Virginiatown Road, which still stands today. Belle Fagg Fowler is on the far left.

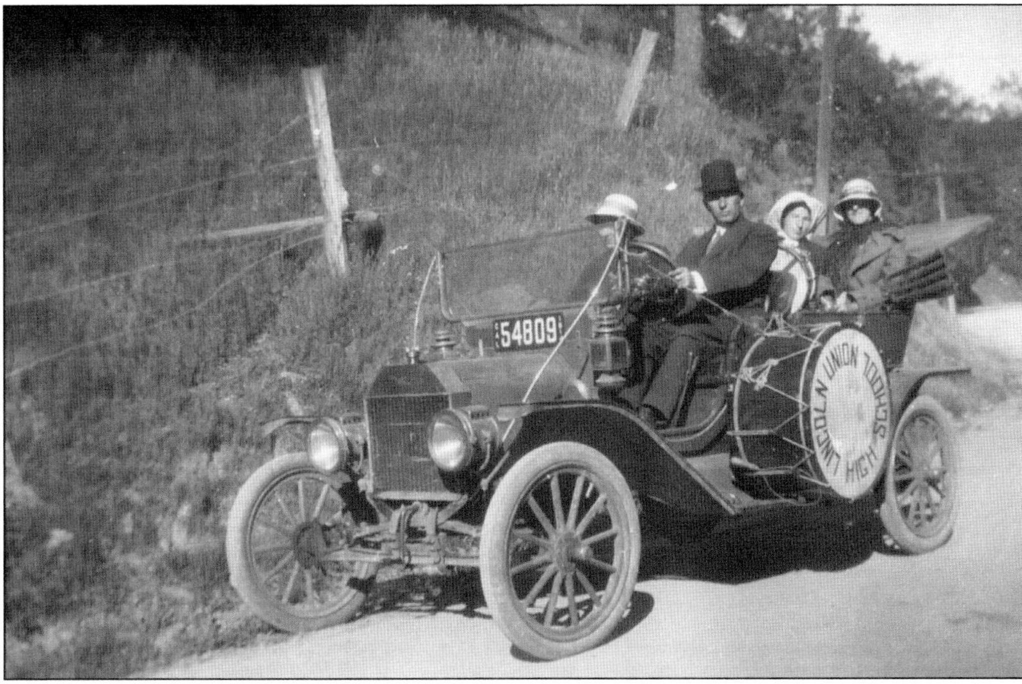

In this 1914 photograph, Eugene Fowler (Robert Eugene's father) is behind the wheel. He always drove a Dodge "machine." Eugene married Myrtle Maring. Myrtle's grandparents, Nicholas and Marie, natives of France, came from Ohio in 1851 and mined in the Ophir/Gold Hill area, where they soon established a fruit ranch. Myrtle's father, Albert Maring, also operated the successful ranch. Eugene managed the Silva-Bergthold Nursery, which became the Fowler Nursery in 1912.

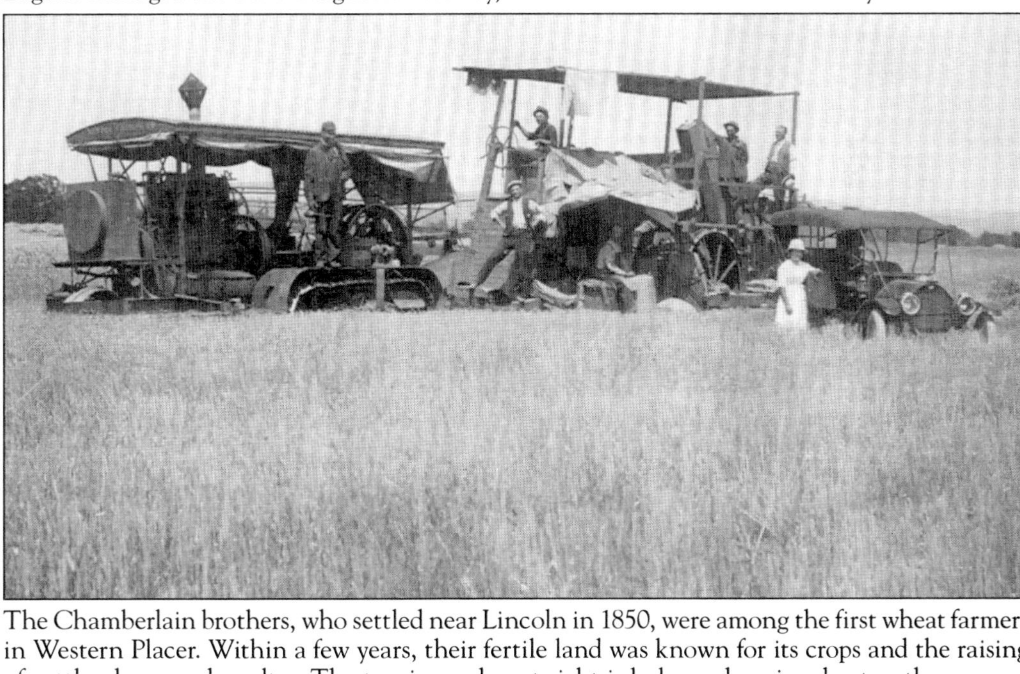

The Chamberlain brothers, who settled near Lincoln in 1850, were among the first wheat farmers in Western Placer. Within a few years, their fertile land was known for its crops and the raising of cattle, sheep and poultry. The touring sedan at right is hubcap-deep in wheat as the men on the Chamberlain ranch take a break from work on the thresher.

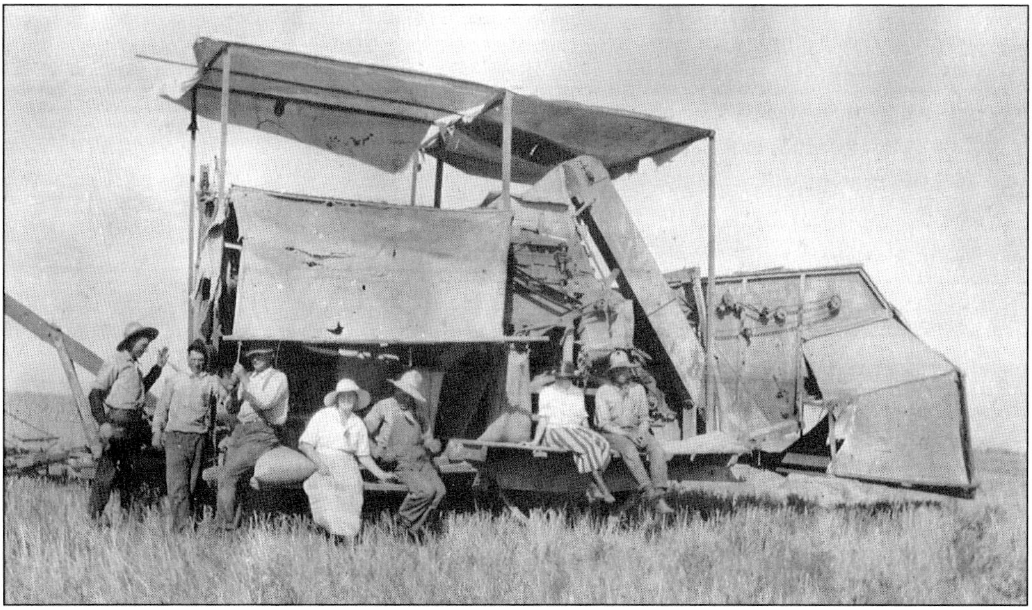

David McCartney, born in Ireland in 1864, came to Western Placer via Canada in 1883. He began work on the well-known Whitney Ranch south of Lincoln, and was the foreman by 1890. In 1895, he left the ranch and began farming 960 leased acres on his own, then expanded to 3,000 acres of grain. He bought part of the Reeves Ranch and raised cattle, horses, mules, and turkeys. Taking a break from harvesting are, from left to right, Ted McCartney, two unidentified, Jessie Dillian, Dee McCartney, unidentified, and Wilson McCartney.

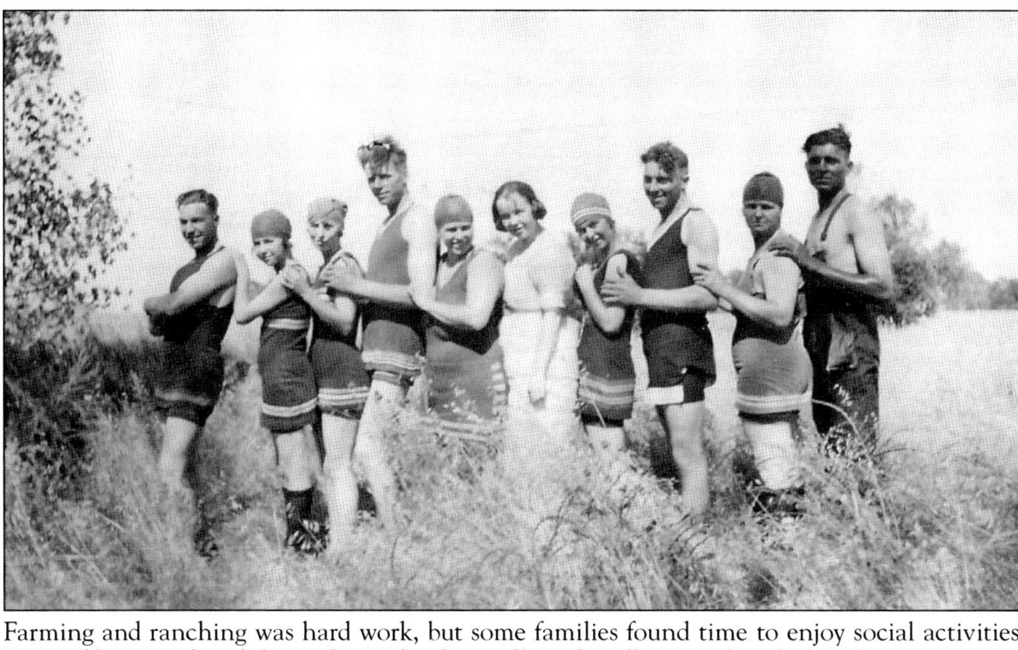

Farming and ranching was hard work, but some families found time to enjoy social activities. Pictured here are, from left to right, Richard Leavell, Freda Dillian, unidentified, Wilson McCartney, unidentified, Mary French, Ora Dillian, Ted McCartney, Jessie Dillian, and Dee McCartney. This photograph was taken in the early 1920s at Coon Creek, north of town.

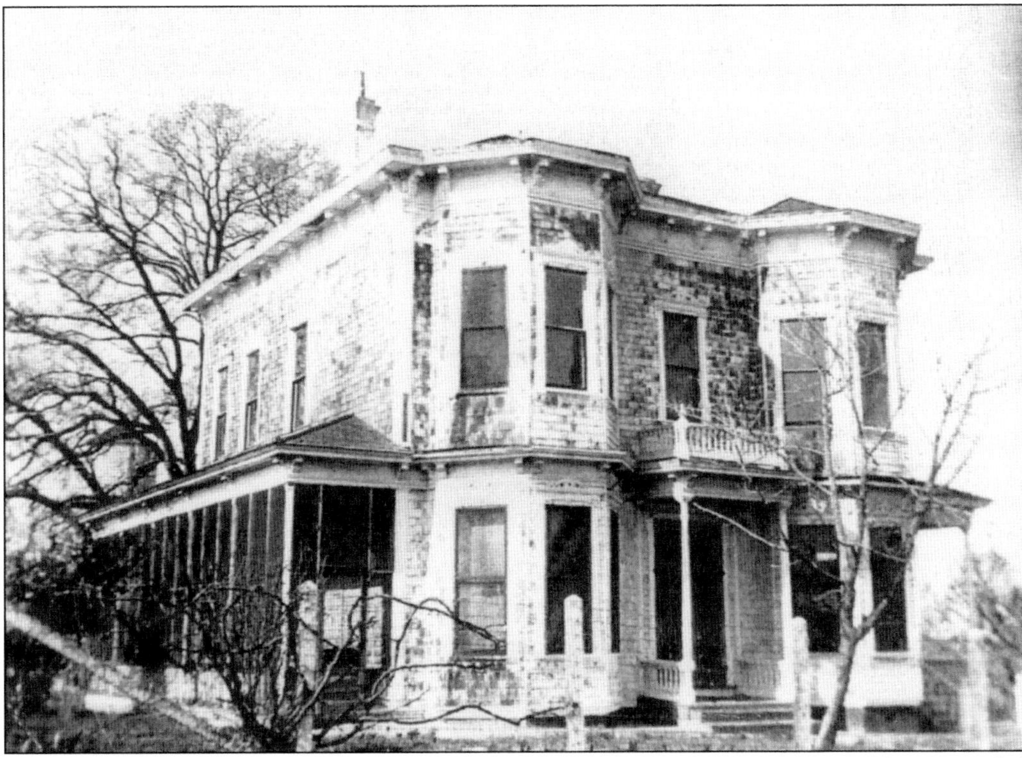

This photograph shows the Albert Gladding house many years past its prime, after it was left vacant. Gladding was interested in agriculture and in the late 1890s purchased the 1,400-acre ranch on Coon Creek that once belonged to E.J. Sparks. Gladding produced grain, stock, and fruit. He was also active in the city of Lincoln; as one of the founders (in 1902) and president of the Bank of Lincoln, he worked to get Lincoln incorporated. He was a leader in organizing the Lincoln Union High School and a member of the first board of trustees. A new high school was built in 1907 during his tenure as trustee.

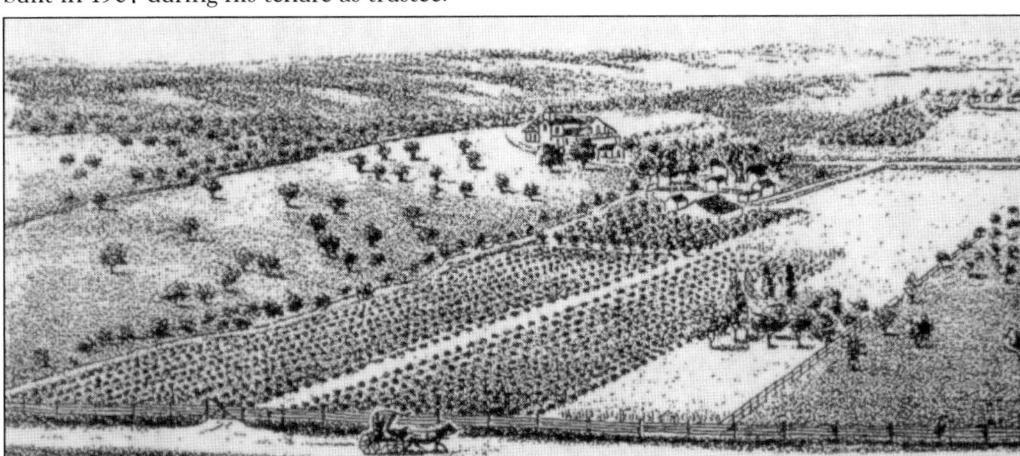

This is a drawing of the James R. Nickerson Ranch—located on Doty's Ravine, three miles northeast of Lincoln—as it looked in 1852. As mentioned in the introduction, Nickerson's first-rate vegetables, fruits, and wines were well known and highly sought. The Ragsdales are descendants of James Nickerson.

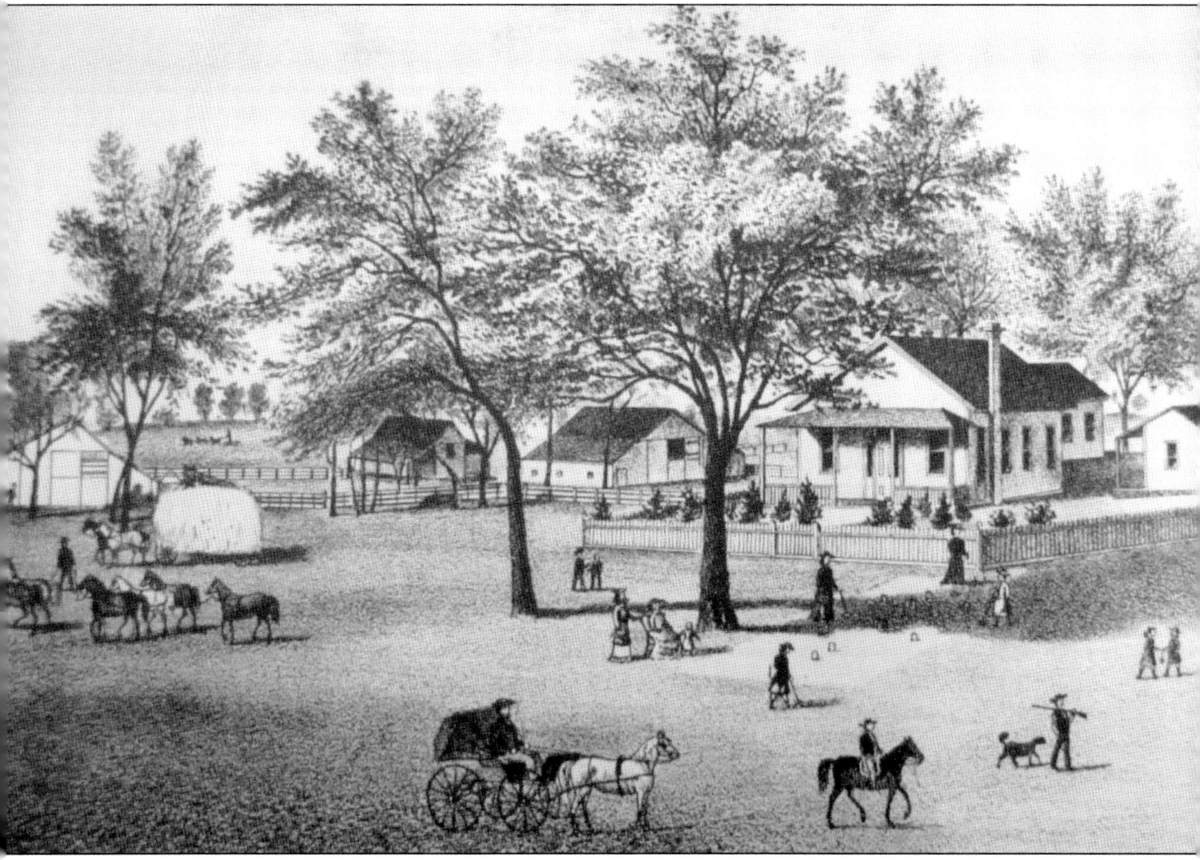

Peter Ahart came to California in 1852 and successfully engaged in mining until 1857, when he bought the ranch depicted here. For years, he pursued the business of raising and dealing in cattle, then turned his attention to sheep. Some Ahart descendants continue to raise sheep and cattle on the land he purchased. He married Ursula Prudence Ragsdale, daughter of William B. and Sarah W. Ragsdale.

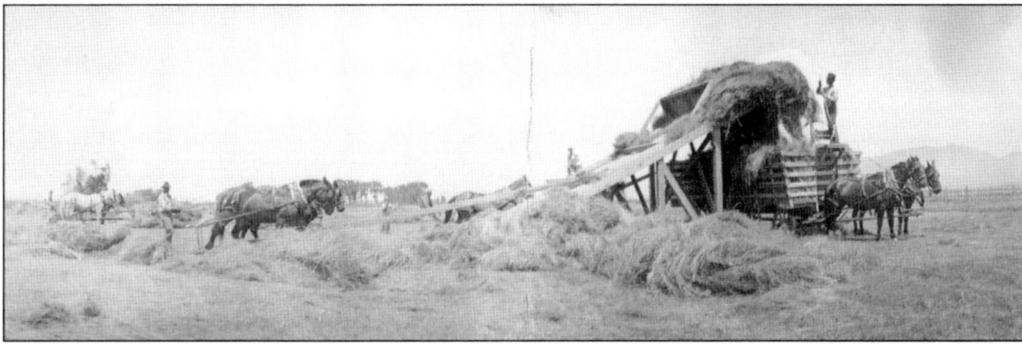

The Maloney ranch was started by James Maloney Sr., who came to the area in the 1860s. He was born in 1842 in Ohio. In 1888, Maloney was listed in the *Placer Herald* as being one of the major wheat producers in Western Placer. His son Charles was also a rancher and a trustee for the Central School District. These men are harvesting wheat on the Maloney ranch.

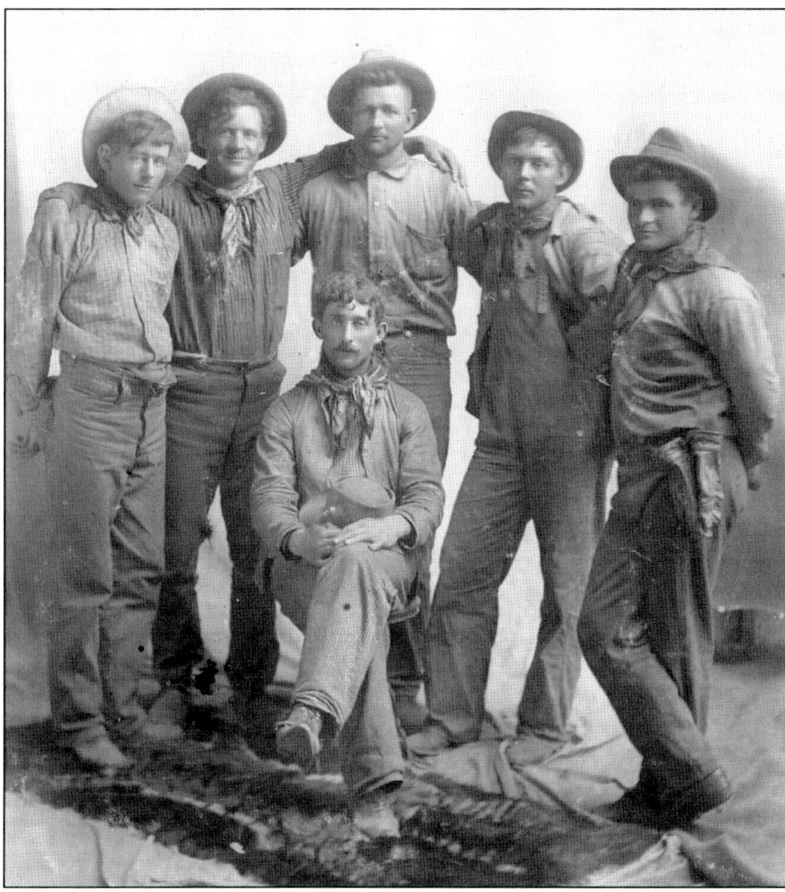

Charles Maloney was born in Lincoln in 1885 and was the father of Vivian (Maloney) Ahart. Vivian married Tom Ahart, combining two of Lincoln's pioneer families. The rancher sitting among his fellow workers is an unidentified member of the Maloney family.

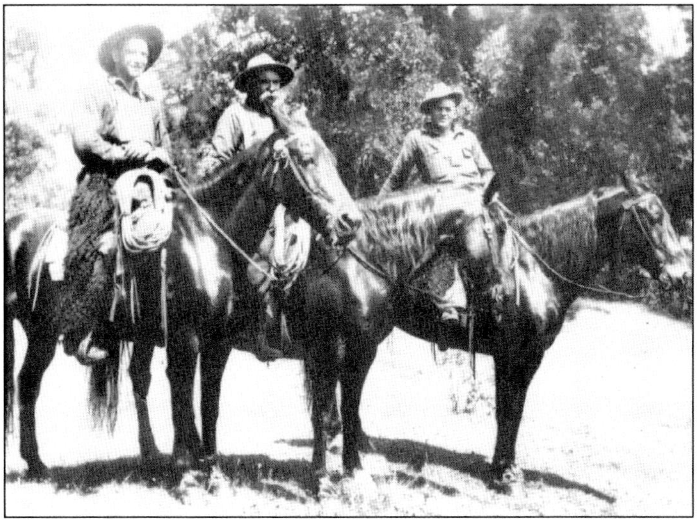

The riders in this 1919 photograph are Harold or Hal "Buck" Murch (left), George Cirby (center), and Lloyd "Dusty" Reeves. Lloyd Reeves was descended from Joshua Reeves and Margaret Purcell. Joshua Reeves was born in Ohio in 1829 and came to the Gold Hill area to mine. Margaret arrived in the 1850s with her parents. By the 1880s, Joshua Reeves had 1,400 acres of land and was one of the top five wheat producers in the county.

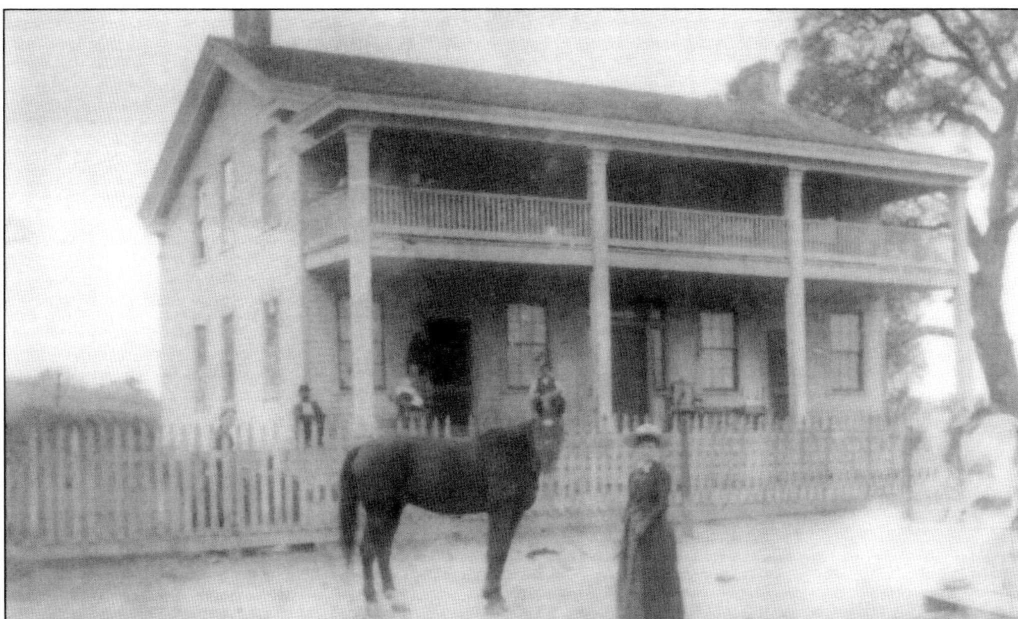

Oliver Perry Richardson came to California in 1850 with his wife, Sally, and in 1864 the family settled in Coon Creek. They bought a ranch that included the famous Colonial House, a wayside inn on McCourtney Road that was a social center in the 1850s and early 1860s. One of the Richardson's 12 children, Mattie (standing by the horse), married Walter Wiswell, and they operated the large ranch for many years. Their descendant Robert Wiswell Jr. is the fifth generation of the family to live on the property. The Colonial House burned down in 1890.

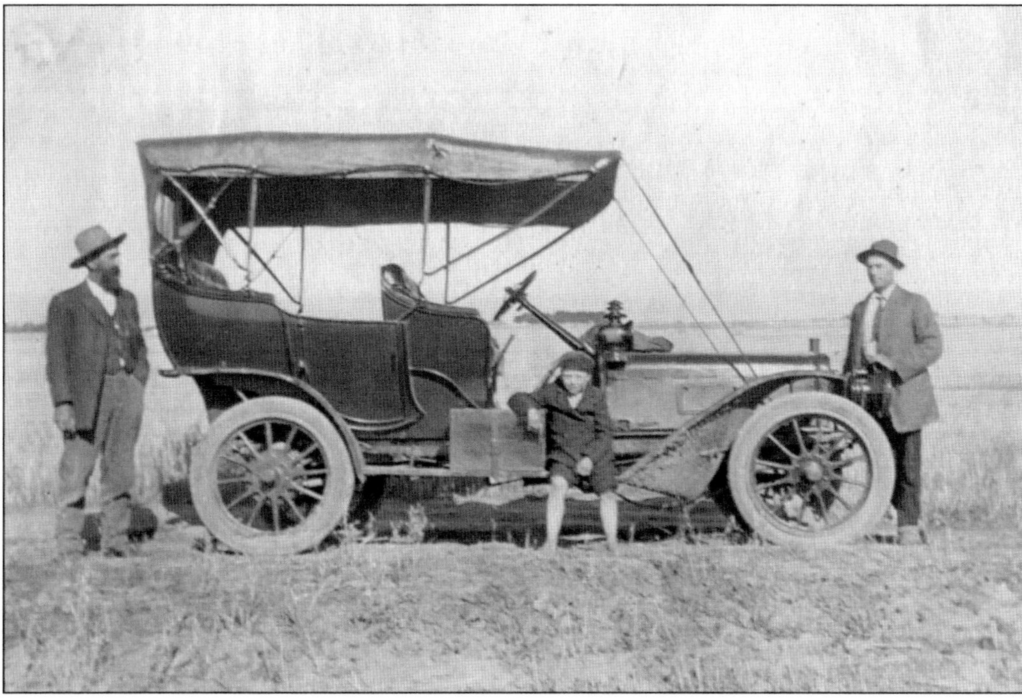

The gentleman at left in this photograph is Herb Freeman, and his brother William Freeman is at right. The young boy sitting on the running board is William's son Wes. Herb and William married sisters Thelma and Edith Williford, respectively. The family lived on farms on Kilaga Springs Road.

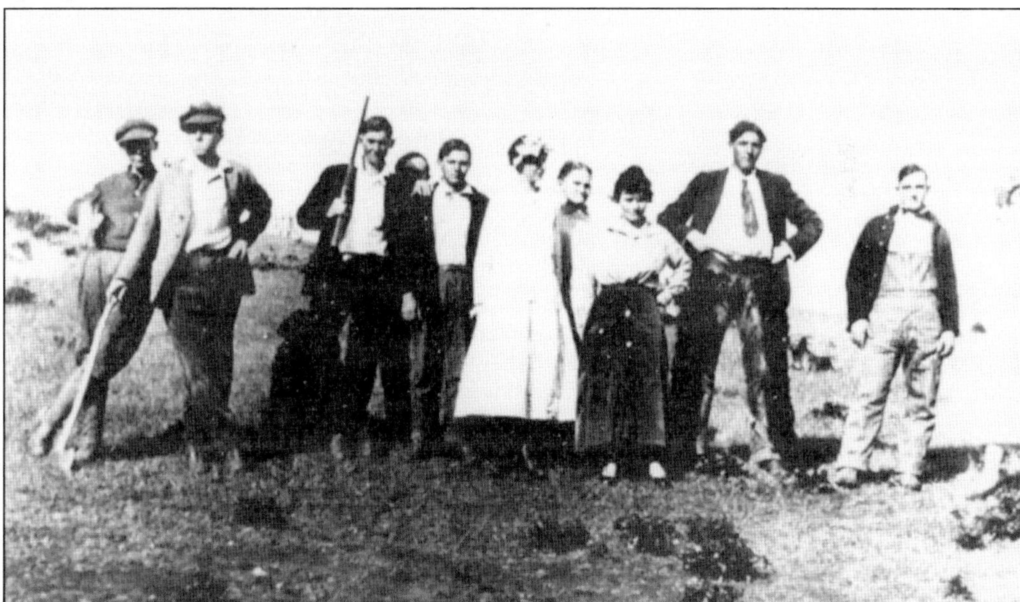

This group is taking a break from farming for a day of fun. From left to right are two unidentified, Onnie Freeman, Joe Merz, unidentified, Edith Williford, unidentified, Blanch Hodgson Murch, Harold Murch, and Art Merz.

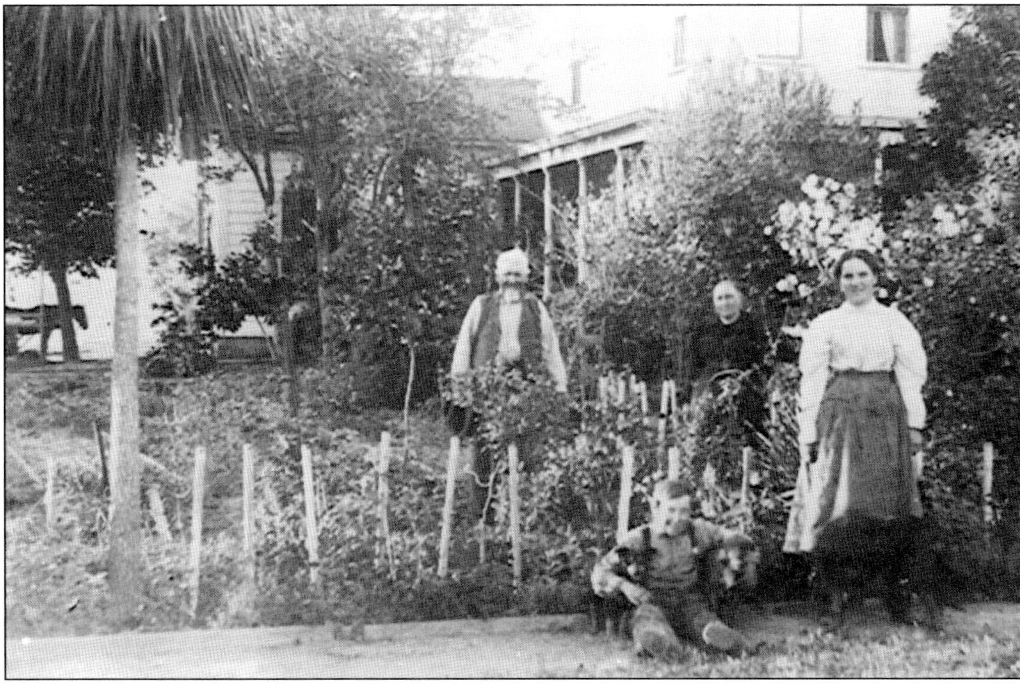

Henry Nader and his wife, Bertha (in dark dress), arrived from their native Germany in the early 1860s. At the time, the family name was spelled "Nather" but pronounced as "Nader"—Henry grew tired of the confusion and changed the spelling. Nader settled in the Coon Creek area and purchased a Daneville general merchandise store from John Ziegenbein in 1869. He soon turned to farming his large ranch which, in 1884, contained 805 acres. Henry Sr. is standing at left, and Henry Jr. is sitting with the dogs.

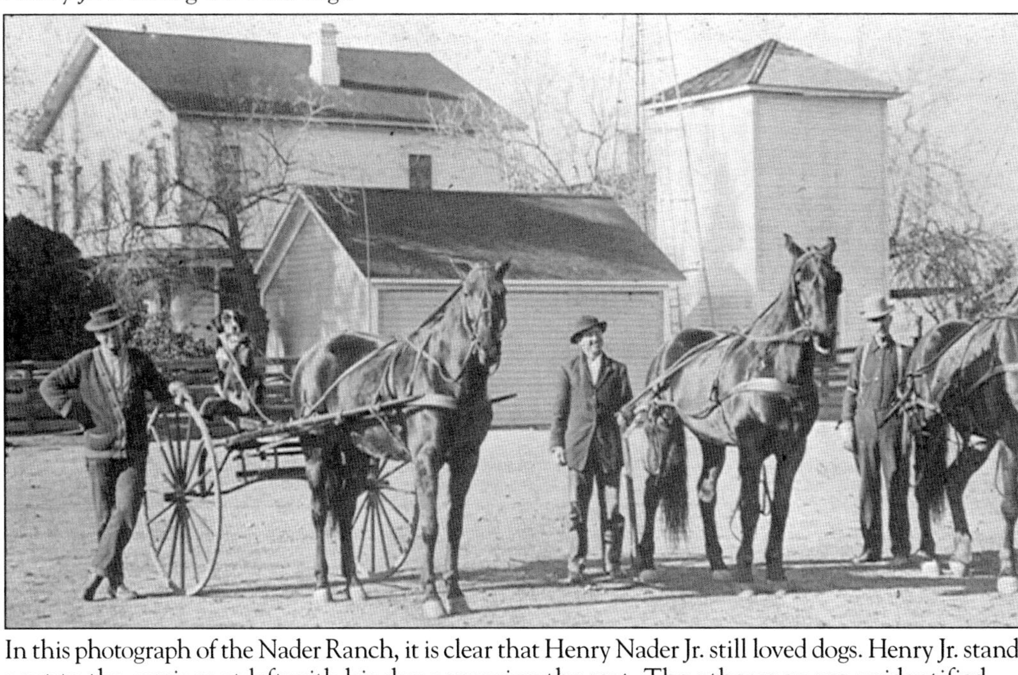

In this photograph of the Nader Ranch, it is clear that Henry Nader Jr. still loved dogs. Henry Jr. stands next to the carriage at left with his dog occupying the seat. The other men are unidentified.

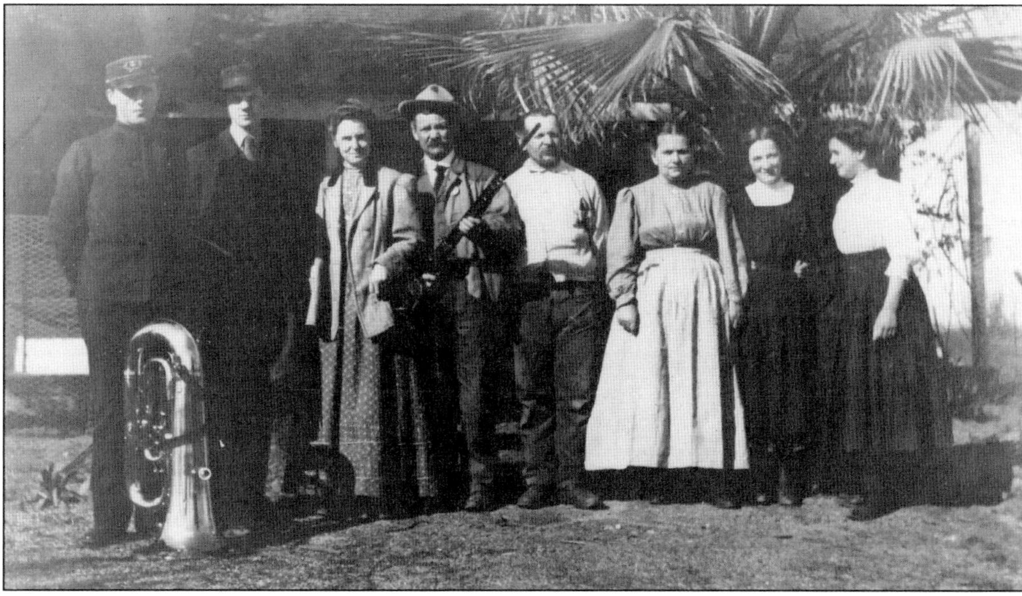

Pictured here is the Bohme/McCrary family. From left to right are Emil Bohme (with tuba), Godfrey Johnson, Mrs. Johnson, Mr. Johnson (holding shotgun), Ernest Bohme, Selma Bohme, Madeline Johnson, and Mina Bohme McCrary. Members of the local Clinton family are descendants of the Bohme/McCrary family. The photograph was taken in 1909 on their ranch on Wise Road just west of Garden Bar Road in the Mt. Pleasant–Fruitvale District.

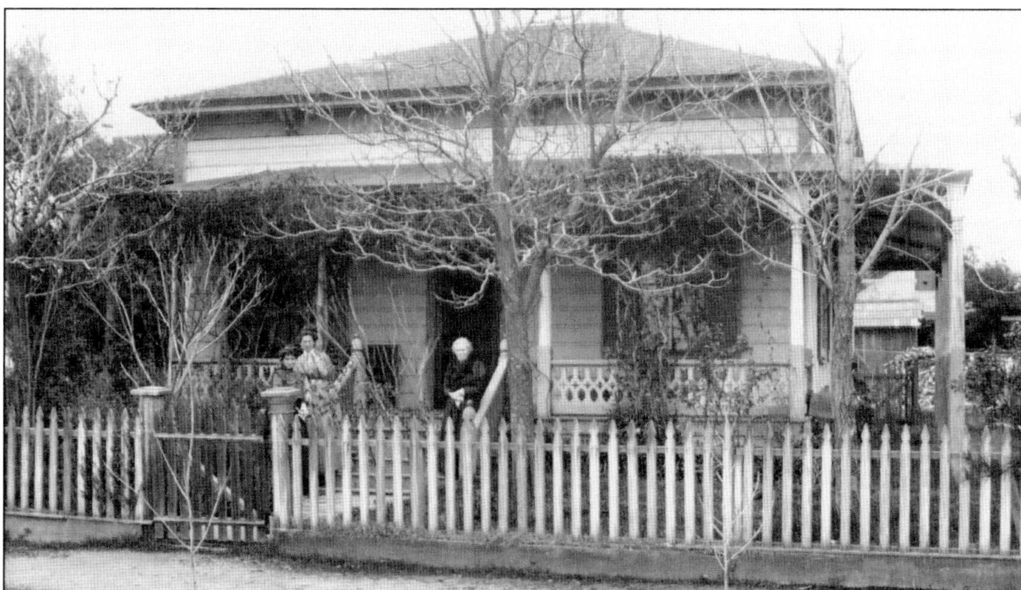

Albert Carlyle Fleming came to California in 1853, went to Gold Hill briefly in 1861, and finally settled in Lincoln in 1870. The Flemings were associated with the railroad, the post office, and several businesses in Lincoln. The Fleming farm was established northeast of the present-day intersection of Gladding and Fleming Roads. This is the Fleming home, located on F Street between Sixth and Seventh Streets. From left to right are Kathleen Maitland Fleming, Elizabeth Agnes Fleming, and Eliza Higgins Fleming.

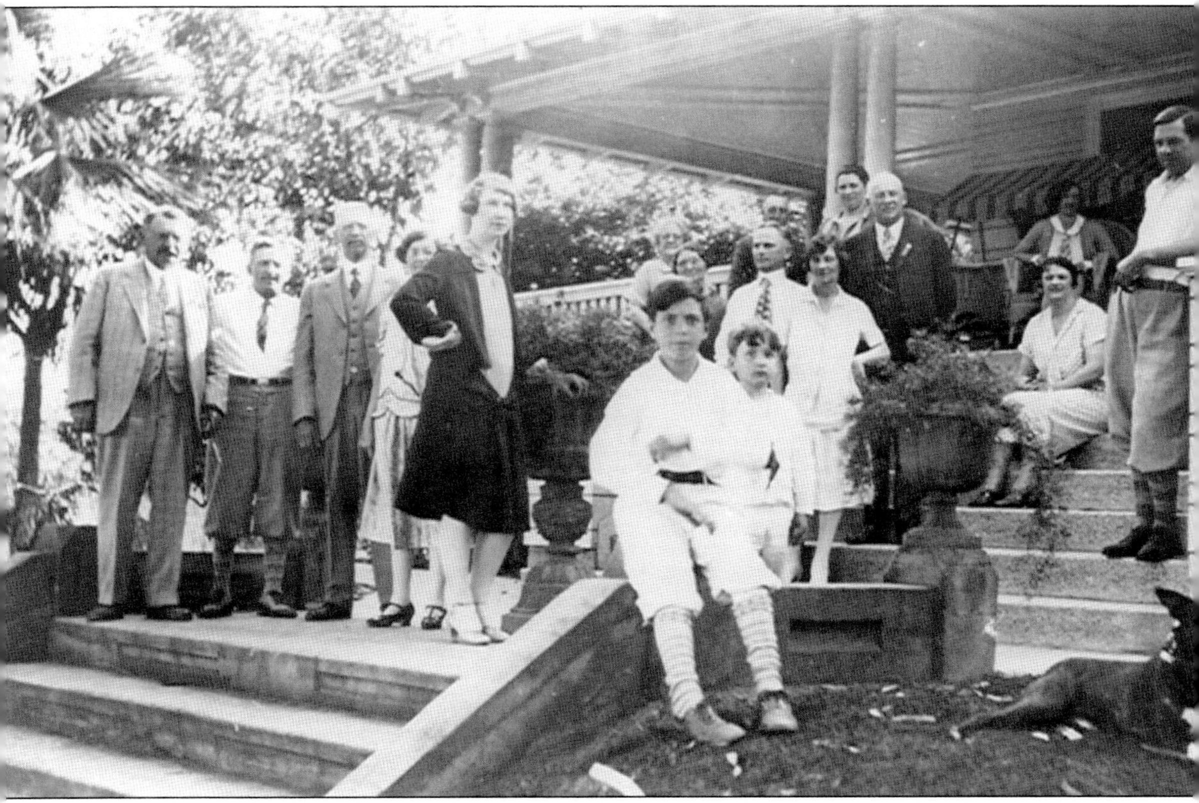

This photograph was taken at the Walter Jansen home on the northwest corner of Fourth and J Streets. From left to right are H.P. Jansen; unidentified; Walter Jansen and his wife, Emma; and Tillie (Jansen) Bird. H.P. and his wife, Christina (not pictured), had two daughters, Tillie and Anna. Anna became Anna Reed. Walter's son, Walter K., is standing on the far right, and his wife, Ann, is in the very back in the sweater. The young boys in the foreground are Jarol and Kay, sons of Walter K. and Ann. This gathering was held for the occasion of Walter Jansen being in Lincoln for 50 years and to honor his business partnership with Lincoln's farmers and ranchers.

Five

Businesses and Buildings

The phrase "build it and they will come" is certainly the case when it comes to the development of Lincoln. After the town was founded in 1859, many of the pioneers who were in the area—mostly miners and farmers—began opening businesses like hotels, grocery and dry goods stores, and blacksmith shops. These merchants were primarily from the northeast part of the United States, with a few coming directly from Europe. The traditions they brought with them involved close-knit families and communities.

When the trains arrived in Lincoln, so did more people. Some new arrivals saw the need for additional businesses, including restaurants, theaters, more grocery stores, feed and grain suppliers, butcher shops, drugstores, bakeries, saloons, banks, and more.

Lincoln became a prosperous town with many successful merchants. With wooden buildings, the threat of fire was always present. Many merchants were forced to rebuild several times because of fire losses. The fire of 1883 claimed all four of the original hotels near Fifth and G Streets. The Exchange Hotel burned to the ground in spectacular fashion in 1886. Gladding, McBean suffered two major fires, and the Cannery burned to the ground in 1946. A number of brick buildings were erected after wooden structures burned down; these brick buildings served as a buffer against the spread of future fires, and they are still standing today. Family homes were not as threatened, as the wide streets and ample space between homes usually kept fires contained to one home at a time.

The Gladding, McBean "pottery," as it was often referred to, was Lincoln's largest employer, and its founders were very generous to the town of Lincoln. They donated (or gave at cost) building materials to projects in Lincoln such as the Carnegie Library, the high school, the grammar school, the civic auditorium, the women's clubhouse, McBean Swimming Pool, and the veteran's memorial building.

As the town grew, so did the need for structure and rules. Although the town was essentially founded in 1859, the incorporation of Lincoln did not take place until 1890. The establishment of a town government gave Lincoln permanence and a sense of security. Many successful merchants were also involved in the politics of Lincoln and served in various capacities to help form and run the town. They constructed homes and raised families and were proud of the town they built.

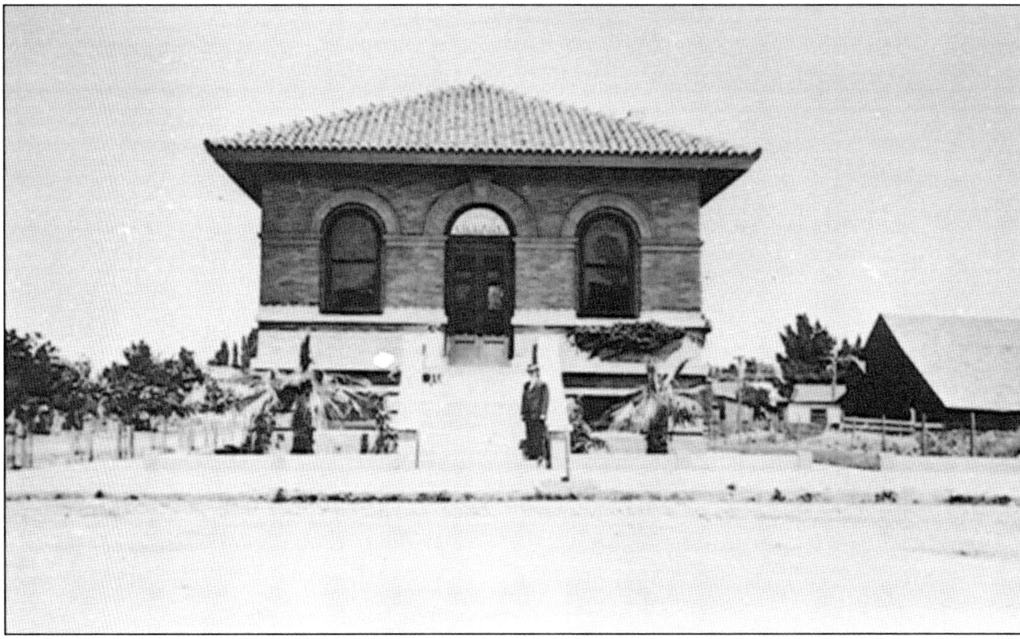

Shortly after the town of Lincoln was established, a reading room was created. This room moved around and was once housed in the Simple Pleasures building on Fifth Street. In 1904, the city began to support the reading room with tax funds, and in 1906, the city established a board of trustees. One of the board's first actions was submitting an application to Andrew Carnegie for funding for a new library. In 1908, the application for a Carnegie grant was approved in the amount of $6,000, and the town raised an additional $3,000. The bricks used in the library's construction came from Gladding, McBean. The cornerstone was laid on April 3, 1909, and the Lincoln Public Library opened at the corner of Fifth and F Streets on September 1, 1909.

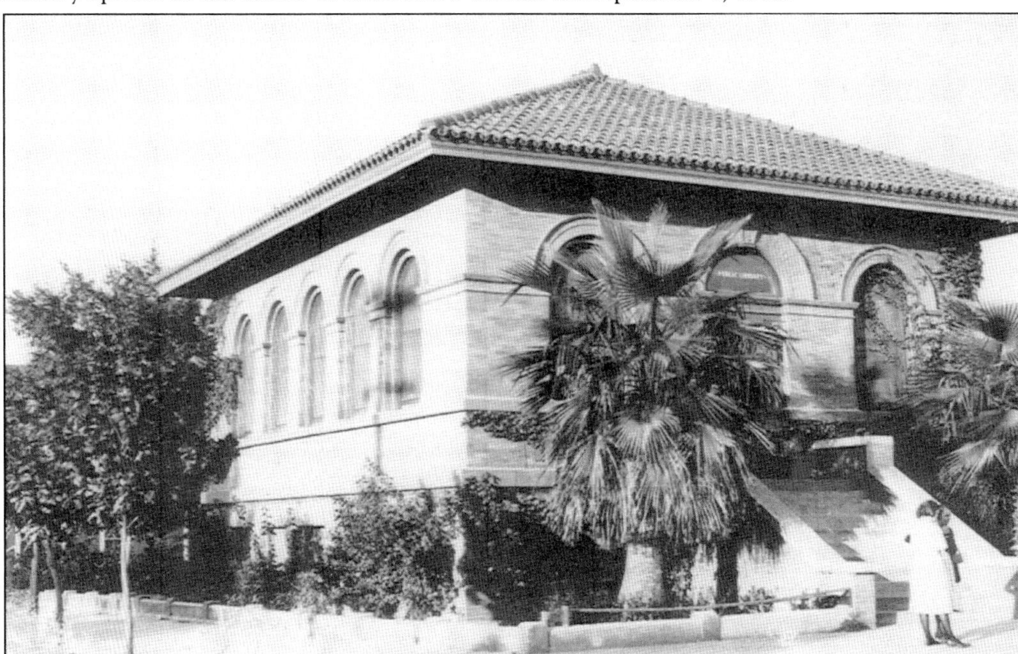

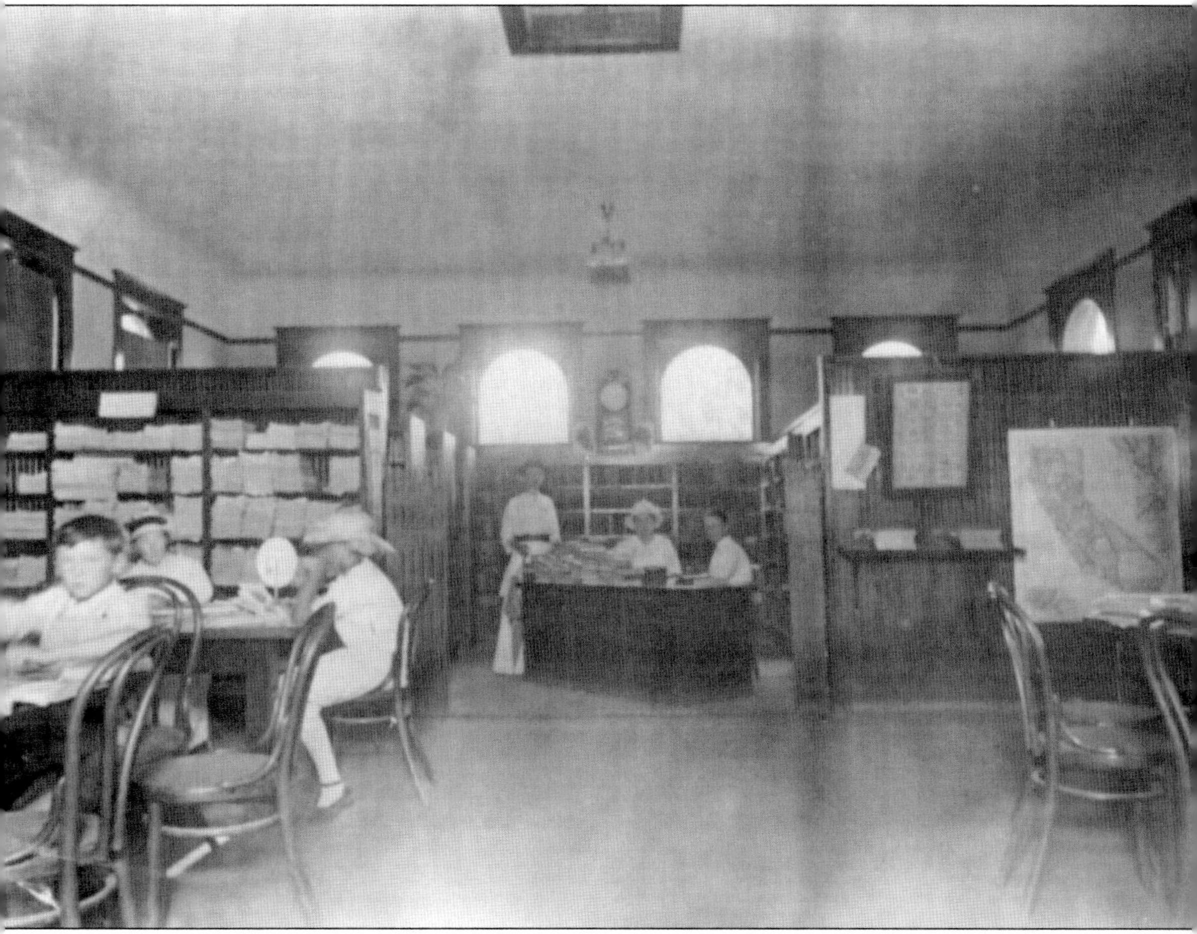

This photograph from inside the Lincoln Public Library shows several residents reading. The interior of the library has not changed much since it was built. The librarian's desk in the center has been relocated, and there are a few more shelves and books, but the integrity of the interior remains the same.

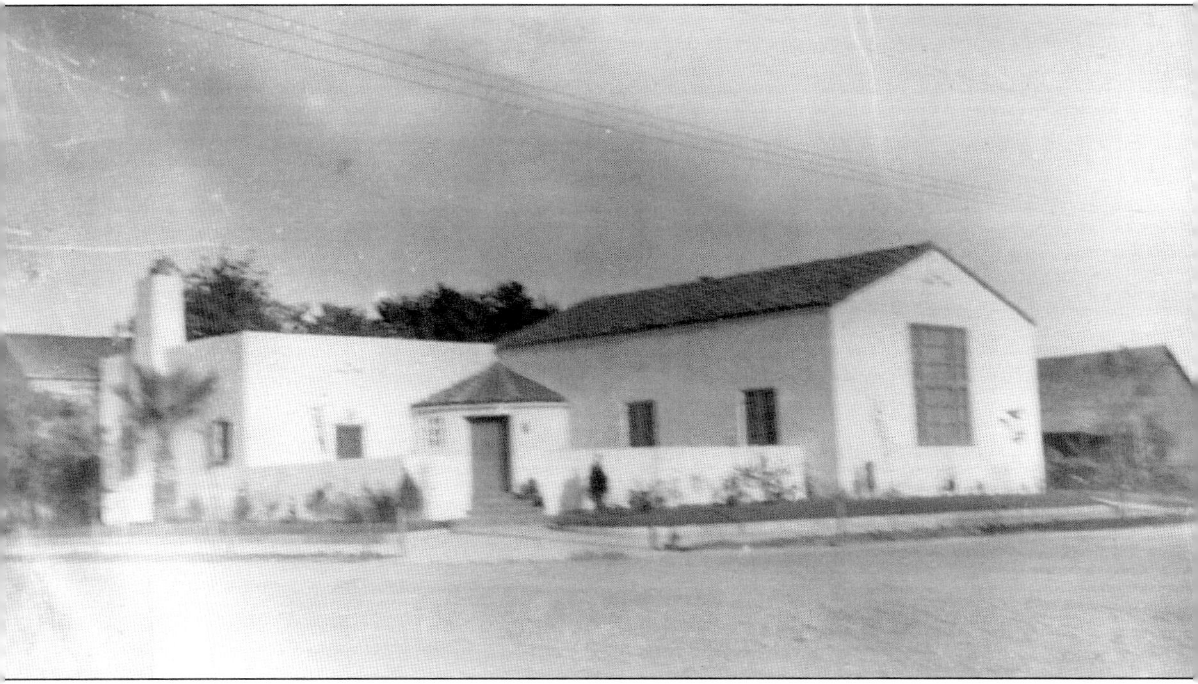

In 1867, Chauncey L. Hotchkiss (ancestor of the Leavell, Fuller, and Van Dyke families) purchased the lot on the southeast corner of Fifth and E Streets. The Hotchkiss home stood into the 20th century. Walter Jansen eventually acquired the land and, in 1923, presented the corner to the Lincoln Women's Club, which appointed a building committee composed of Emma Williamson, Carrie Gladding, Clara Hayt, and Marguerite McCullough. Gladding donated $3,000 as a memorial to her mother. Gladding, McBean gave $1,300 worth of building materials. Other gifts from members amounted to $3,500. The total cost of construction in 1923 was $11,860. Groups and individuals could rent the hall, which is a great place for large social gatherings and is still in use today.

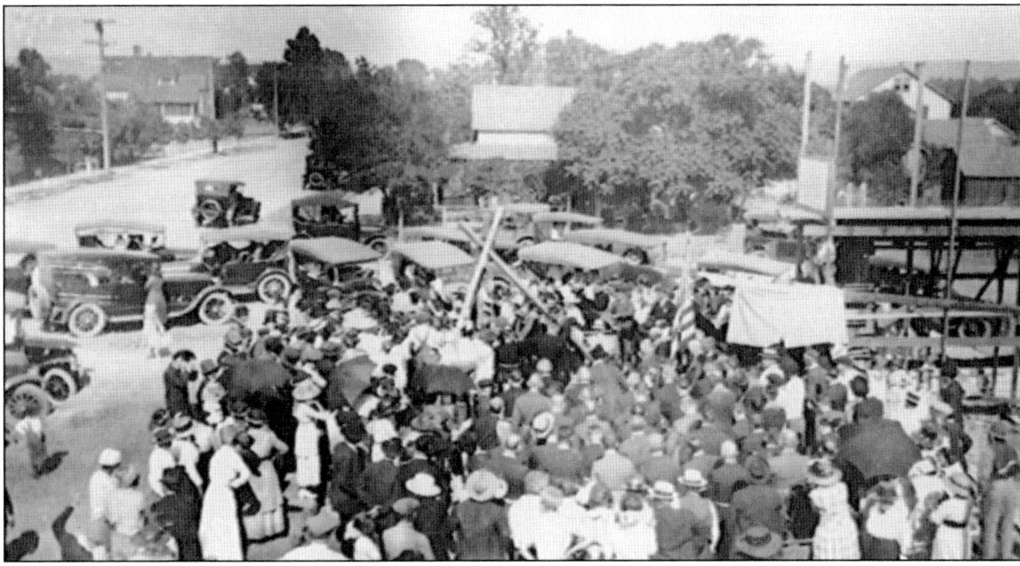

The only building to occupy the site of the civic auditorium before the start of the 20th century was the home of Galusha Gray. Gray was a pioneer in Virginia(town) and Fox's Flat, two mining towns several miles east of Lincoln and up the Auburn Ravine. Gray owned Lincoln's first water system and served as councilman and mayor. This 1921 photograph documents the placing of the cornerstone for the auditorium.

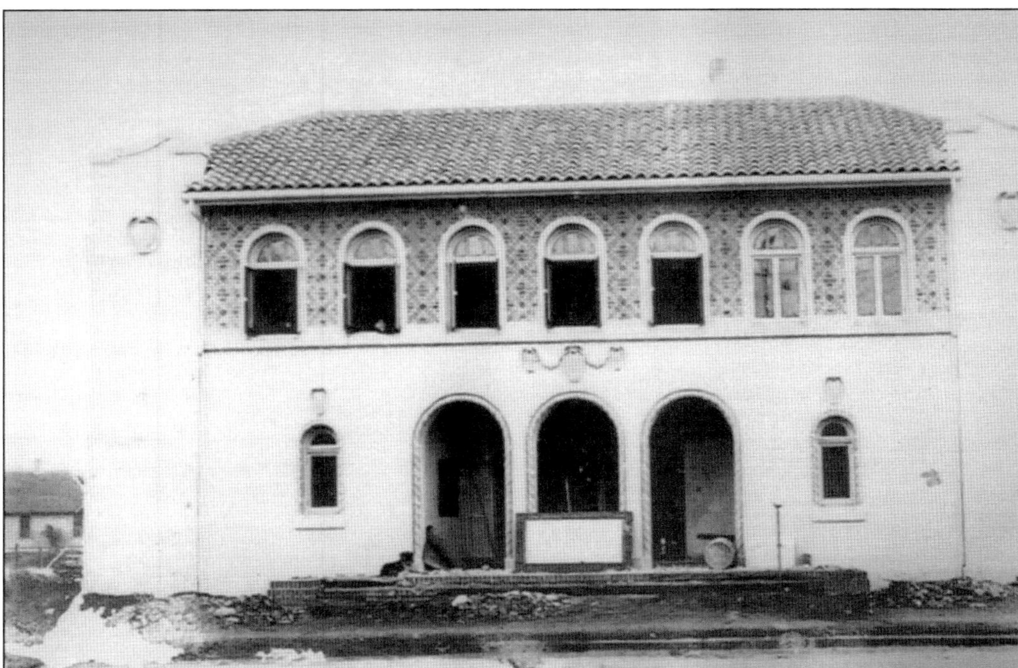

After the town purchased the site from Galusha Gray, it passed a bond issue in 1919 to build a civic auditorium for $22,890. The building had a large stage at the south end, a balcony, a projection booth, restrooms, and hat-check rooms. Many events were held in this building because of its great amenities. It was remodeled in 1972 for use as city government offices, but was returned to its original state in 2013.

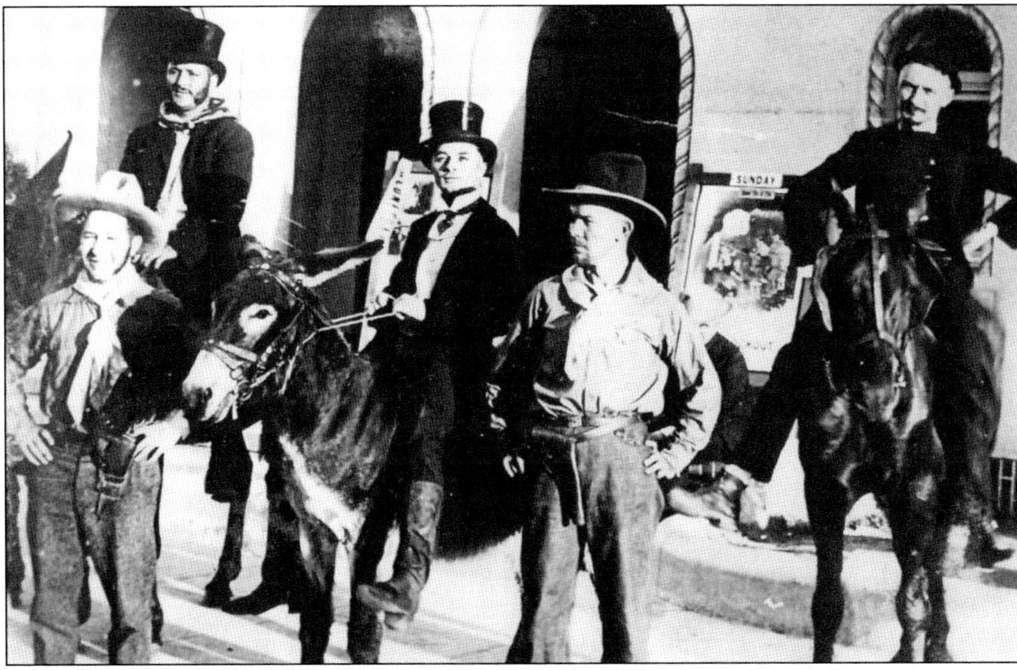

This 1920s photograph was taken in front of the civic auditorium. From left to right are Sam Goldine, Walter Cory, Ed Wyatt, Elmer Beermann, and unidentified. Based on the billboards in the background and the men's attire, it appears that they are advertising a play taking place in the auditorium.

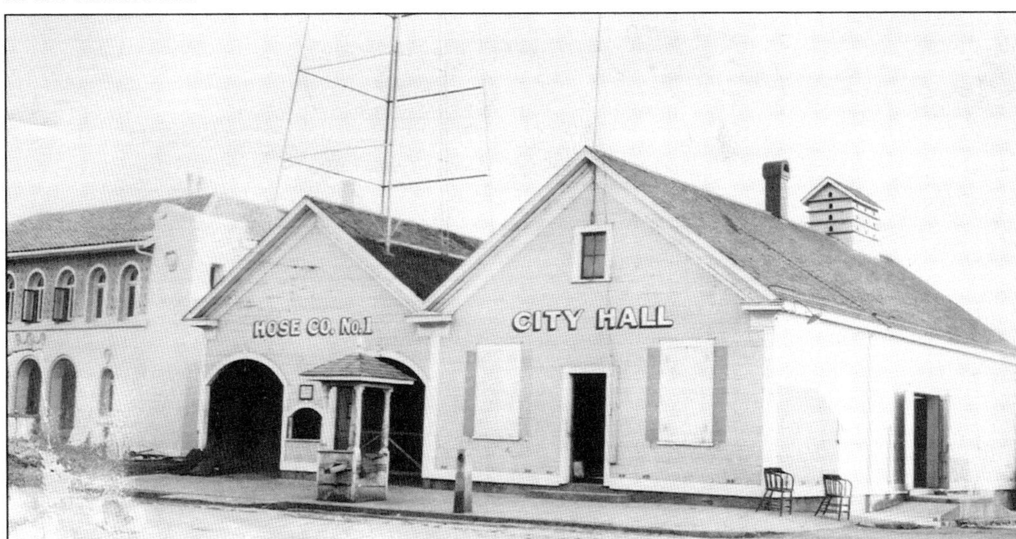

Lincoln's City Hall and firehouse were located on Fifth Street next to the civic auditorium, in the present-day location of the Veteran's Hall. Although fires caused damage to structures in Lincoln, the wide streets and spacious sites usually limited fires to a single block. After Lincoln's largest fires, Gladding, McBean brick, stone, and terra cotta were used to replace or add to buildings in the downtown area. The brick and terra cotta buildings served as barriers to the spread of fires. Because of this and the creation of the fire department soon after the town incorporated in 1890, many second-generation wooden buildings were preserved.

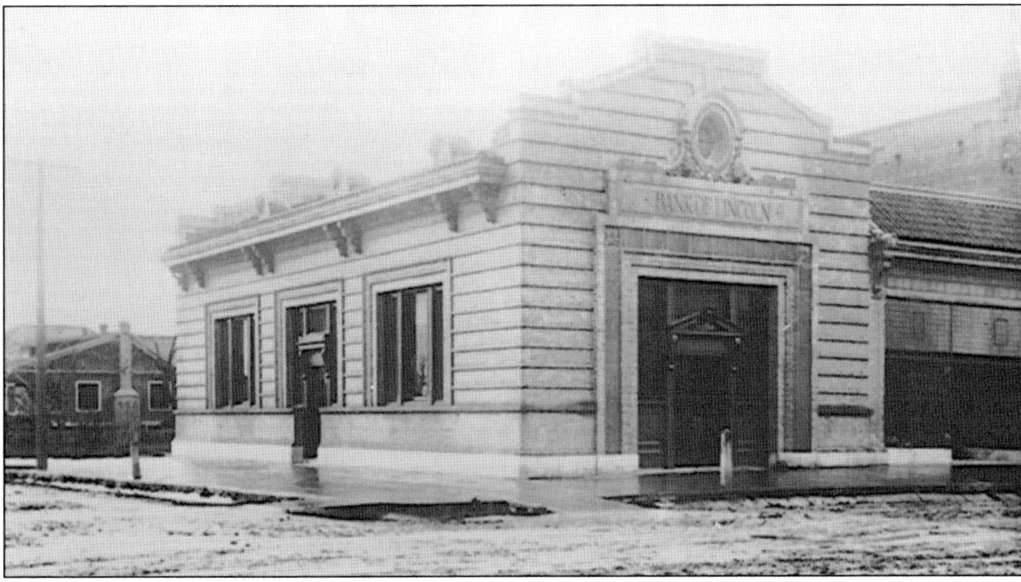

The International Order of Odd Fellows (IOOF) and Masonic lodges purchased the lot on the southwest corner of Fifth and F Streets in 1862. They built a two-story wooden structure used by both lodges from 1862 to 1864, then only by the Masons from 1864 to 1867. Both lodges then met next door in the new IOOF building. In 1867, Richard Fuller bought the old lodge, which burned down in 1895. In 1911, the new Bank of Lincoln building was erected on this site.

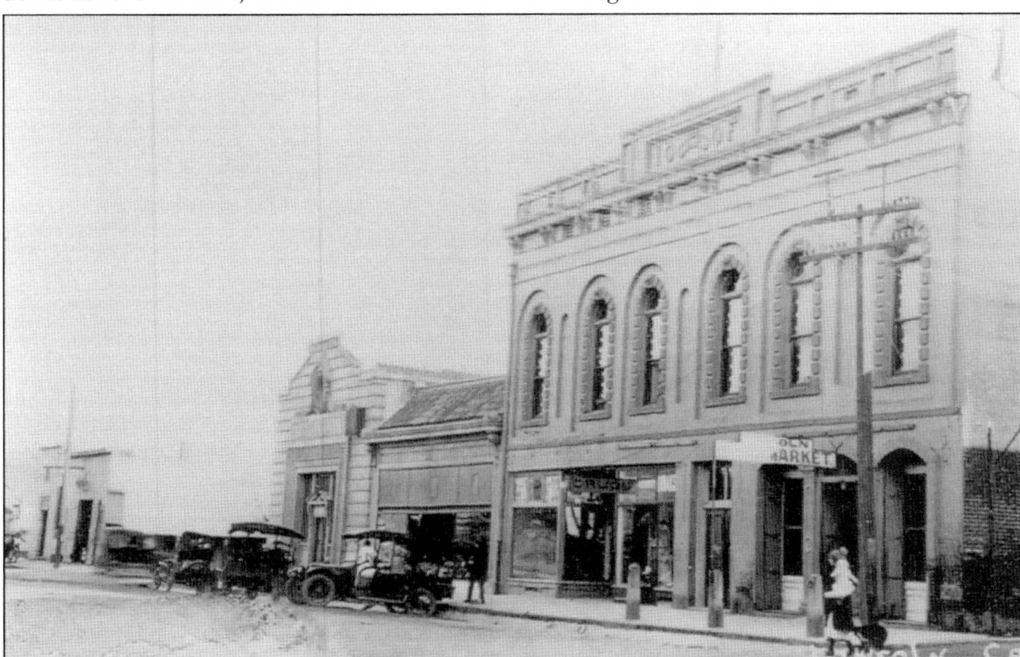

In 1864, the Odd Fellows acquired the lot at 625–645 Fifth Street and constructed a two-story brick building on the site. It was dedicated on December 8, 1864. The Odd Fellows and the Masons met upstairs, and the downstairs housed a store. Joseph Dallman's dry goods store used the space up to 1900, and at the turn of the century, it housed Fiddyment and Louis Leavell's general store. In 1905, the IOOF expanded the building to its current size.

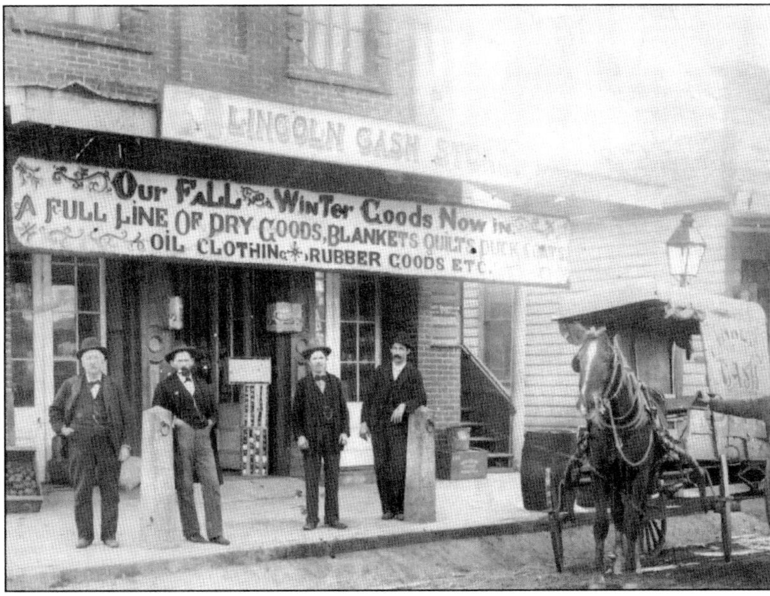

In this photograph of the IOOF Building, Dr. William Finney stands at far left; the other three men are unidentified. The Lincoln Cash Store behind the four men dates the picture to 1913. The store was owned by A.E. Grey, A.C. Crosby, and Edward A. Grey. C.E. Finney, the son of Dr. William Finney, owned the store from 1905 to 1913.

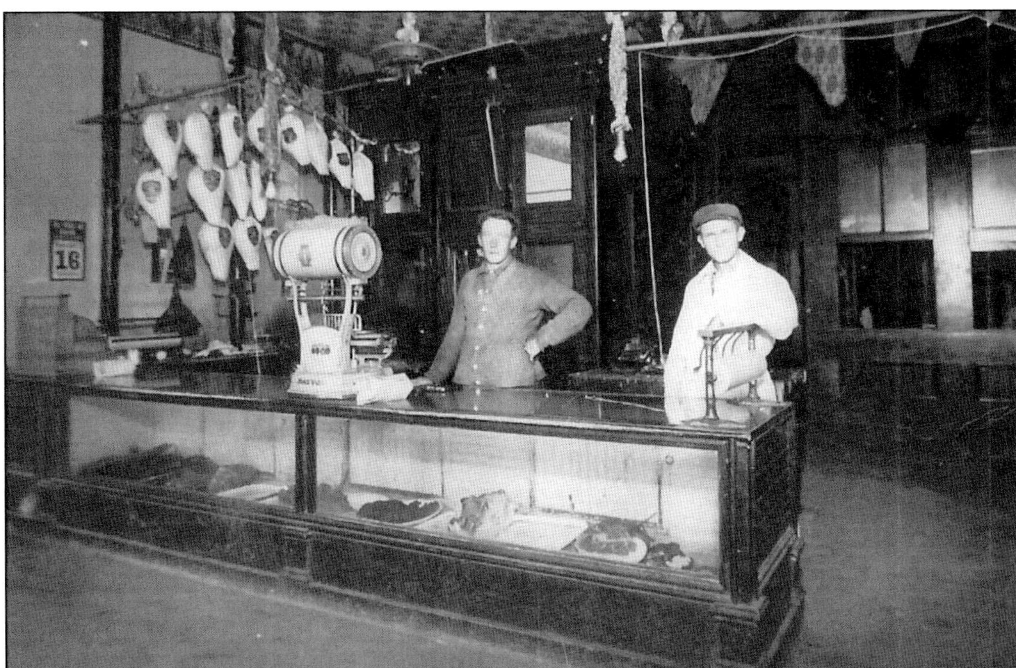

Charles F. Beermann started a harness shop on the northwest corner of Fifth and F Streets in 1880. Beermann was active in city government, serving as treasurer beginning in 1892. This picture shows Charles's sons Elmer (left) and Carl, who operated this meat market in the IOOF Building from 1909 to 1930. Elmer ran the meat market by himself from 1930 to 1950. Charles's daughter, Millie, married James E. Wyatt Jr., and they had five children: Charles, Fred, Woodrow, Pershing, and Verna. Kathy Braden and Robert Moore were Elmer's grandchildren.

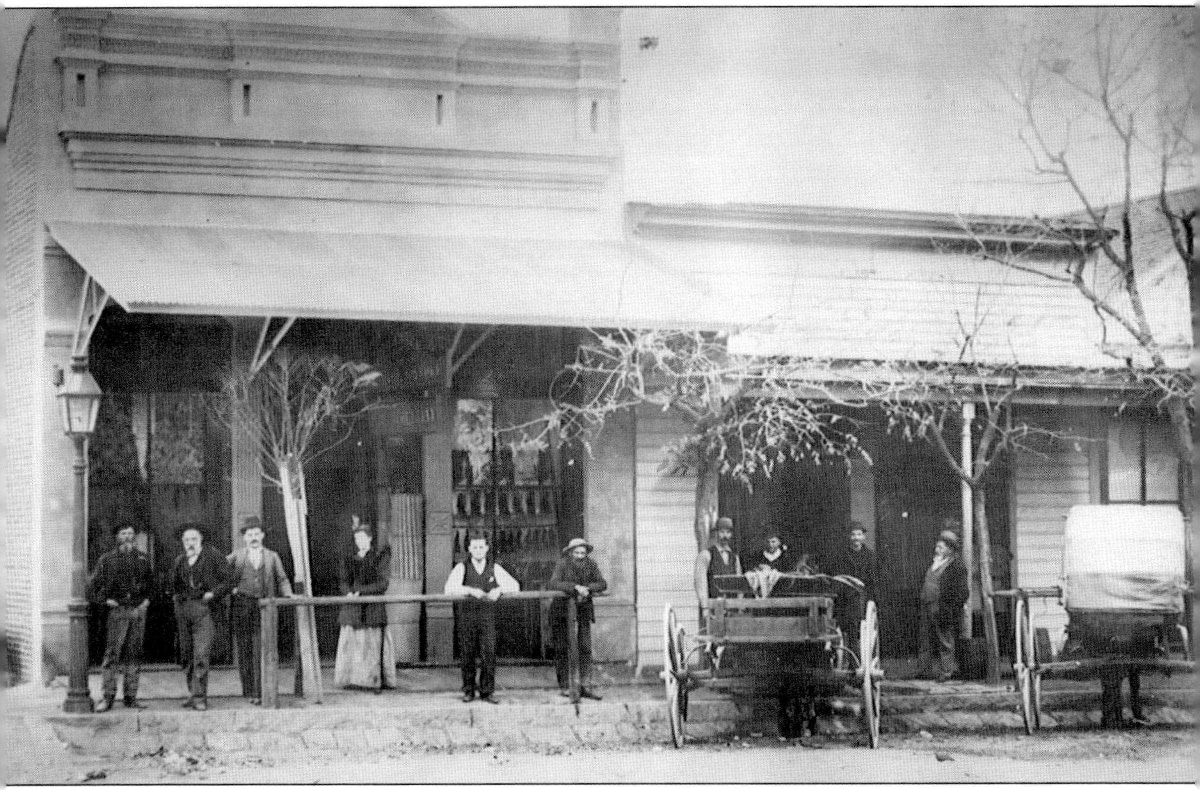

In the early 1860s, attorney John Cannon used a small wooden building at 644 Fifth Street. In the 1870s, attorney Peter Singer, and then Chris Hoppert, took over. In 1892, Hoppert constructed a new building (pictured), known as the Hoppert Building, on the site. A few businesses that used space in the Hoppert Building in the early days included Levy and Levitt's Farmers and Mechanics Store, W.P. Adams' Sonora Meat Market (which was taken over by W.J. Wyatt), L. Spurgeon's saloon, and Roy McCrary's pool hall and dairy bar (which was open from 1920 to 1945).

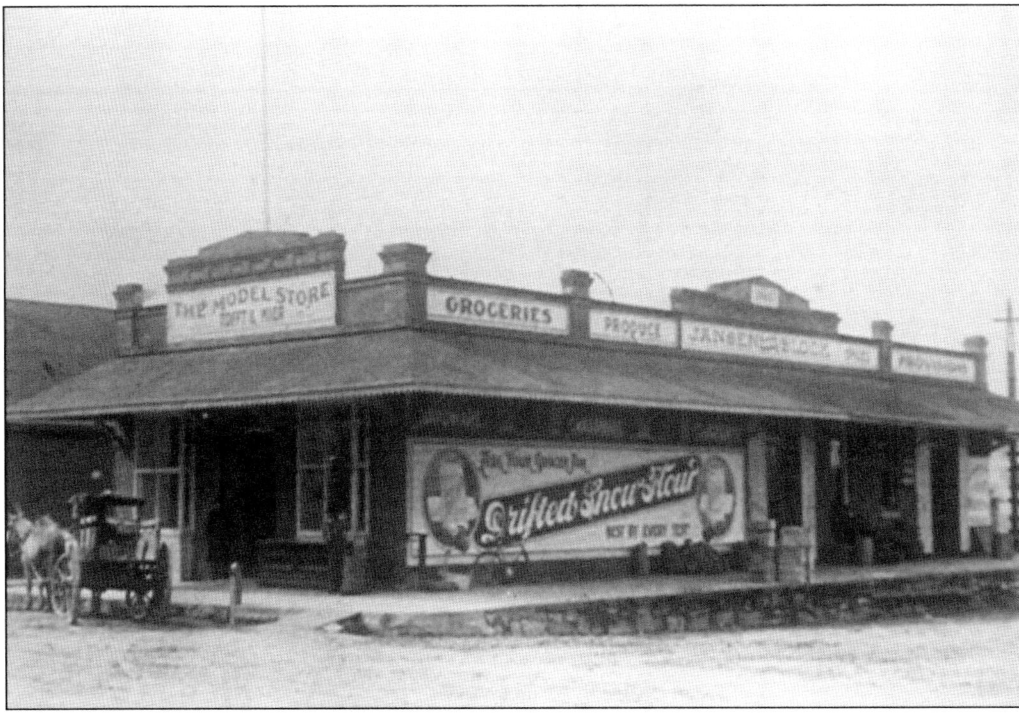

The Butterfield Building, located on the southwest corner of Fifth and G Streets, housed J.E. Jute Tofft's Model Grocer (from 1908 to 1912), and Fred E. Brown's grocery (from 1917 to 1920). Lincoln's founder, Charles Wilson, had a wooden frame building in this location in the early 1860s, and Wilson's brother-in-law, Henry Rood, operated the building as Rood's Hall. By 1879, Stephen and Melissa Burdge ran a boardinghouse here known as the Hotel Burdge. It burned down in 1883. Gladding, McBean then built a brick store on the site, and in 1887, C.H. Butterfield bought it, and it became the Butterfield Building. Some grocery stores once located in the building include Rochdale Store (1903–1905), Tofft and Kier (1907–1908), Frank Fergus (1913–1916), and O.A. Allison (1916–1917). R.J. Tofft Hardware was in this location from 1918 to 1931.

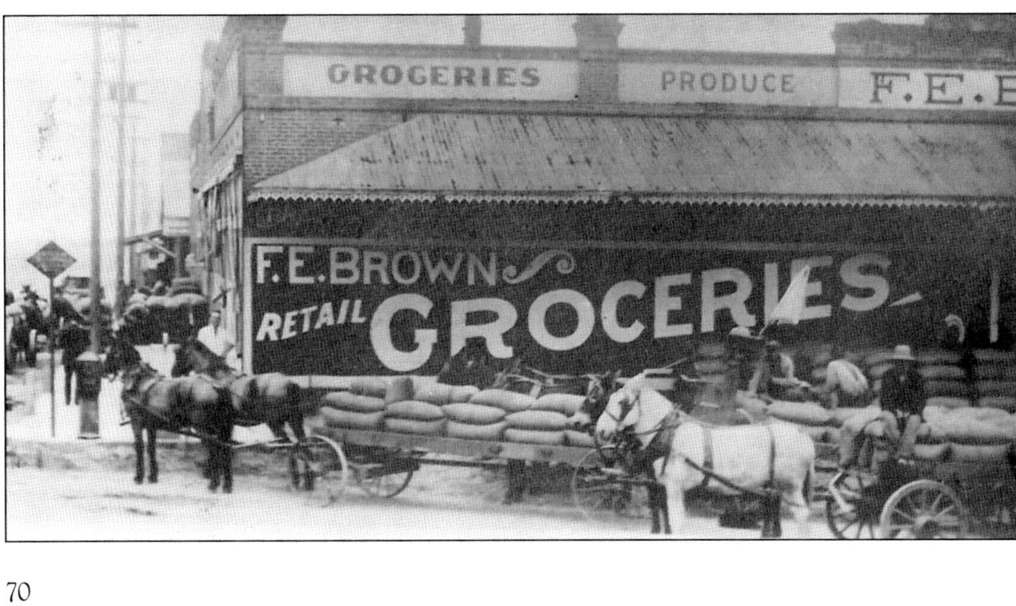

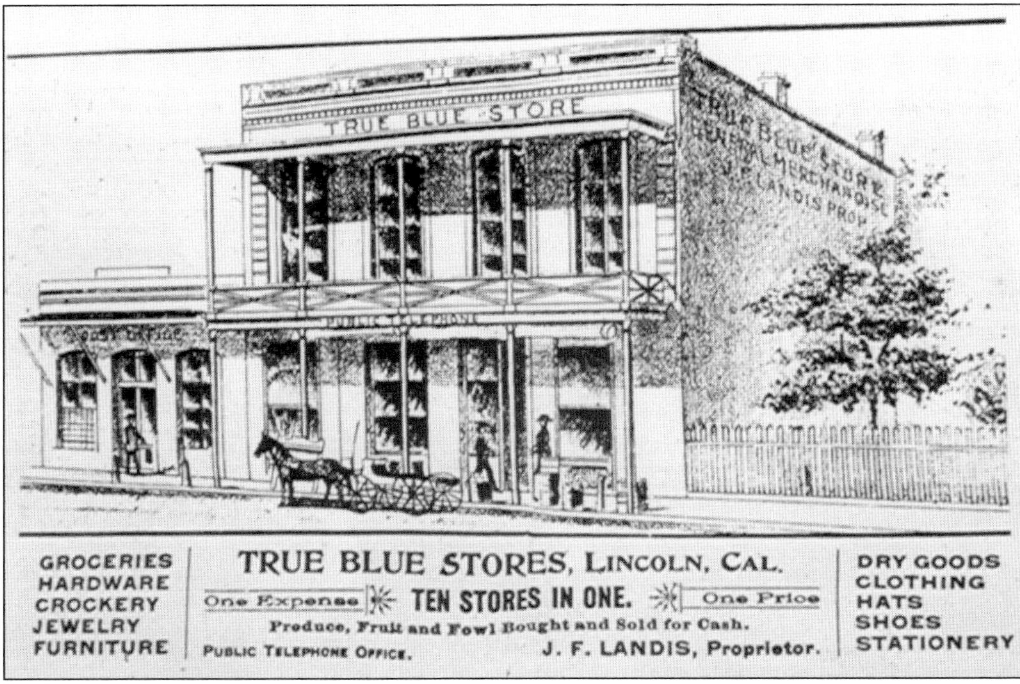

These are early pictures of what would later be referred to as the Emmada Building, located at 531–537 G Street. Good Templar's Hall was erected on this site in 1860 as a two-story brick building. Lincoln's first grammar school was housed here in 1864. The first owner was the Independent Order of Good Templars, a temperance organization. They built the Good Templar's Hall on this site in 1860. In 1875, the building became Grangers' Hall, and in 1880, Peter Ahart bought it. There was always a store on the ground floor, and meetings and social affairs were held on the second story. In 1892, John Landis used the entire building for his general store, the True Blue Store. The building housed Ingram and Mason hardware store until it burned down in 1919.

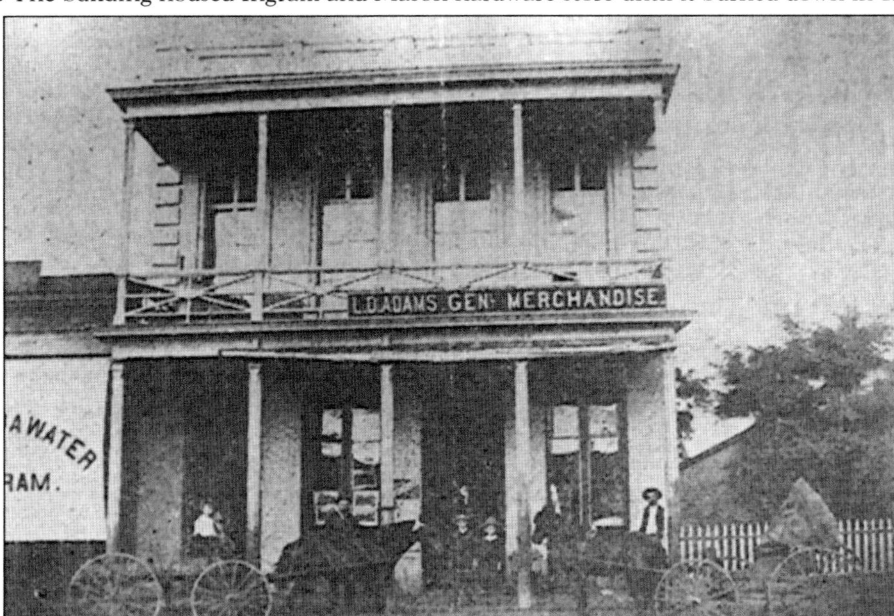

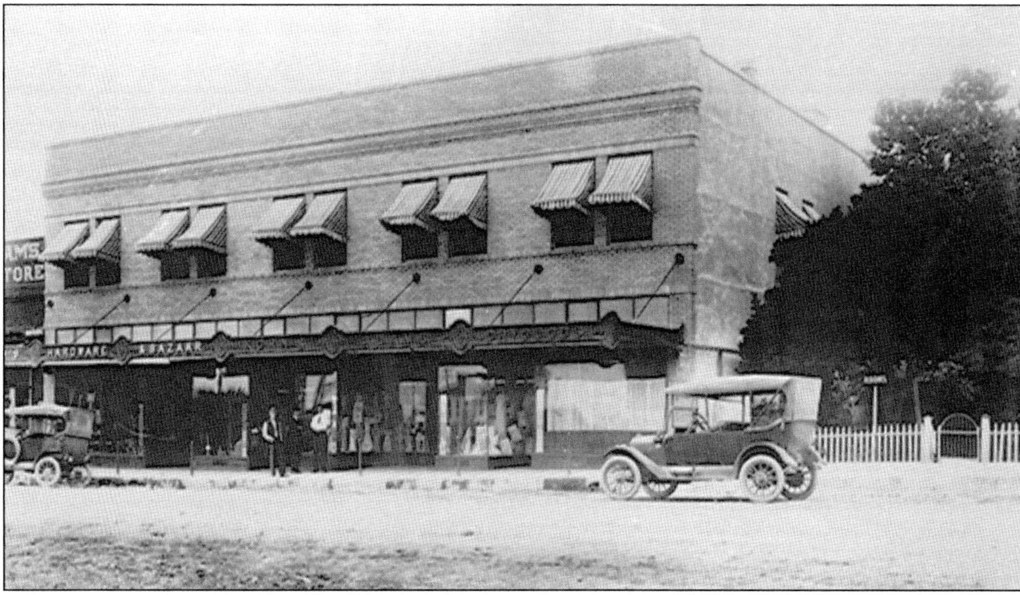

This photograph of the Emmada Building was taken during the time it was the L.D. Adams general merchandise store, from 1891 to 1903. In 1913, the building was expanded by owners Williamson and Ingram and named Emmada after their wives, Emma and Ada. The older part of the building (537 G Street) housed Ingram and Mason hardware (1913–1918), Tofft and Johnson groceries (1918–1929), Owen and Ingram groceries (1929–1933) and Wyatt Hardware (1933–1983). Address 531 G Street housed department stores, most notably Demas Department Store (in partnership with a Mr. Short for a time).

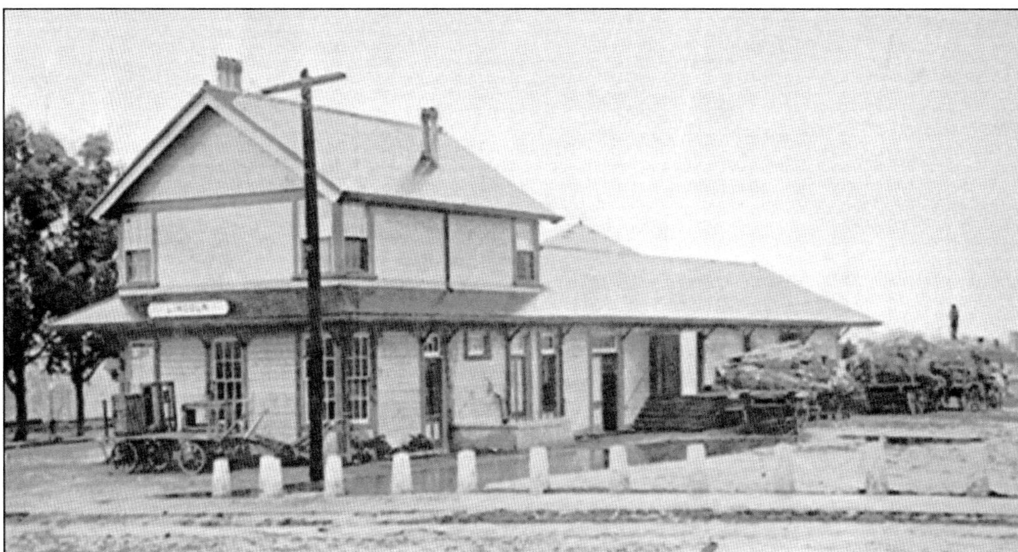

The train depot was kept busy shipping out various products grown in and around Lincoln. In this image, trees on wagons are waiting to be loaded and shipped from a local nursery. Many farmers and ranchers used trains to transport goods throughout California and the United States. The first Lincoln depot was built in 1861 and replaced by the one pictured here in 1893. The first railroad to come to town was the California Central, then the Oregon & California, then the Central Pacific, and, finally, the Southern Pacific Railroad.

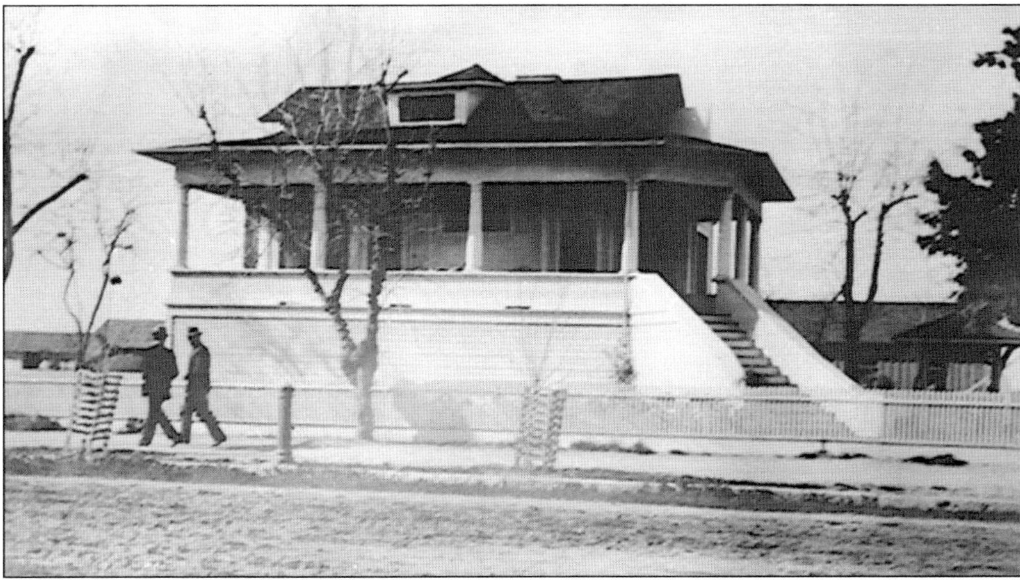

This is the George D. Williamson home, which he built for his family around 1890 on Fourth and F Streets. Gladding, McBean then purchased the house in the late 1920s or early 1930s, and it was referred to as the Gladding, McBean Club House. The company would use the house as a place for out-of-town guests to stay. Pottery superintendents were also allowed to live there from time to time. A cook and caretaker lived on the premises.

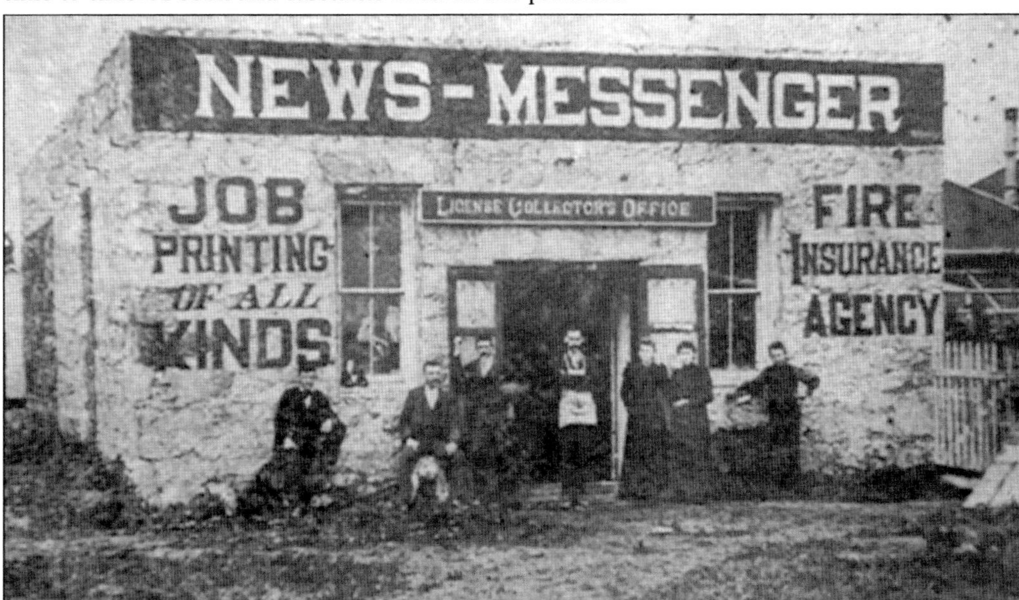

Many Western Placer towns had newspapers prior to 1880, and the citizens of Lincoln frequently made it known that there should be a local paper. In 1887, publisher J.H. Austin launched the *Lincoln Gazette*, but it only lasted a few weeks. Other short-lived newspapers include the *Lincoln Recorder*, the *Lincoln Ledger*, *Cyclone Newspaper*, and the *Reporter*. This photograph was taken in 1892, when the *Reporter* became the *Placer News Messenger* and then the *Lincoln News Messenger*, which is still published on a weekly basis. Publication began in this stone building at the intersection of Fifth Street and the railroad.

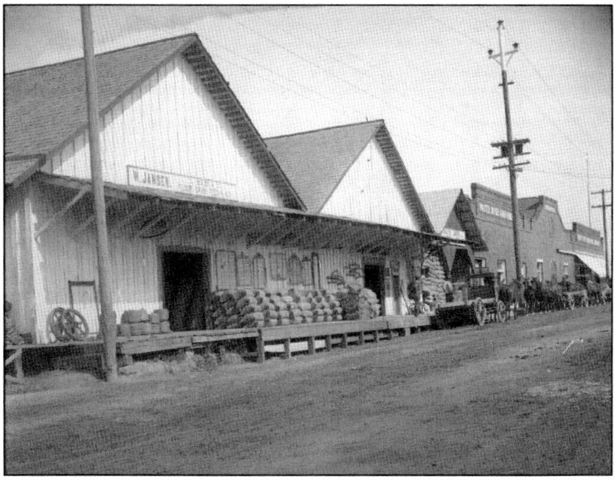

The Logan Livery Stable was initially built in the middle of the G Street block by Harford and Stauffer in 1846. Various changes of owners took place, and in 1876, it burned down. The lots were purchased by George Aldrich, who built the twin warehouses after 1880. In 1890, Butterfield operated the two buildings as grain warehouses. The Buckeye Milling Company, owned by partners J.T. Howard and Walter Jansen, was founded the same year and moved into the twin warehouses in 1892. In 1894, Jansen bought out Howard.

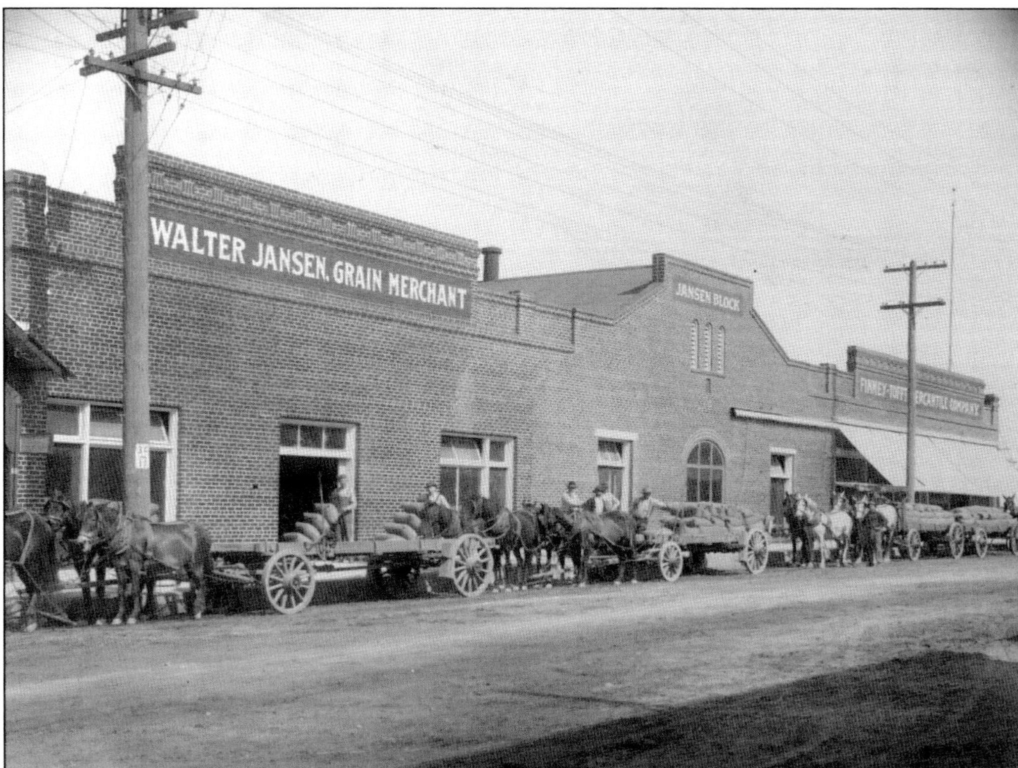

Newspaper articles about the wheat belt of Western Placer appeared in 1881. The wheat area was approximately 10 miles long and stretched from the Bear to the American Rivers and from the foothills to Sutter County. About 128,000 acres averaged 18 bushels per acre. Much of the wheat went through Lincoln's longest-lasting agricultural business, Walter Jansen Grain Merchant. After 1900, Jansen's business grew to include the entire block—300 feet of frontage on G Street between Fourth and Fifth Street. The complex was known as the Jansen Block; it is still in use today.

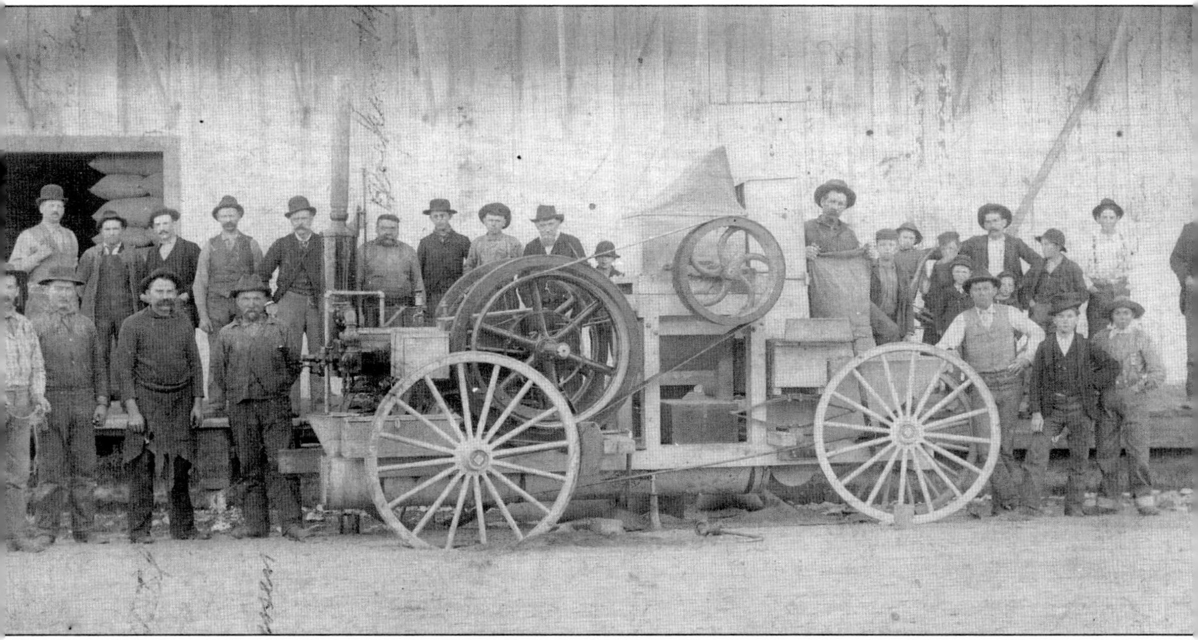

These interested spectators are surrounding an early grain crusher. Evidently, this barley roller was built at Walter Jansen's in 1902. Not everyone is identified, but the crowd contains people with last names like Ahart, Andresen, Brown, Hughes, Luce, Shoffer, Sparks, and Wortel. The night watchman, Murphy, is at far right.

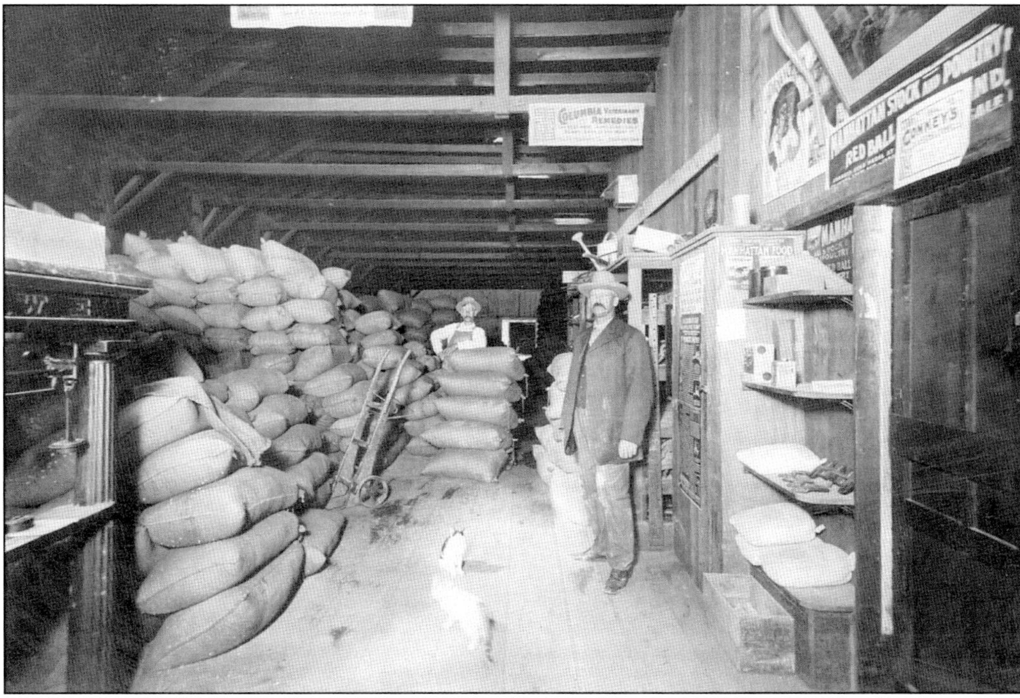

Walter Jansen came to Lincoln from Denmark in 1877 at age 15. He followed his older brother H.P. Jansen and lived the rest of his life in Lincoln. Walter spent 11 years working on farms, but in 1888, he shifted to the grain business and found a good opportunity to work for wages. His business became Jansen's, and, eventually, Walter Jansen and Son. The corner of one of the three scales used in the plant is at far left next to the grain sacks in the above image; the scale now stands in the Lincoln Area Archives Museum. The other photograph was taken in 1915 and shows Walter Jansen in his office with his dog Ty.

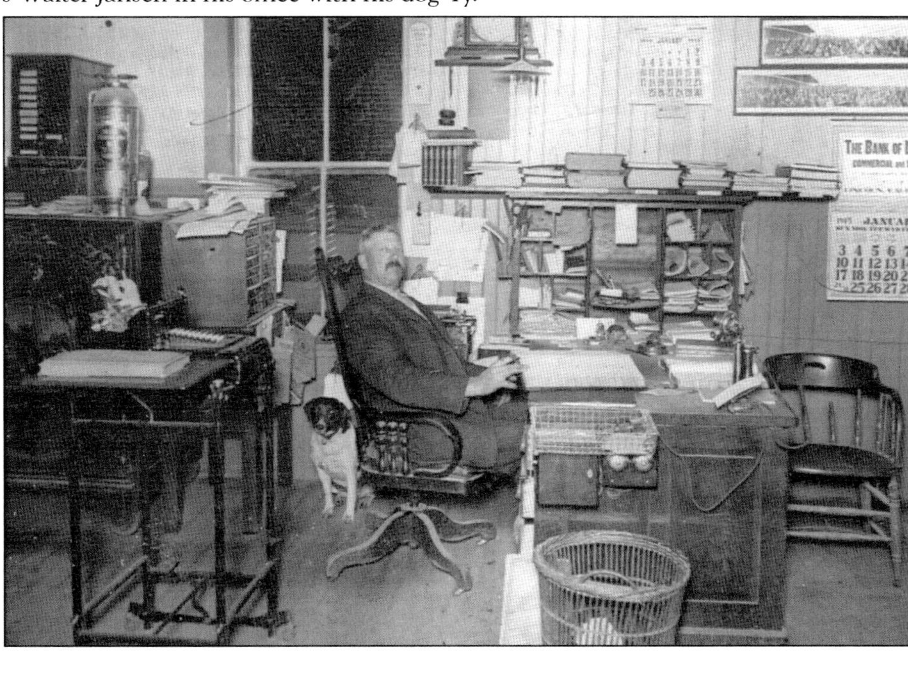

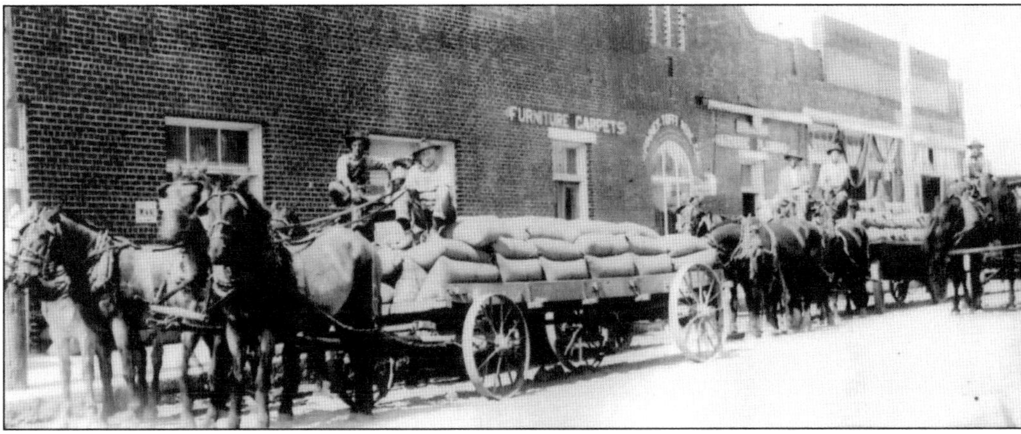

These wagons from Moore ranches are bringing in a crop of grain to Jansen's. Alf Shane is the ranch hand (far left) sitting next to Tom Moore on the first wagon; Royal Fredrick Moore and his brother Charley Moore are in the second wagon. Tom was a cousin of Royal and Charley's; both families' descendants still farm in the area.

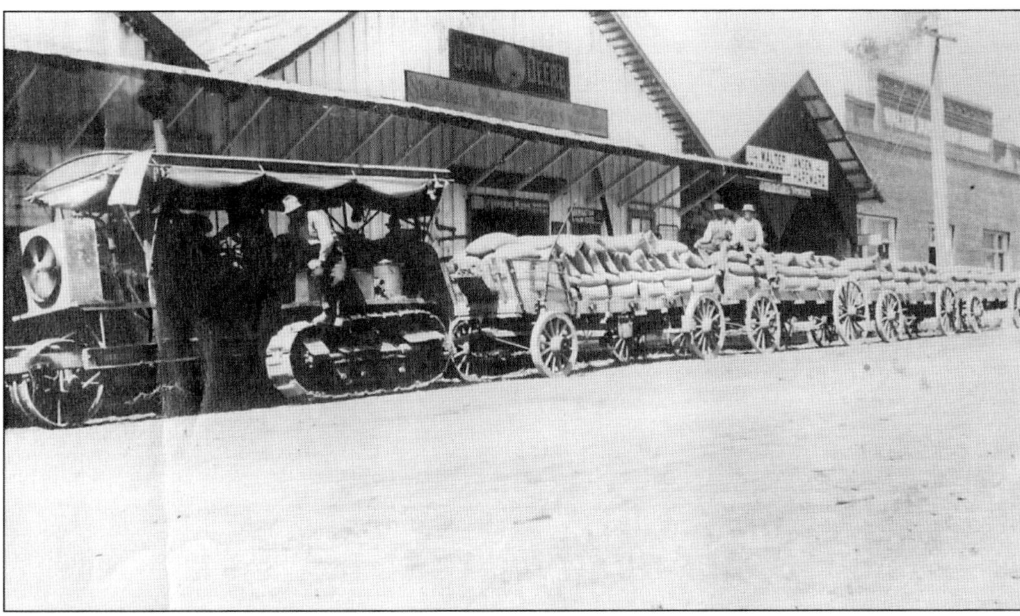

In this image, Peter Crough's tractor, with wagons full of grain sacks, waits to unload in front of Jansen's. Grain was brought to Jansen's from the fields, cleaned and processed, then repacked for shipment. The sign underneath the John Deere sign reads, "Studebaker Wagons & Buggies sold by Walter Jansen."

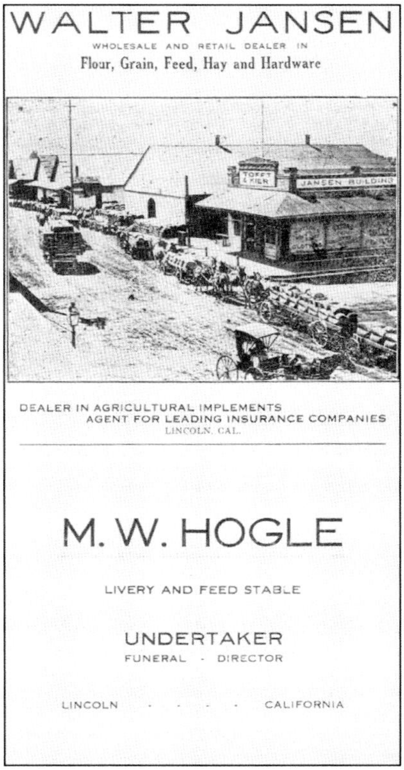

In 1900, Hill and Hughes owned a mortuary at 453 G Street and a livery stable at 447 G Street, across from Jansen's. The businesses were taken over by M.W. Hogle and Bishop (and then by Hogle by himself). W.F. Farnsworth purchased the mortuary business in 1939 and operated it until well into the 1950s. Ann Hogle married Walter K. Jansen in 1916.

This c. 1910 image shows the fully stocked shelves at Tofft Grocery, located on the southwest corner of Fifth and G Streets. The Tofft family engaged in the grocery and hardware business for several generations and were very successful. They were able to gauge the wants and needs of the community they served.

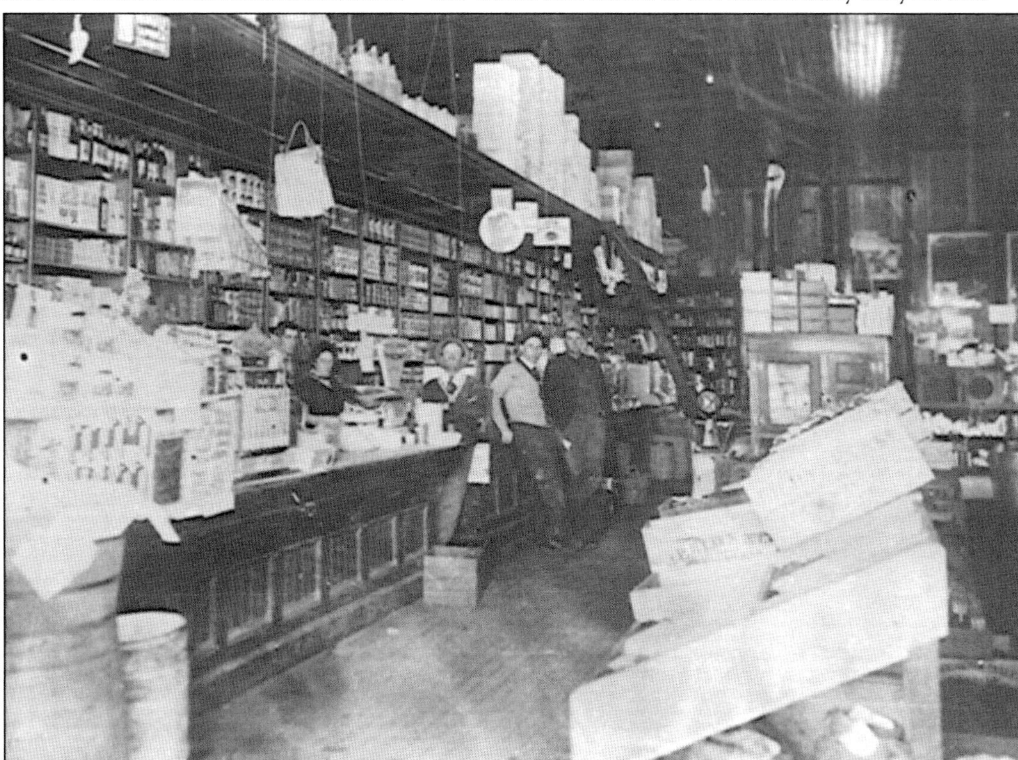

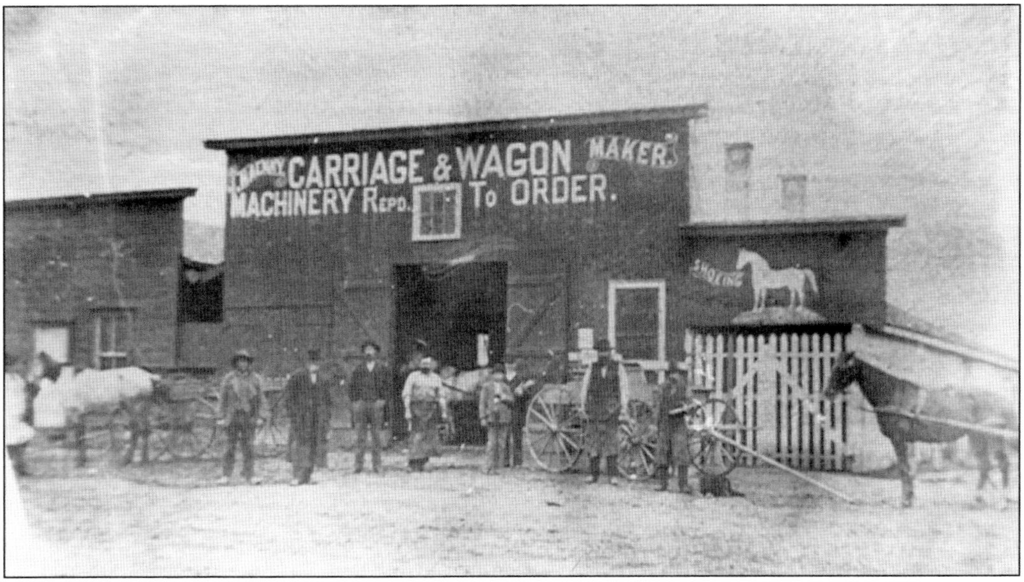

There were quite a few blacksmiths in Lincoln over the years, and many of the smithies changed hands a few times. The main shops in Lincoln were at four principal sites. John Haenney's (pictured) was on the southeast corner of Fifth and F Streets, James Hickey's was at 570 Fifth Street (next to the library), John Neville started his shop at 629 G Street, and Fred Wortell's was at 447 G Street from 1900 to 1950.

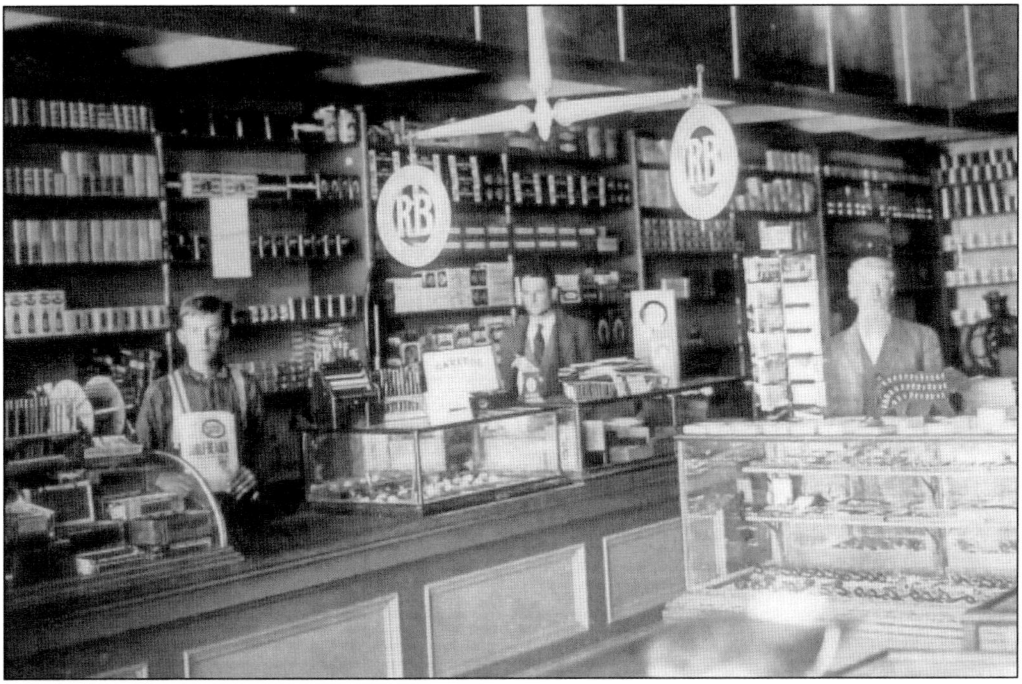

Sparks Variety Store was in business from 1911 to 1913 and was located at 519 G Street. William "Buzz" Sparks is standing at center, and his father, William M. Sparks, is standing on the right. Sparks was a variety store and newsstand.

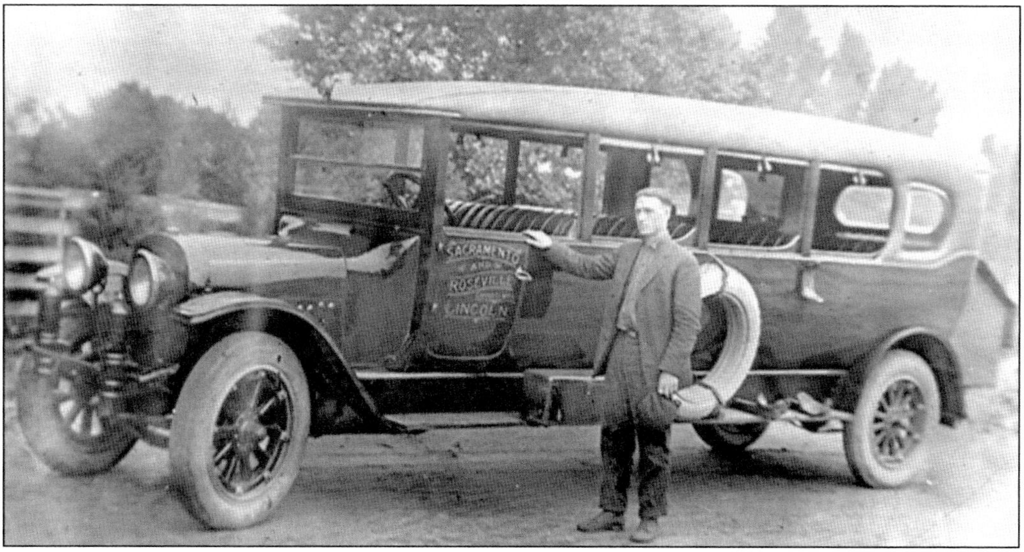

With the increasing number of new automobiles, Lincoln was proud to have an "auto stage" line that began in 1914. W.W. Wall was the proprietor of this pioneer line that operated between Lincoln, Roseville, and Sacramento. Stages left daily from Leveque's Store on G Street, and returning stages left from Sacramento's Windsor Hotel, the last of which left at 11:30 p.m. Jerry Seifert is the man standing by the stage.

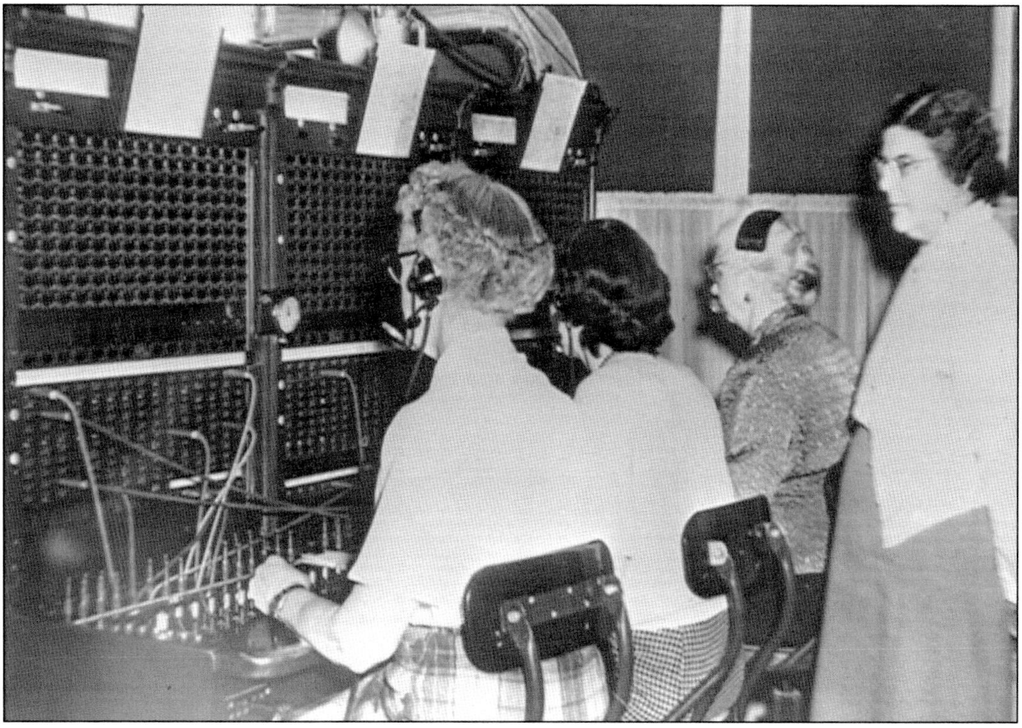

In the 1890s, long-distance telephone service was made available to the residents of Lincoln and rural communities. The first office was located in the True Blue Stores and conducted by John Landis and Sons. Laura Landis, daughter of James and Bertha C. Landis, was the first "telephone girl." This photograph shows Gertrude Dixon supervising telephone operators.

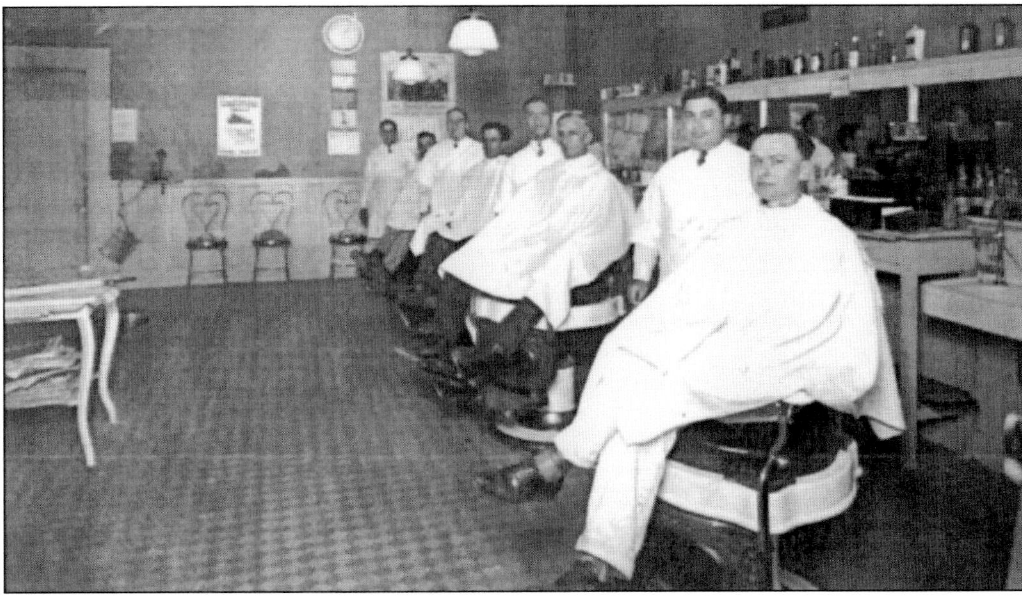

William Airo started working at Harry Richardson's barbershop in the Hotel Burdge in 1917. After working at the pottery for a while, Airo opened his own barbershop across the street in McCrary's Pool Hall at 544 Fifth Street. The shop was called, at various times, The Square Deal Barber Shop, Deluxe Beauty and Shaving Parlor, and Deluxe Barber Shop. William Airo was followed in business by his son, William Airo Jr. The Airos are descendants of pioneers Heitor Airo and John Casina.

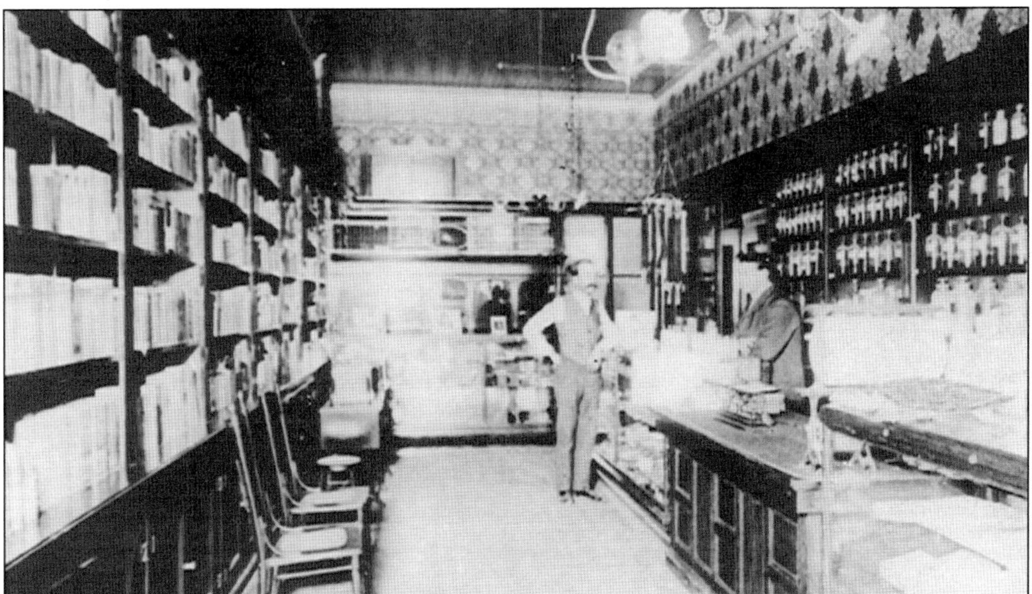

The Ingram Drug Store at 543 G Street was in the Ingram family for 75 years. William Ingram (left) and his son William D. are pictured here inside the store. Ingram was not the only drugstore in town; John Alexander opened a drugstore at 627 Fifth Street in 1916 and continued in the same location until 1945, and Arthur Leavell began a drugstore at 680 Fifth Street in the 1890s and operated it until 1906.

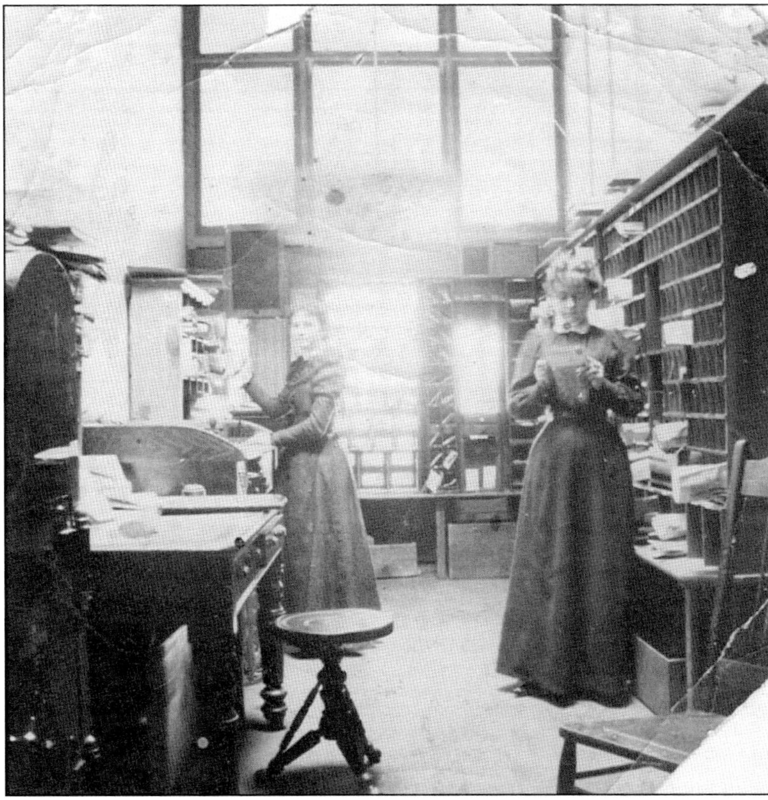

In the 1870s, William Ingram was Lincoln's postmaster, and the post office was part of his store. He held the position for over 25 years and was also a town trustee for over 20 years. The unidentified ladies in this photograph are busy sorting mail. In 1899, Ingram became the town telephone agent, and there was a public phone booth in his store.

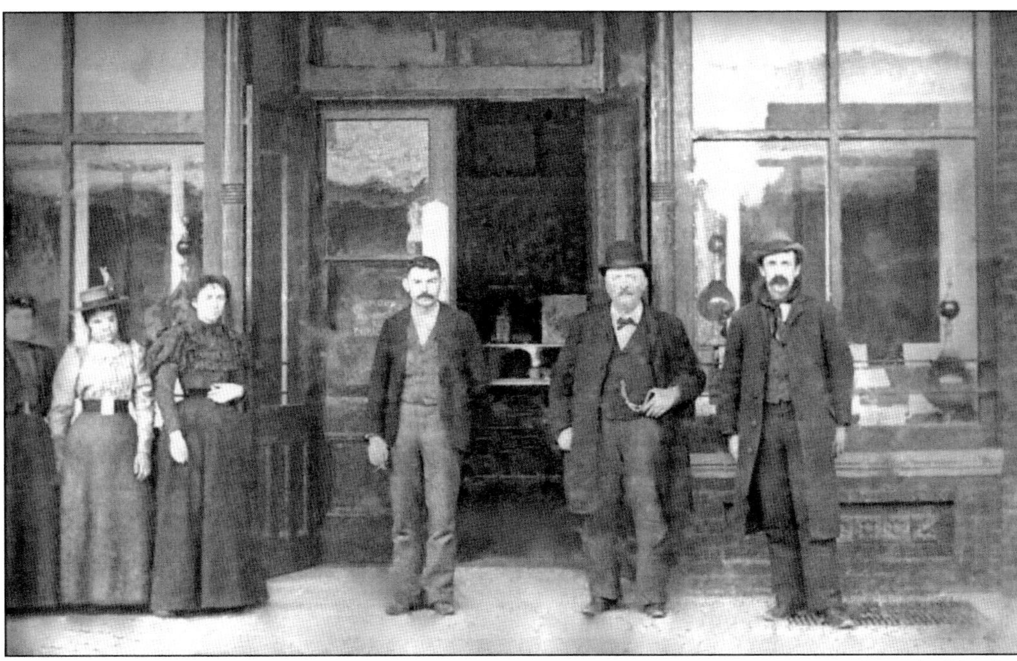

This photograph was taken outside the Ingram Drug Store. The women are only identified by first name—May, Rose, and Kitty. The men are, from left to right, P.L. Moore, Dr. William Norman Finney, and Charles Gladding, one of the original founders of Gladding, McBean.

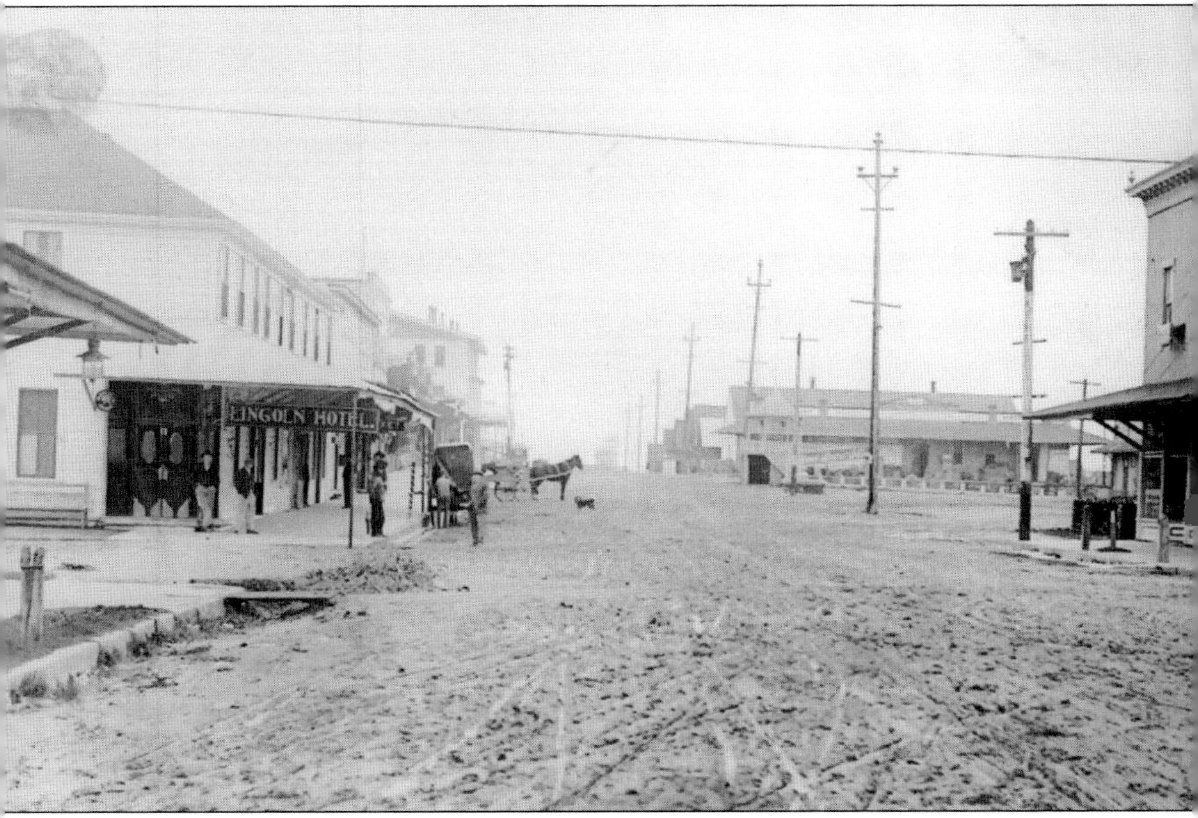

This photograph looking north down G Street shows muddy, unpaved streets. The two-story Lincoln Hotel, at left, was on the southeast corner of Sixth and G Streets and was initially built and owned by Murdoch McCrimmon. It was called the Parry House from 1888 to 1892, when G. Parry leased it. In 1893, the hotel became the Exchange Hotel when J.H. Dixon and Mrs. C.W. Harris took over. Fire claimed the hotel in 1896, and McCrimmon rebuilt, naming his new structure the New Lincoln Hotel. There was a store, office space, and a bar on the G Street side of the newly rebuilt hotel. The True Blue Hall is across the street at right. Farther down the street on the left is the three-story Hotel Burdge.

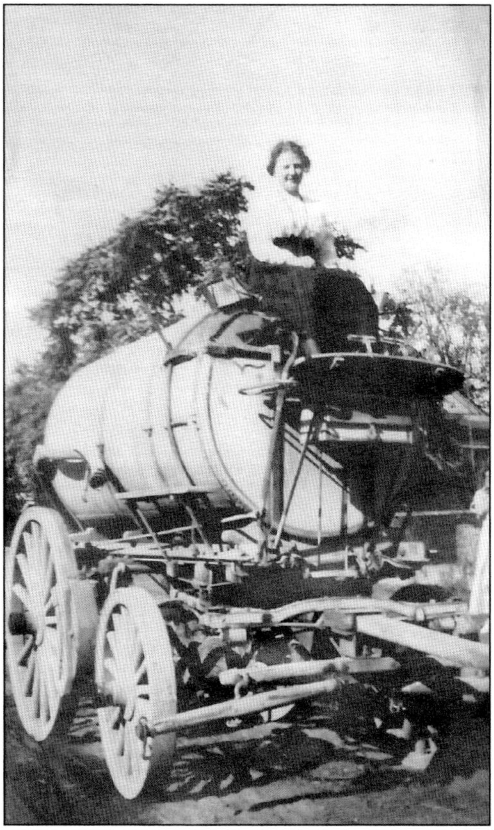

The Lincoln city council voted to pave the streets in 1918. Water trucks, like this one, were used to keep the dust down on the dirt streets. Viola Alspaugh, daughter of Isaac Alspaugh and granddaughter of early settler Benjamin Alspaugh and his wife, Susan Hall Alspaugh, is seated on top of a water truck in this 1921 photograph. Viola married Edward Bates Russell Sr. in 1924.

The Lincoln Saloon was possibly in the Lincoln Hotel, at Sixth and G Streets, across from the "Opera House" in the True Blue Hall. The sign at left announced that "this bell will ring five minutes before the curtain raises," which allowed patrons time to get to their seats for the show.

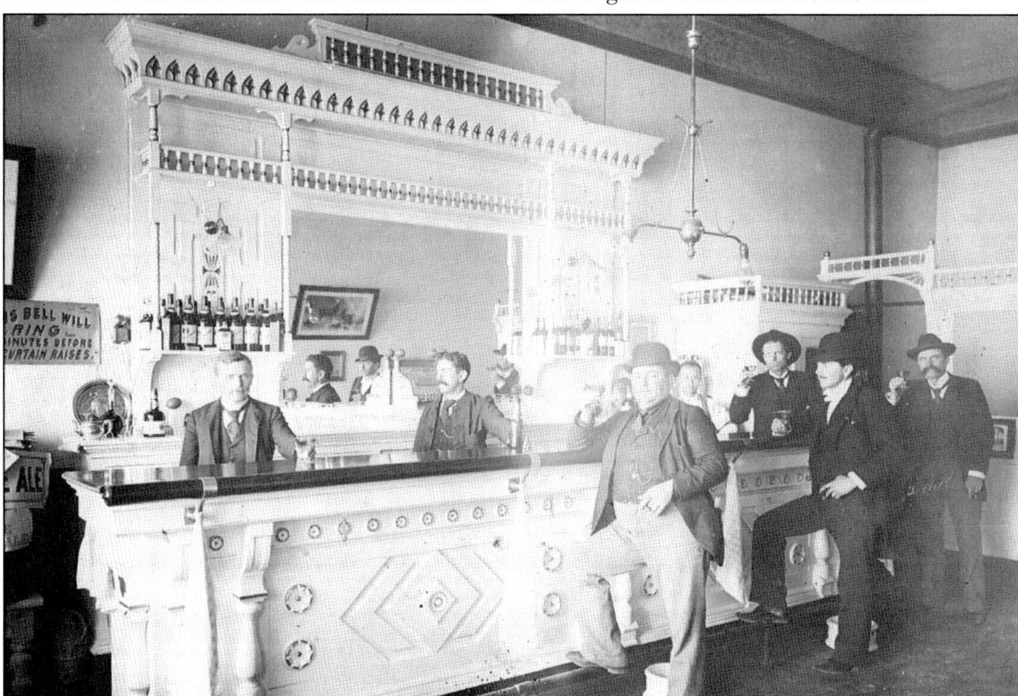

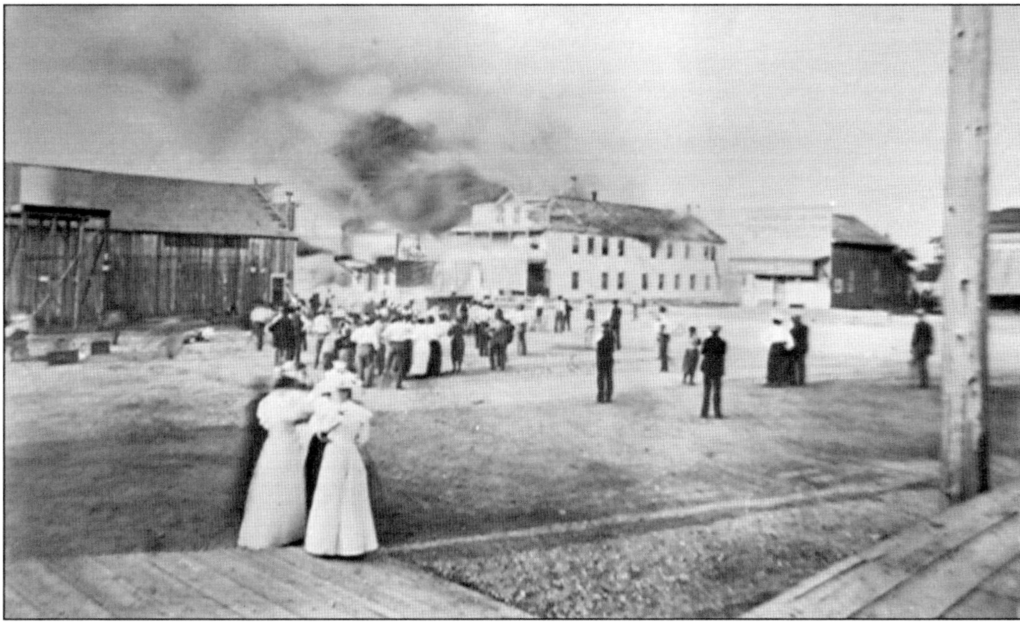

The fire of 1883 destroyed Lincoln's four original hotels, all of which were located near the intersection of Fifth and G Streets. Some businessmen, like Murdoch McCrimmon, did not let fires discourage them. After losing hotels in the fires of 1883 and 1896 (pictured), McCrimmon continued to build. His third hotel, the New Lincoln Hotel, managed to escape being destroyed by fire.

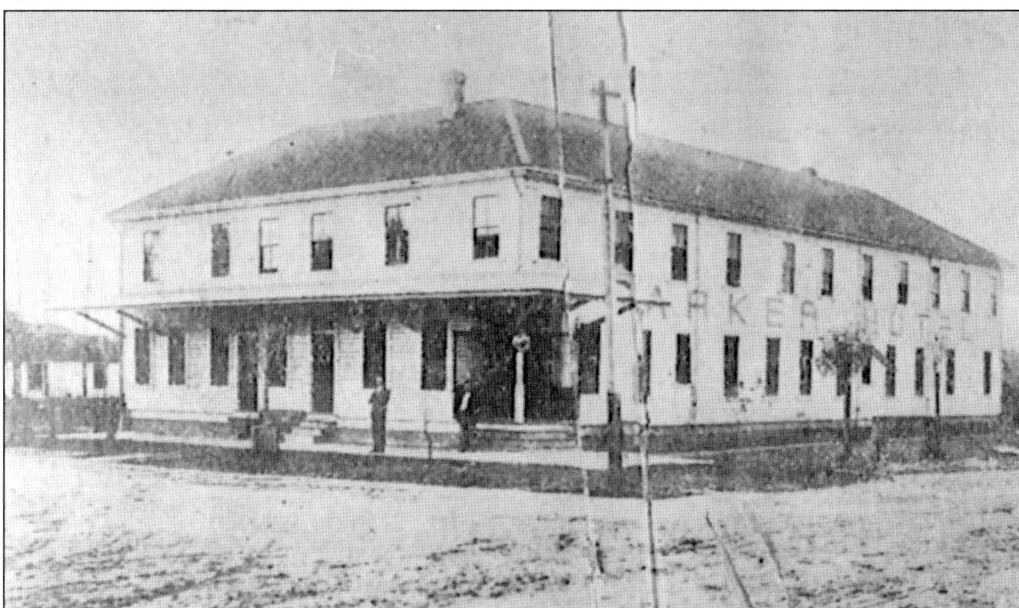

The Parker Hotel, built in 1904 on the southwest corner of Seventh and F Streets, was the only hotel built in Lincoln between 1900 and 2013. There were no buildings at this location before 1900, as Charles Wilson held onto the property in case there was a revival of coal mining. From 1900 to 1925, the Lincoln Hotel and the Parker Hotel housed many Europeans who worked at Gladding, McBean. Eventually, many bought homes of their own and became part of the Lincoln community.

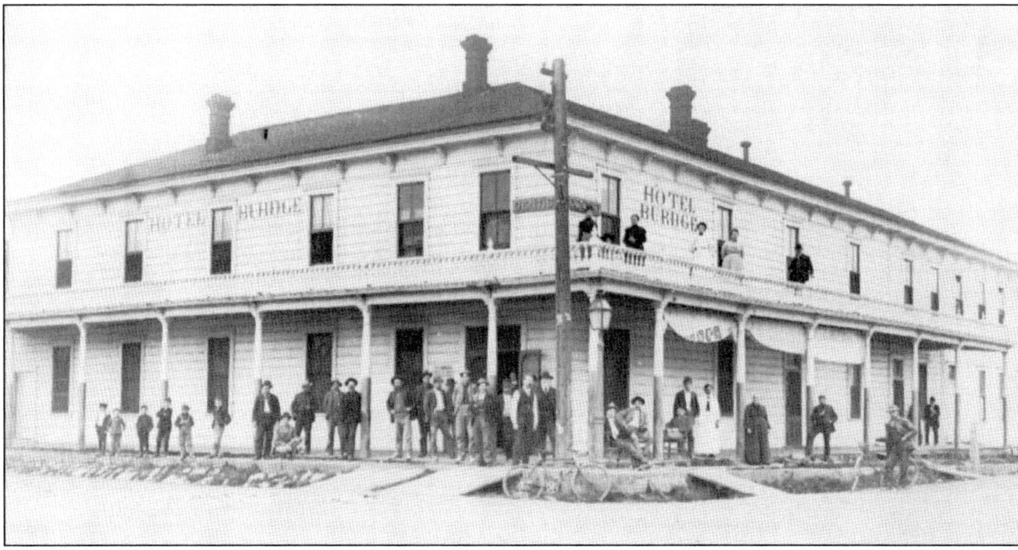

John Chapman built the Phoenix Hotel (later known as Logan House) in 1860 on the southeast corner of Fifth and G Streets. The saloon there is said to be the first business to open in Lincoln. Lincoln's largest fire occurred on July 11, 1883, and destroyed both Logan House and the saloon. Stephen Burdge and his wife, Melissa, then built their two-story Hotel Burdge there.

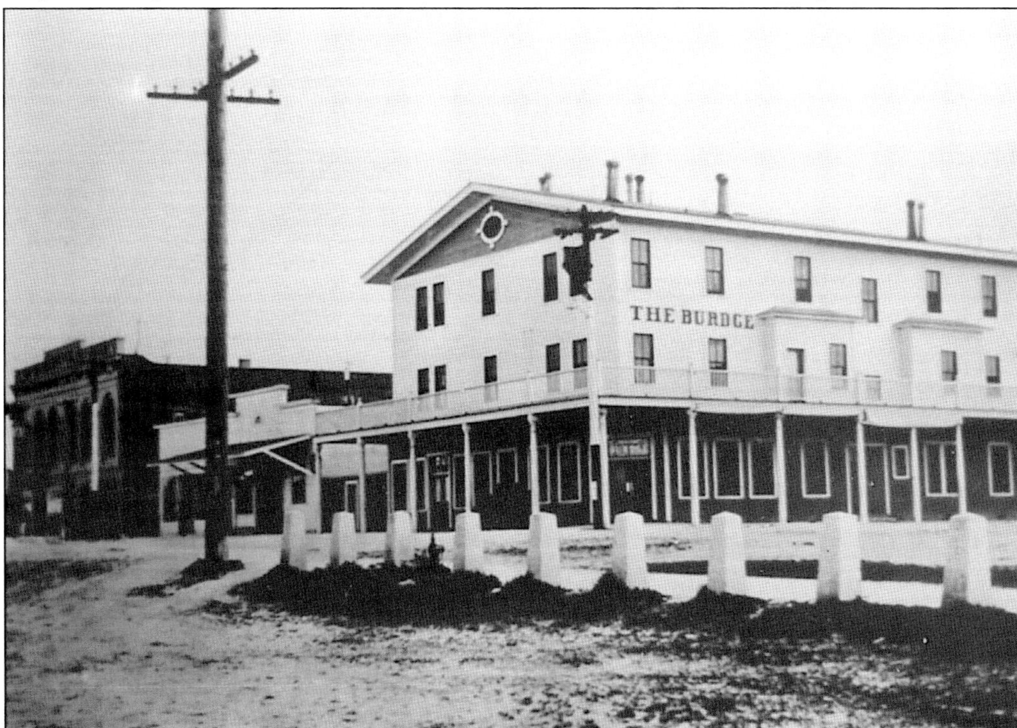

Between Christmas night and the early morning hours of December 26, 1904, fire struck again and destroyed the Hotel Burdge. The owners, Stephen and Melissa Burdge, rebuilt the hotel as a three-story building. The hotel building stood until it was torn down in 1940 to make way for the Standard Oil Service Station.

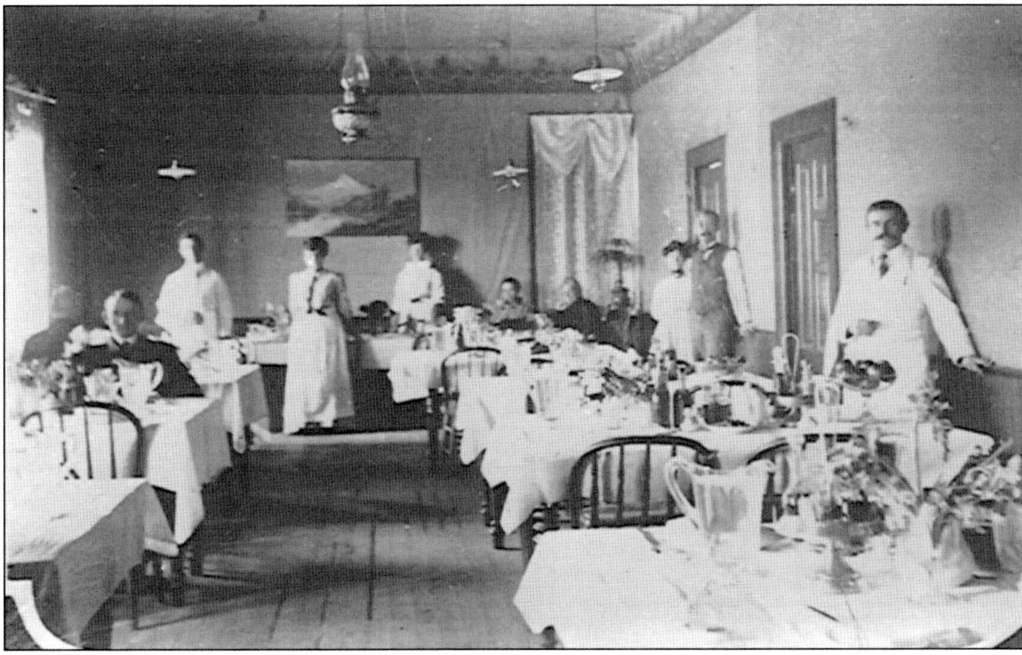

This is a photograph of the dining room in the Hotel Burdge. A hotel was on this site from 1861 until 1940. The hotel's original dinner bell is on display at the Lincoln Area Archives Museum.

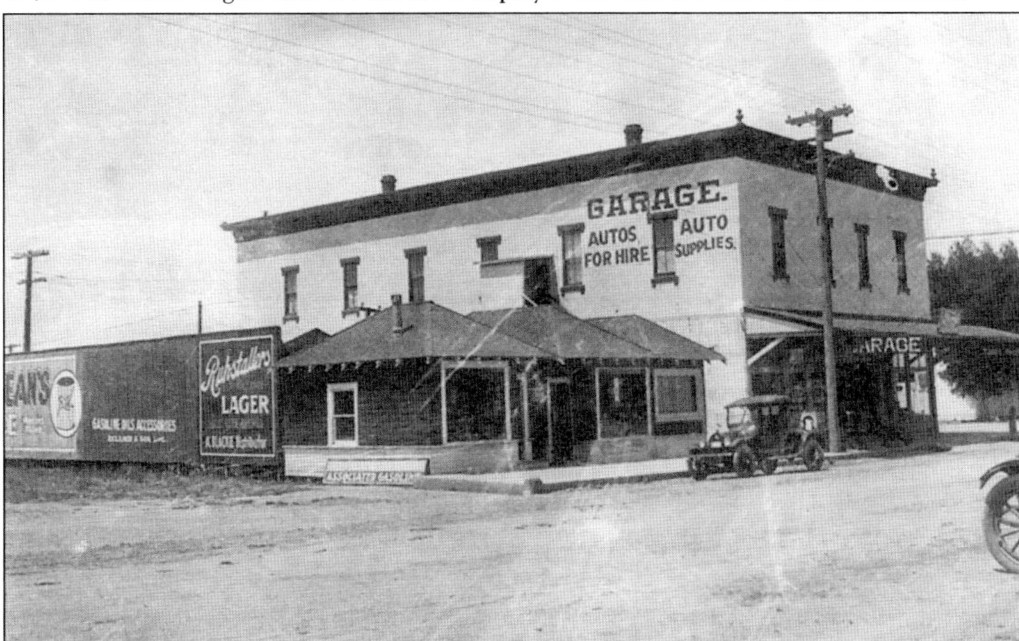

The True Blue Hall was located on the southwest corner of Sixth and G Streets, across from the New Lincoln Hotel. The two-story building is seen here at right. In 1908, the *News Messenger* announced that films would be shown there on a regular basis. When movies came to town, the hall became the Photo Theater. The hall was also called the Lincoln Opera House and was the focal point of Lincoln's entertainment for many years. Dances, plays, school graduations, vaudeville shows, and meetings were held there.

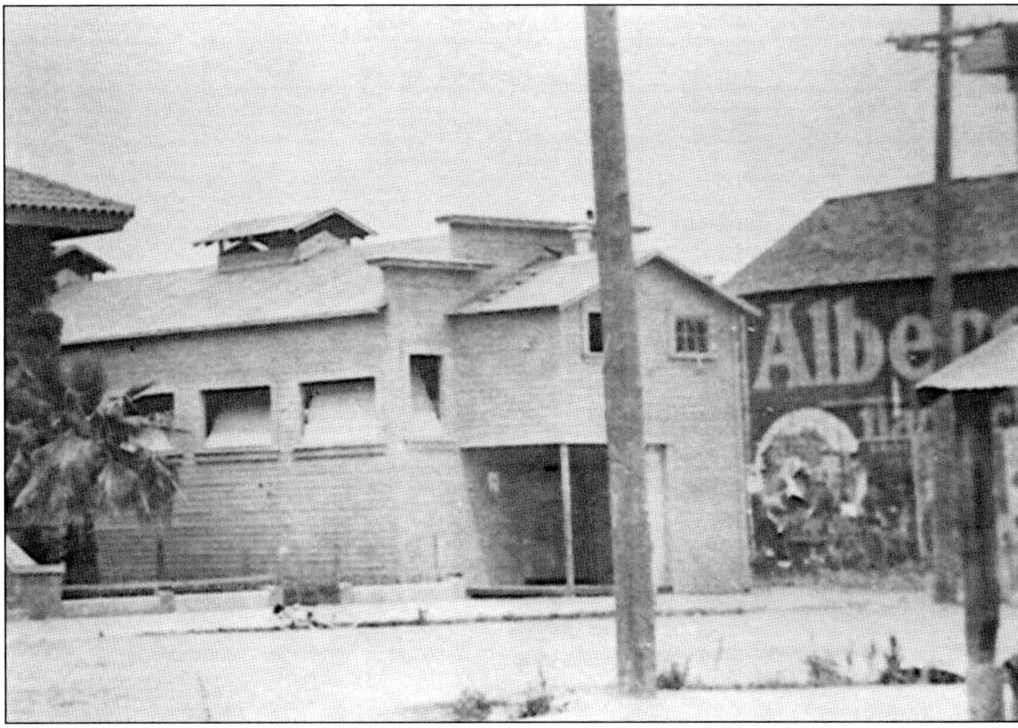

The Aerdome Theatre, pictured above with a corner of the Lincoln Public Library showing at far left, was built on Fifth Street by George Luce and co-owned by Grant Allen—the partnership of Luce and Allen. The theater opened in the 1920s and, according to the *Lincoln News Messenger*, was well patronized and showed a high class of pictures. The first film shown at the theater was *Behind Closed Doors* with Hobart Bosworth. Luce, pictured below, came with his parents and grandparents to Lincoln as a young boy in 1866 and grew up to become a carpenter and contractor. He was the building contractor for the three-story Hotel Burdge that opened in September 1905. He married Levia Hinman, and his daughter, Alice Naomi, married into the pioneer Boyden family.

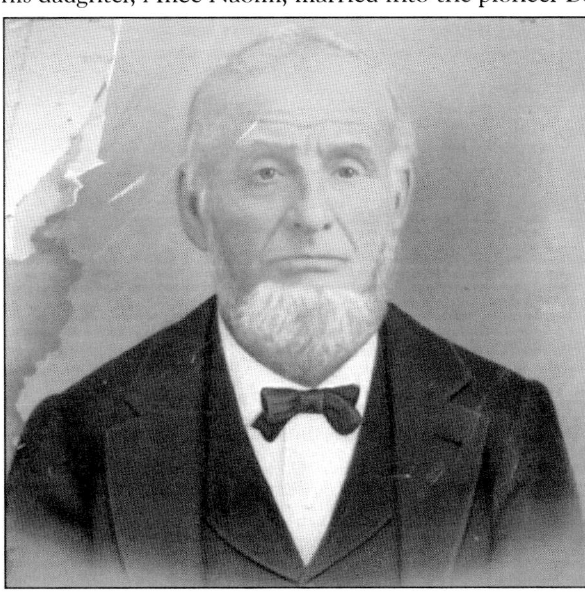

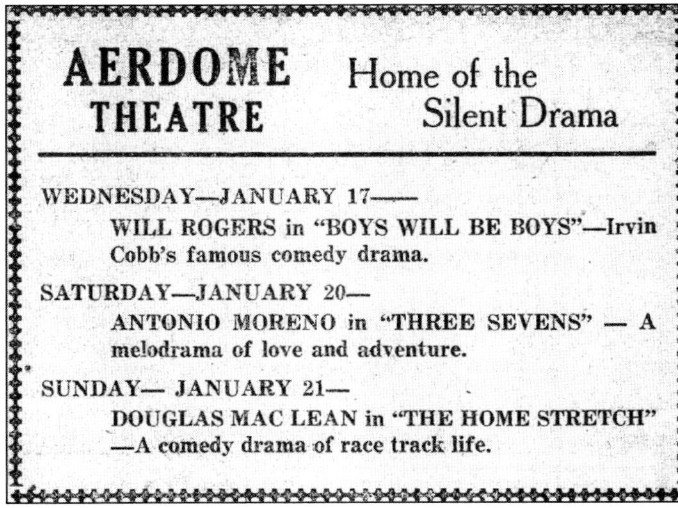

AERDOME THEATRE Home of the Silent Drama

WEDNESDAY—JANUARY 17—

WILL ROGERS in "BOYS WILL BE BOYS"—Irvin Cobb's famous comedy drama.

SATURDAY—JANUARY 20—

ANTONIO MORENO in "THREE SEVENS" — A melodrama of love and adventure.

SUNDAY— JANUARY 21—

DOUGLAS MAC LEAN in "THE HOME STRETCH" —A comedy drama of race track life.

This January 1923 newspaper advertisement shows a playbill for the Aerdome Theatre. According to newspaper articles, (George) Luce and (Grant) Allen, owners of the Aerdome Theatre, were presenting good movies and making an effort to obtain the best pictures possible. The price of a ticket was nominal, and the owners often lost money in order to show the latest and most expensive movies to the community.

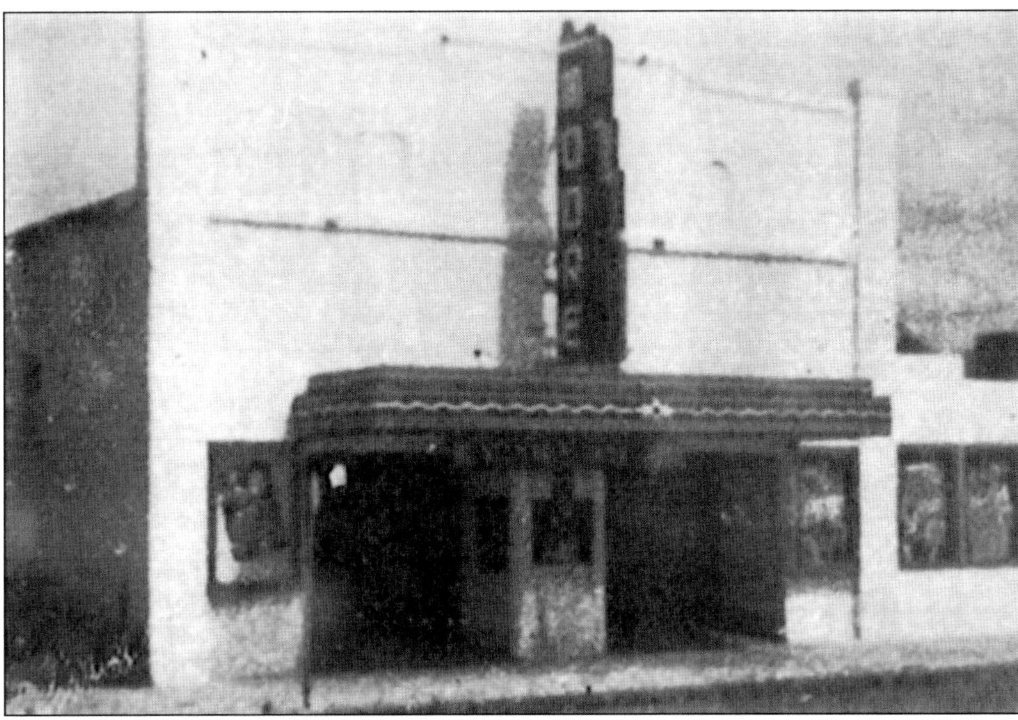

In 1926, John Moore purchased the Aerdome Theatre building and reopened it under the name Strand Theater; in 1929, "talking" pictures were being shown there. In 1936, the theater was renamed the Moore Theater. Moore's enterprise was the best known and longest-lasting movie house in Lincoln. It was in operation from 1926 to 1950.

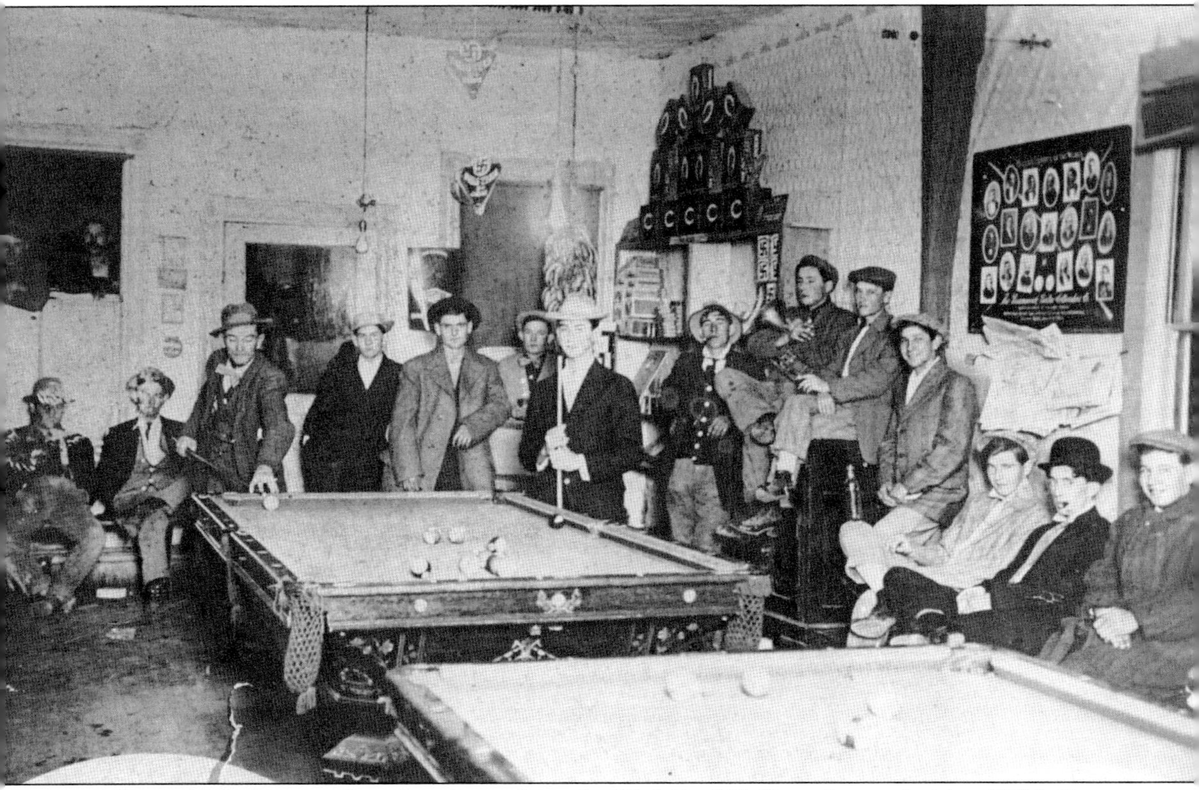

This c. 1910 photograph is thought to show the Club Pool Hall on the south side of Fifth Street, just west of F Street, where Sam Goldeen's store and Tofft Hardware were located. The men pictured are, from left to right, unidentified, Clarence Pardee, Grant Allen, Carl Williams, George Wilson, Tooney Sparks, Harry Williams, Brick Culbertson, Ed Grey Sr., Skip Neville, Fred Laswell, George Warren, Ed Shane, and Coon Culbertson.

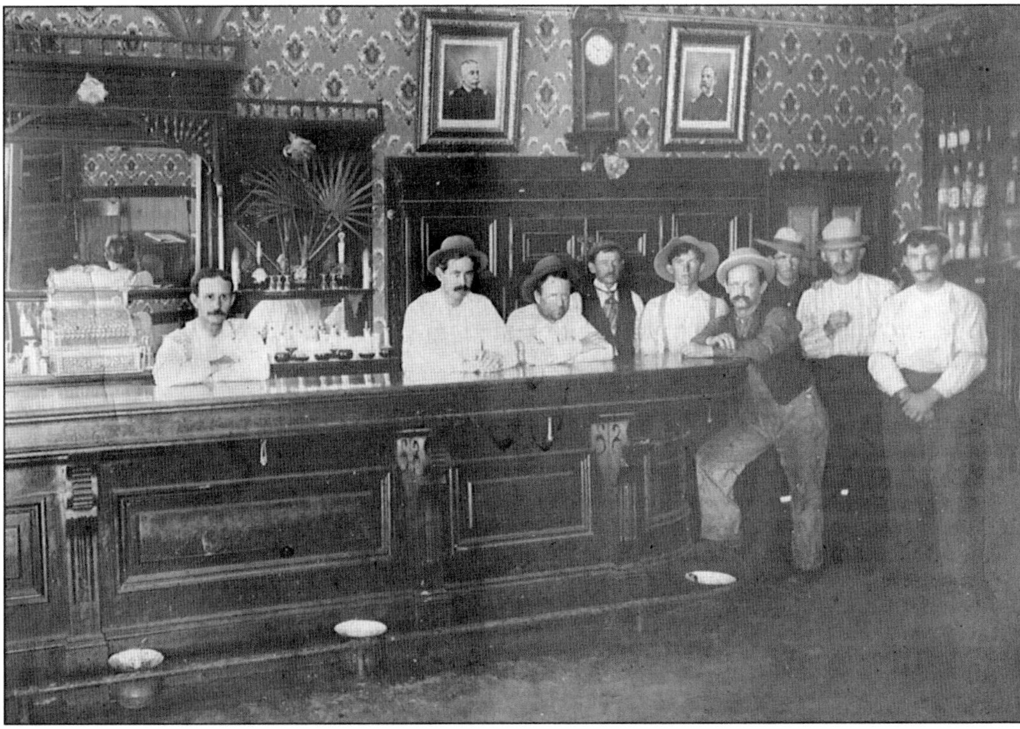

These photographs of Frank Dillian's Bar at Sixth and G Street were taken at different times but both with Dillian behind the counter. Local saloons had billiards, card rooms, and slot machines. Lincoln averaged nine saloons during the pre-Prohibition era (1900 to 1920). This was a limit set by the Lincoln town trustees. No saloons operated legally during the Prohibition years (1920 to 1933). Raids during Prohibition led to the arrests and heavy fining of violators. Most were hotel, restaurant, and poolroom proprietors who were supposedly selling soft drinks.

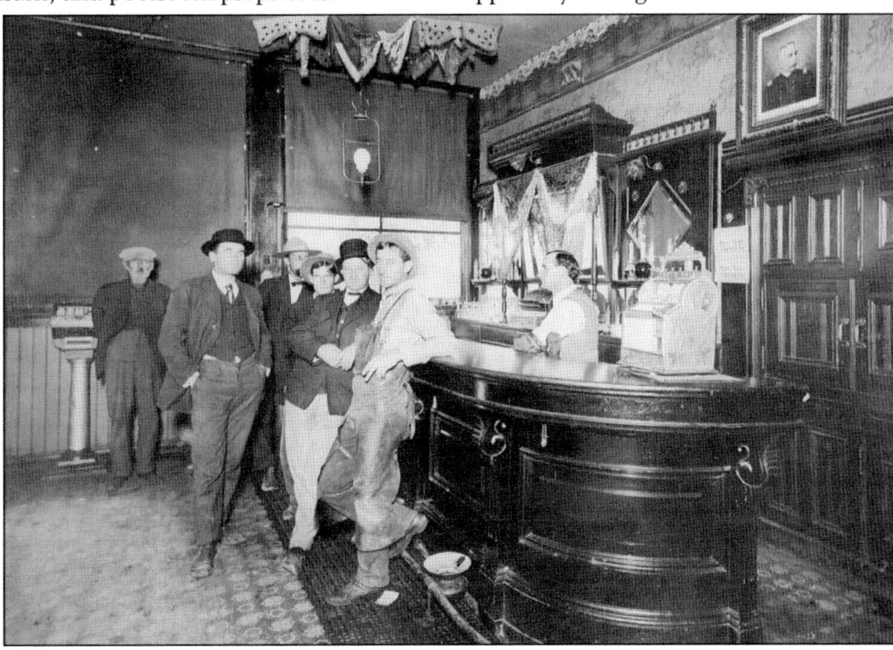

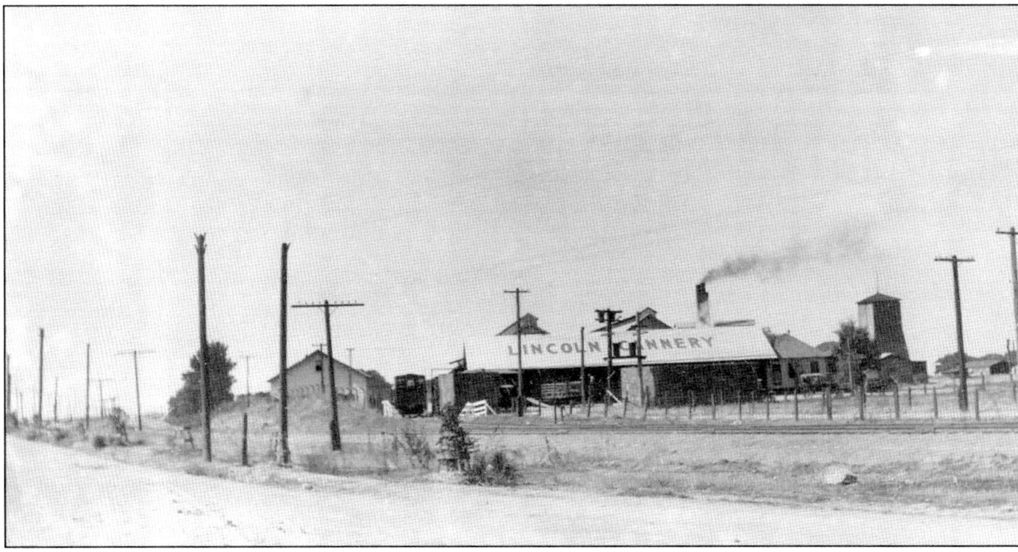

Lincoln's first cannery, known as Lincoln Fruit Packing Company, opened in 1895 in the old railroad depot building that had been moved to Seventh and H Streets. From the onset, the cannery was a success. By the beginning of the canning season in 1897, approximately 75 women and girls were employed there. By 1901, the cannery was four times its original size with an output of 20,000 cans per day.

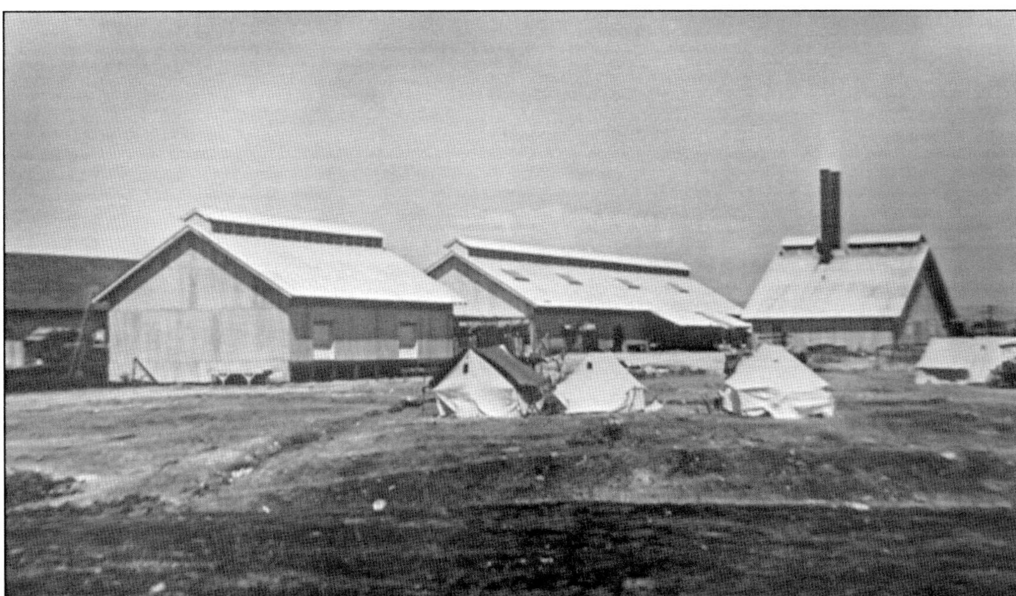

At its peak, the cannery employed over 600 people, many of them housed in a temporary "tent city." In 1903, a large corporation purchased the company, and the entire stock was sold. By 1906, a skating rink opened in the closed cannery's main warehouse. Soon after Lincoln Union High School opened on H Street in 1907, one of the old cannery buildings was used as the girl's gymnasium.

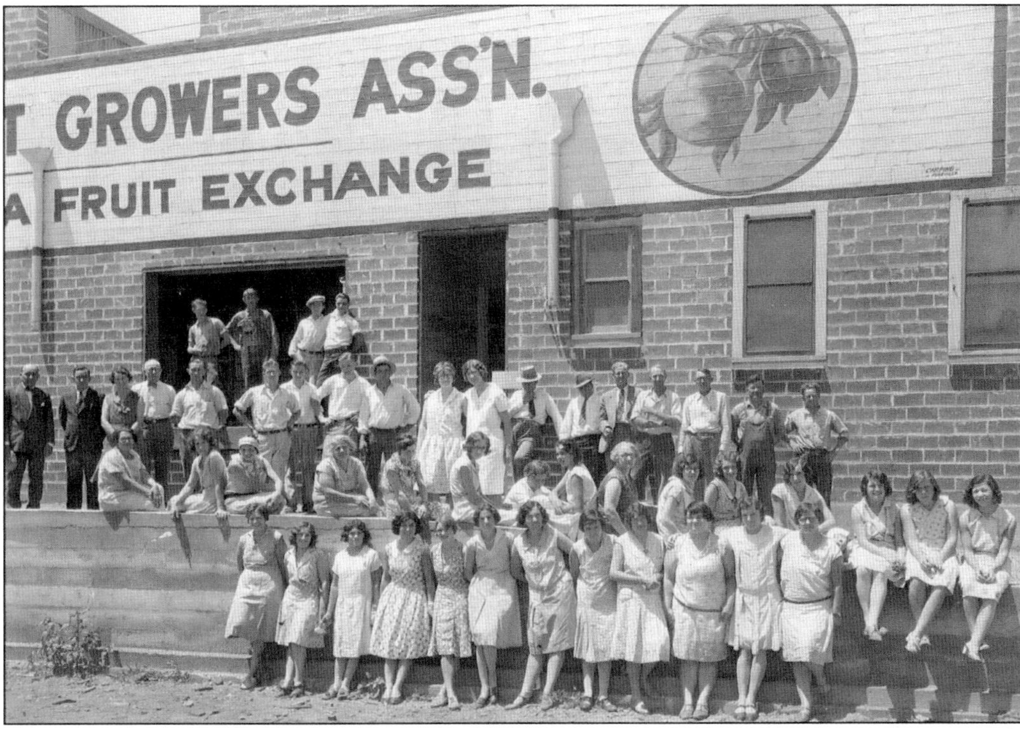

The Lincoln Fruit Growers Association formed at the Fruitvale schoolhouse in June 1910 for the purpose of packing and shipping fruit. They used an old warehouse north of Seventh Street and began shipping in July of that year. The original officers were A. Isaac (Mt. Pleasant), S.W. Hinckley (Mt. Pleasant), L. LaBrie (Fruitvale), Herb Fowler (Gold Hill), and Fred Clark (Mt. Pleasant). The group had 25 charter members. In 1924, they purchased the southwest corner of Fourth and G Streets, where they erected this building in 1930.

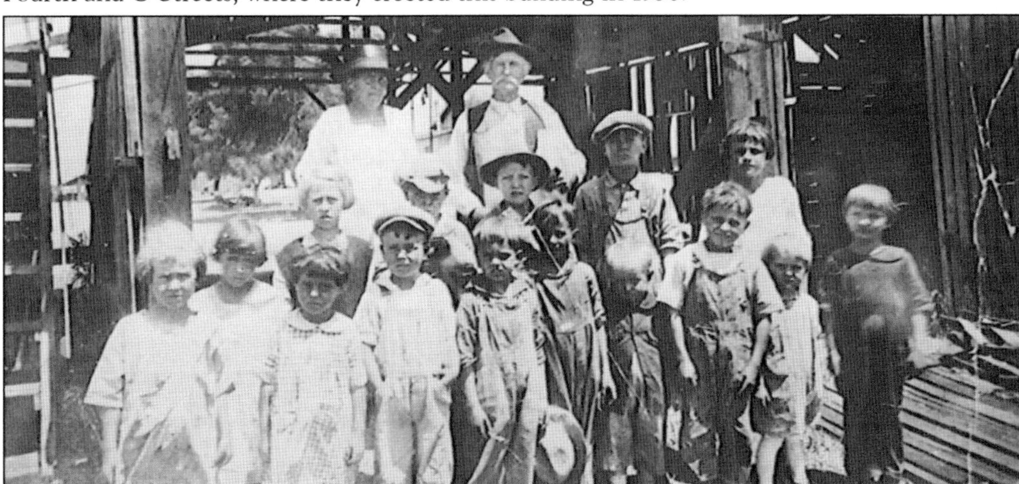

The children of the packing company's employees are pictured here in 1924. They are, from left to right, (first row) Ethel Hansen, Helen Paillex, unidentified, Bill Wyatt, two unidentified, Robert Paillex, Robert Hansen, and two unidentified; (second row) Helen Hansen, unidentified, Fred Christianson, Louis Hansen, and unidentified. Mrs. and Mr. Gordon are the adults behind the children.

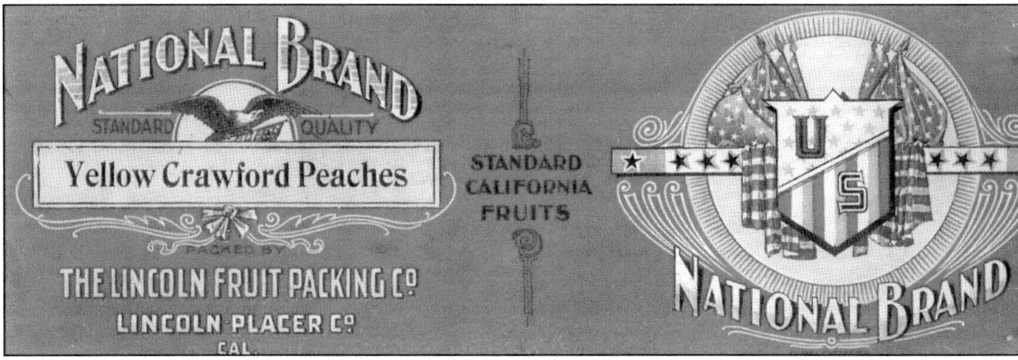

Beginning as early as the 1880s, countless colorfully lithographed paper labels were used to sell fruit of all kinds. These labels were used by farmers, growers, and packing houses to identify and advertise wooden boxes of fresh produce. Not only did the label identify each individual box of fruit, it also had to communicate the appeal of the product so someone would buy it. This made the label an important tool for every packer. Each packer or farmer had a brand to identify their specific shipments. The brightly colored and attractively designed labels soon became the main way to draw attention in the wholesale produce market. The grower's livelihood soon became totally dependent on the crate-end label's reputation for quality. These labels are from the Lincoln Fruit Packing Company.

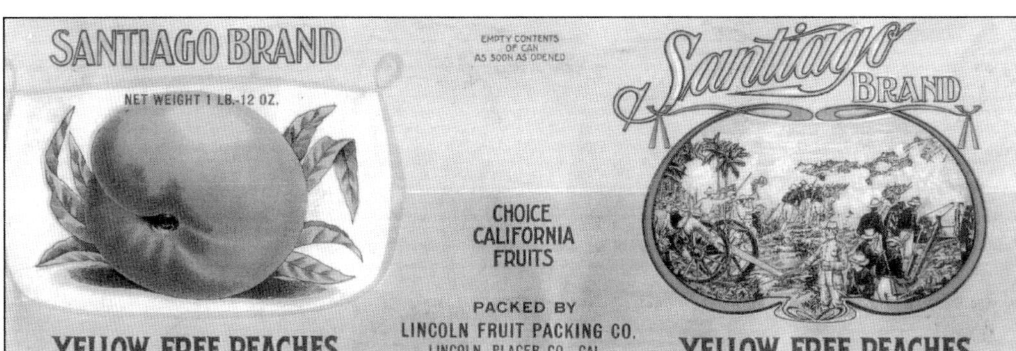

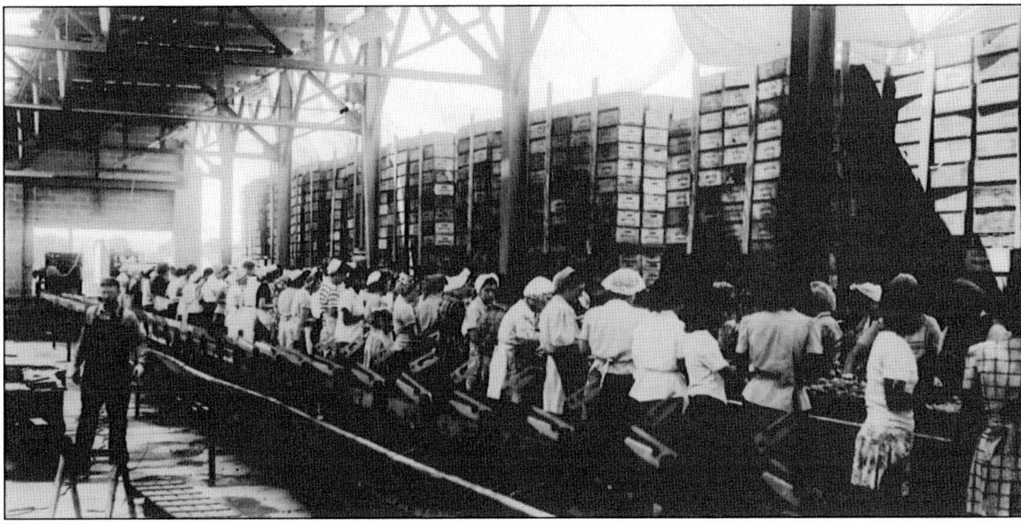

A new cannery was established in 1912, and the new building was dedicated in October 1913. The location was about seven blocks from the previous cannery south of First Street and west of H Street. This was a local cooperative movement, and the articles of incorporation for the Lincoln Packing Company were filed by Antone Fereva, president, and Alfred E. Clark, secretary, of the Placer County Growers Cannery Association.

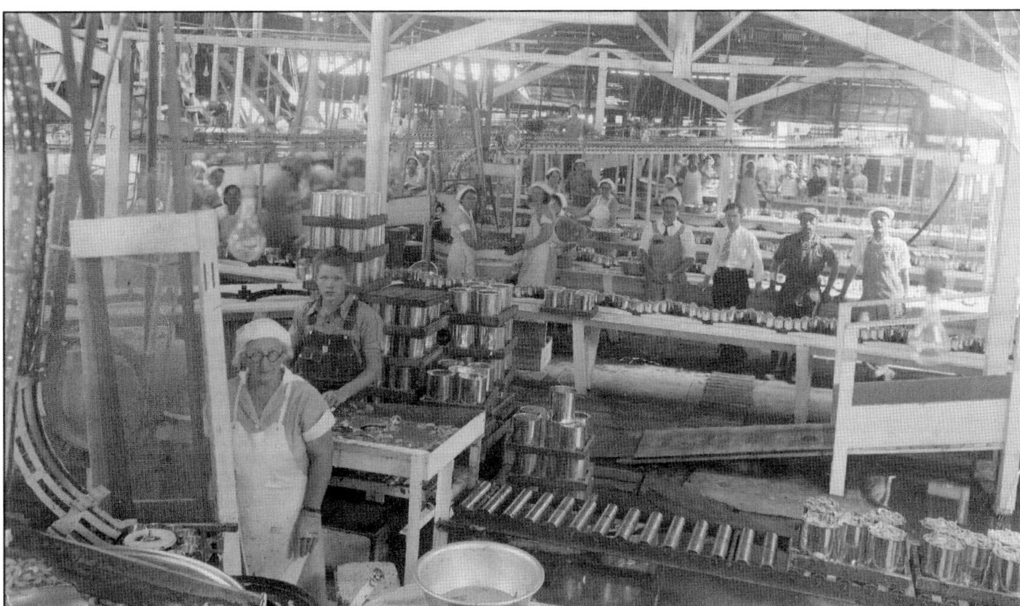

This 1930s photograph shows the inside of the cannery. Lilly Culbertson is in the foreground at left, and Jimmy Sorenson is behind her. The next row of workers are, from left to right, Ramona Padilla, Josephine Orhey, Kenneth Rogers (canning department foreman), Pat Gordon (plant superintendent), Pete Padilla (chief mechanic), and Roy Shields (cook room foreman).

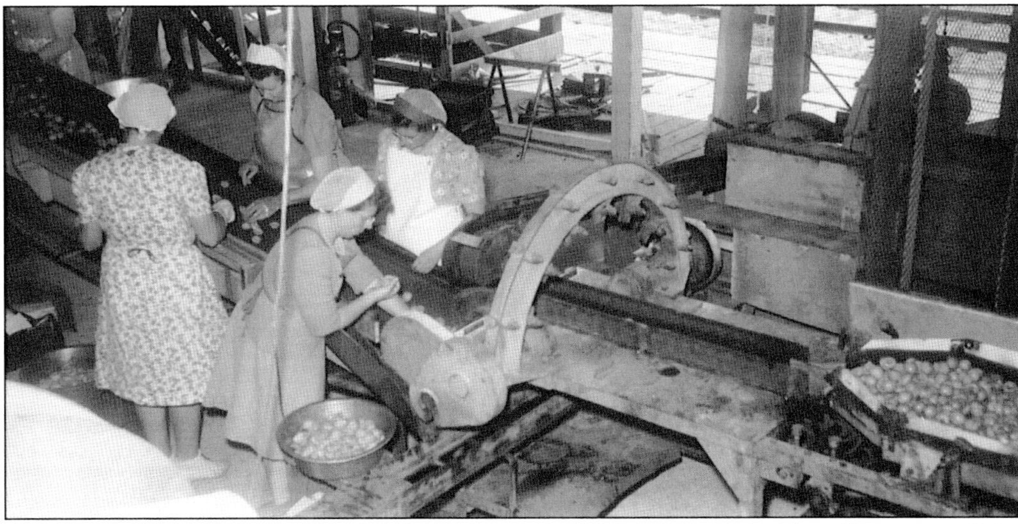

The main products canned in Lincoln were apricots, peaches, fruit cocktail, and tomatoes. Other products were also canned from time to time, including 300 tons of olives in 1924. The cannery owners built a milk-condensing building in the late 1920s from Gladding, McBean terra cotta, and thus began the canning of Holsum Brand condensed milk.

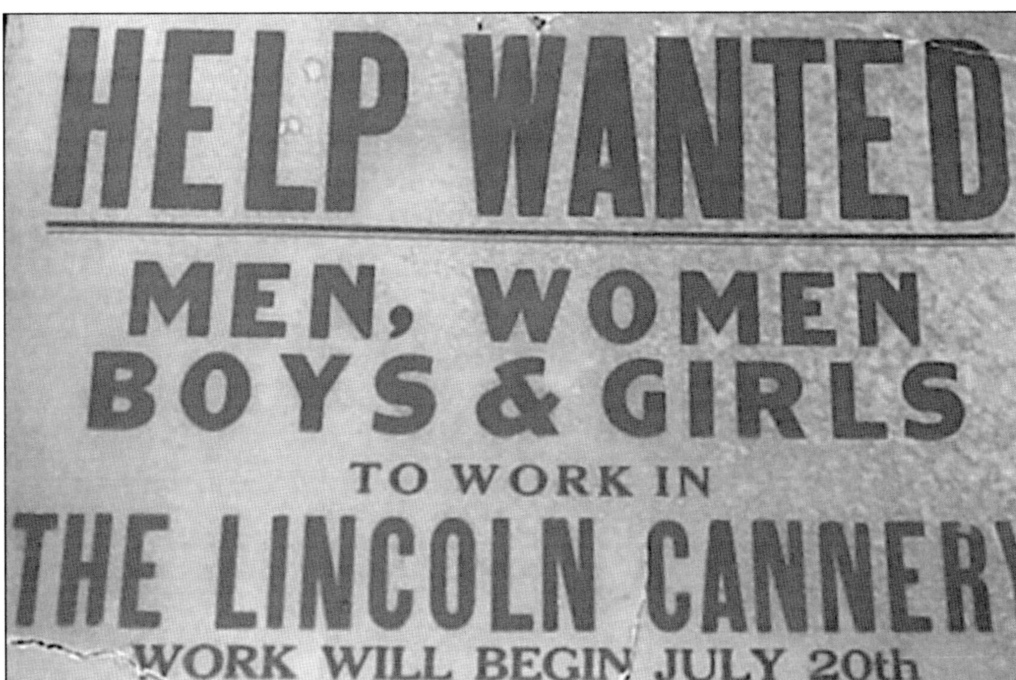

The Lincoln Cannery, also known as the Lincoln Packing Company or the Lincoln Fruit Packing Company, suffered a spectacular fire on July 21, 1946, that destroyed its main plant. This was not only a blow to the canning industry but to the community, whose housewives and students earned money for household and school expenses during the canning season from June through September.

Six

SCHOOLS AND CHURCHES

Educating children must have been important to the pioneers who settled in the area—a conclusion that may be drawn when evaluating the number of schools and school districts that were established in the area as early as 1855. When there were enough children in an area to warrant a school, a district was formed, a school was built, and a teacher hired. The geographic size of the earliest districts was quite large because of the low density of school-age children in most rural areas. For example, Mt. Pleasant School was seven miles away for children living up Garden Bar Road near Bear River. As the population grew, large districts were divided into smaller ones so that younger children would not have so far to walk. Some of the early schools included Gold Hill School, Mt. Pleasant School, Coon Creek/Manzanita, Pleasant Grove, Lincoln School, Sheridan School, Valley View, Central School, Daneville School, New Hope School, Orange Valley, Fruitvale School, and Fair Oaks.

The earliest miners and settlers had little time to be concerned with formal religious affairs, and most of the church-oriented inhabitants considered them a bit loud, rough, and uncivilized. The presence of men of that sort was just a sign of the times in the West. They were accepted because the gold they found brought prosperity to the community and the land they farmed brought food to their tables. As the population grew and started to include families, churches began to appear. Rev. James Hunter, of the Methodist Episcopal Society, held services at various sites, including Gold Hill. History does not record any permanent churches until 1866, when the Union Church was built on Sixth Street between K and L Streets in Lincoln. St. Joseph Catholic Church broke ground for a building around 1881. The Lincoln Methodist Church was completed in 1891, and the Congregational church broke ground in 1890. Three of the four churches were built on Sixth Street, so it became known as "church row."

The Lincoln Methodist Church has 37 stained glass windows, many with humorous captions that have generated a mystery. Local historians, including some who were early members of the church, have been unable to discover the source of the windows, which were installed in memory of ministers and missionaries who traveled West before 1900. Who created the windows? No one knows; however, Peter Ahart paid for them.

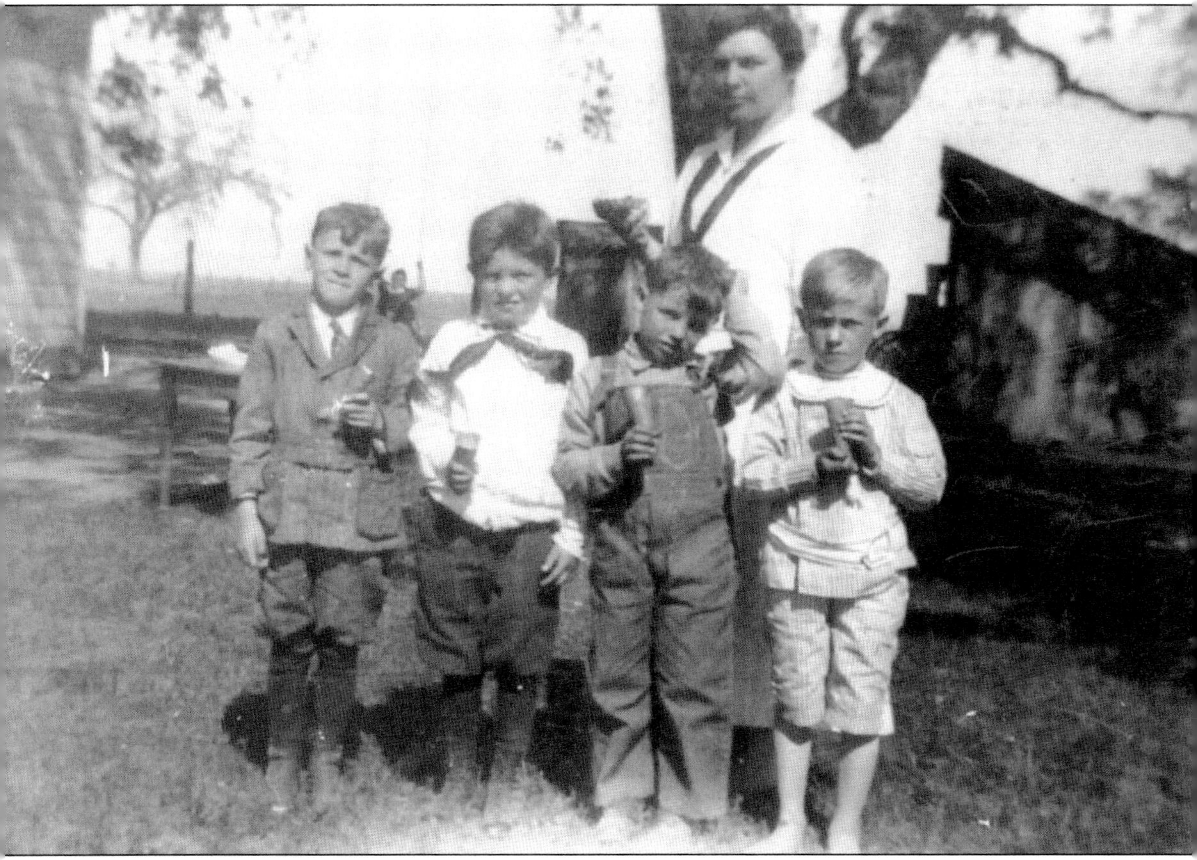

Students attending school in the Central School District, which formed in 1872, are pictured here with their teacher. The land for this first school was acquired from B.C. Peterson for $1. The property was located five and a half miles west of Lincoln on Fiddyment Road. There were no buildings on the property at the time of purchase, but in 1882, accounts in the *Lincoln News Messenger* said that the district had a good schoolhouse well supplied with improved furniture. The school's first teacher was H.C. Curtis. In 1882, G.W. Fuller was in charge of the school, which then had 40 students attending. Three separate buildings have stood on the Central School site. The second schoolhouse, a frame structure with a single wall of windows facing north, replaced the first one in 1920. In 1931, the second school burned to the ground, and a third school was built on the foundation of the second.

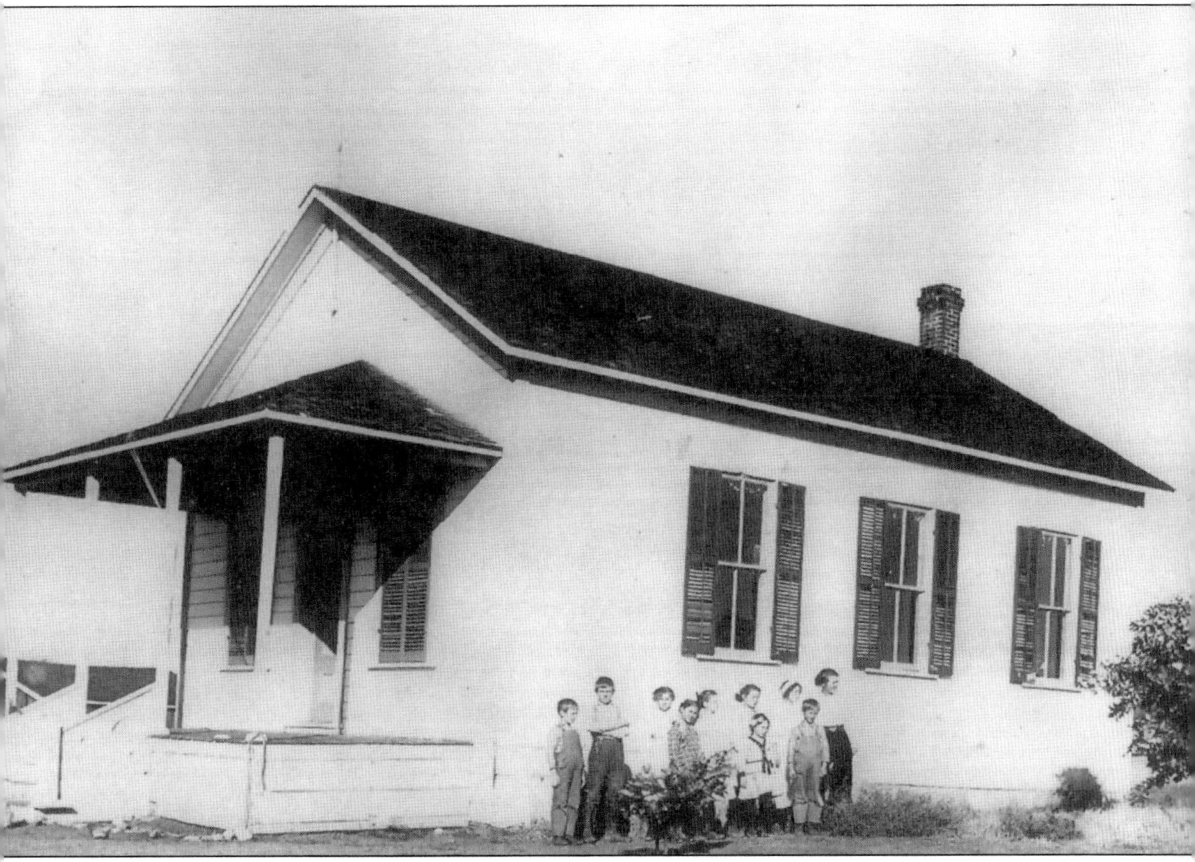

Pictured here is the Daneville school in the fall of 1911. The students are, from left to right, Edwin Williford, Delbert Knudson, Mary Tyler, Eva Tyler, Edith Williford, Thelma Williford, Lenore Tyler, Fred Williford, and Ruth Williford. The teacher (at far right) is Sadie Bickford. O.P. Richardson donated property for the Daneville school. Richardson and Henry Nader were original trustees, and Louis Gage was the first teacher. The school was a few hundred feet north of the northeast corner of the present-day intersection of Big Bend and McCourtney Roads. On February 10, 1893, the school burned down, but it was rebuilt before the fall term began. In 1893, there were 11 students at the school.

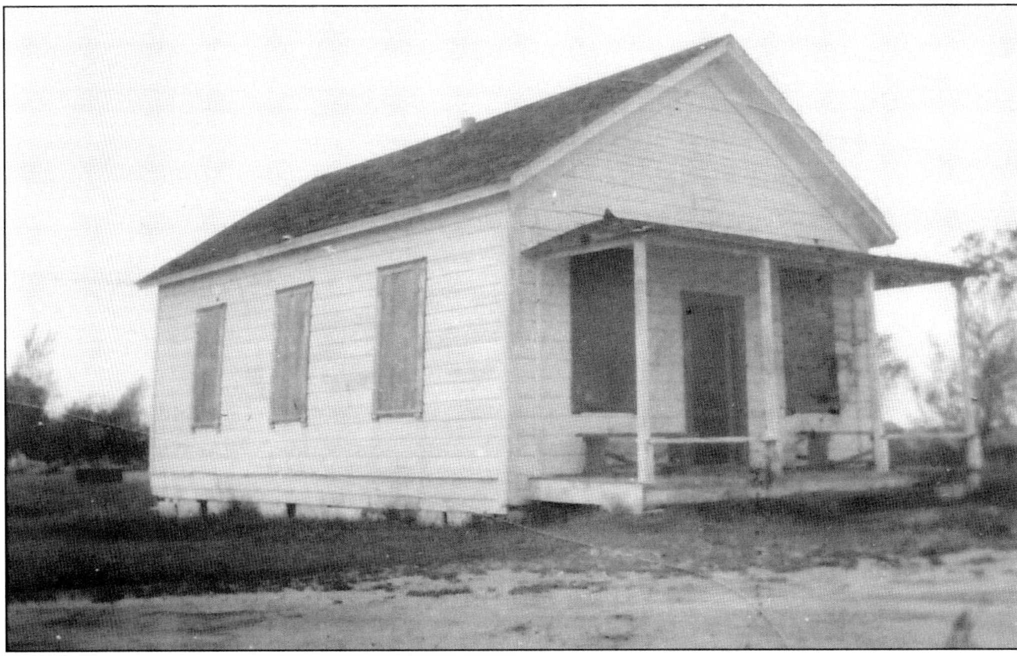

The Fair Oaks School, located on what is now West Wise Road, was built by William Jones and neighbors. The school opened in 1900 and was used until 1935, when it closed due to the lack of school-age children in the district. Maude Mariner was the school's first teacher.

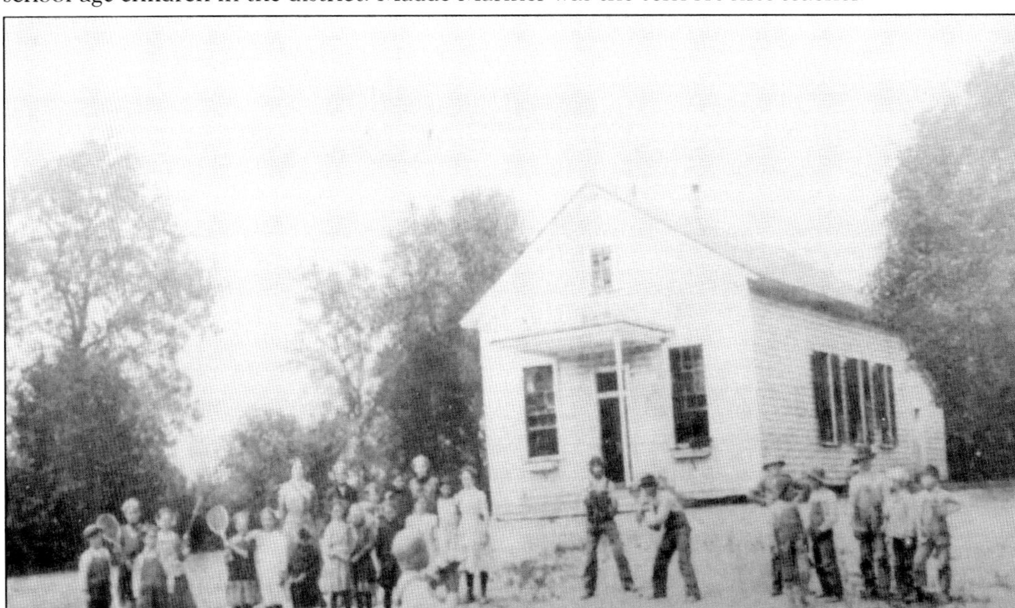

In 1888, a new school district was formed—Fruitvale. Louis Gage was the first teacher. Fruitvale School was a one-room school with two outhouses, one for girls and one for boys. A short time after the school opened, a woodshed and a place to shelter the student's horses were built on the east side. Around 1923, a second room was built at right angles to the west of the first room. Before 1912, a shed roof addition was constructed on the back of the school to accommodate indoor toilets and storage.

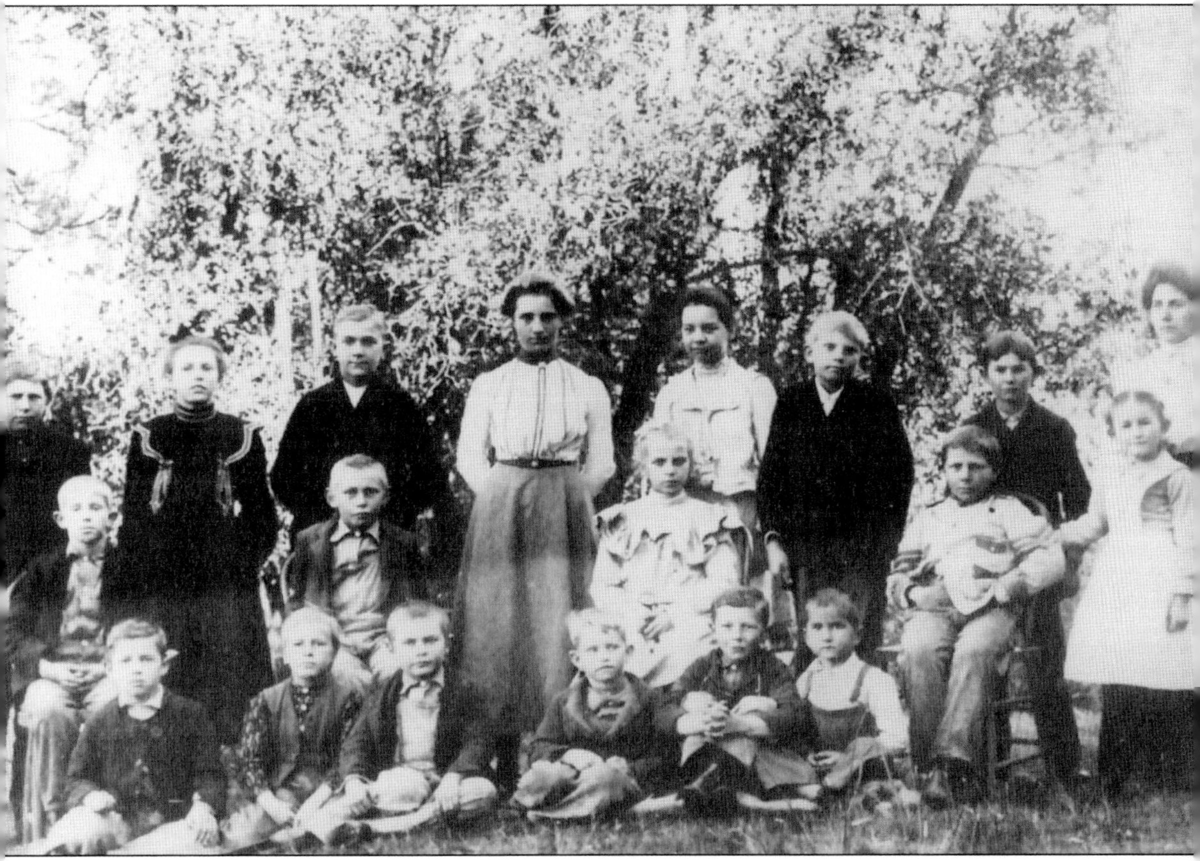

This Fruitvale School picture shows the class of 1905, 1906, or 1907. From left to right are (first row) Eldon Gage, Albert Christensen, Walter Nelson, Martin Nielsen, Chester Leighton, and Albert Muller; (second row) Anders (Bill) Neilsen, Harry Nelson, Frances Fowler, Frank Fowler, and Agnes Freeman; (third row) Lawrence Fowler, Magdaline (Maggie) Neilsen, Clay Fowler, Sophia Christensen Drane, Helen Martin, Christian Neilsen, William Freeman, and teacher Mamie Bartlett.

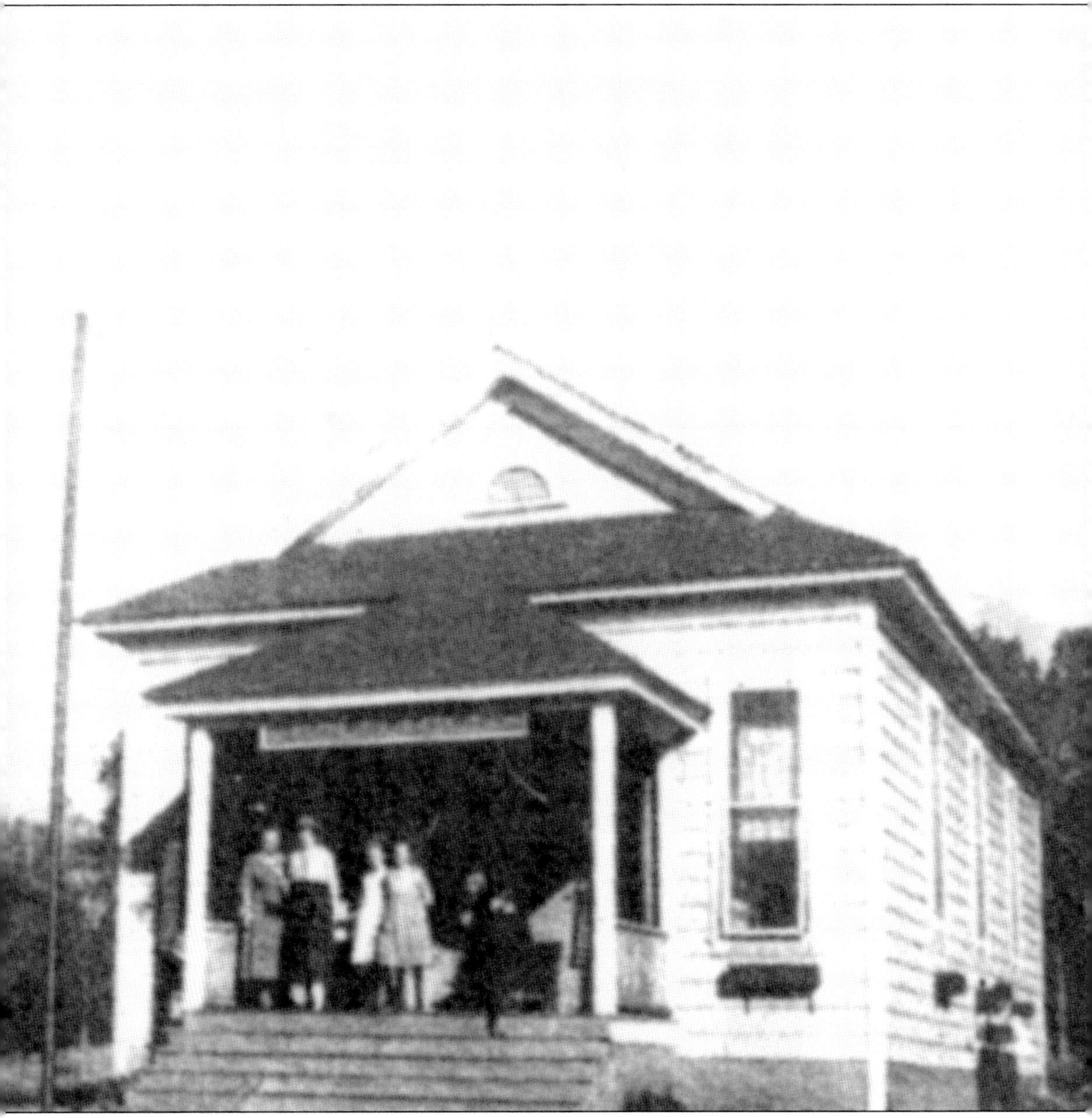

The Masons moved into Lincoln in 1863 from their old building in Gold Hill. The top floor of the building was later removed, and the bottom floor was hauled down Auburn Ravine to near the site of the old town of Oro City. This structure was then properly enclosed and served as Gold Hill's school. In 1901, Antone Fereva donated property on his ranch, just east of the intersection of Gold Hill and Ridge Roads, to the school district for a new school. By the time school was to start, the schoolhouse was not finished, and classes began in Fereva's fruit-packing shed. By 1902, the students were in their new two-room school. The school was used by students until it unified with Lincoln School District in 1946. This picture, taken on March 3, 1930, shows Portia Freed Moss, teacher at Gold Hill School, and some of her students.

On October 5, 1868, the Lincoln School District purchased three lots on the northwest corner of Third and F Streets from George Small for $15. The district soon erected a school building on this site. The need for more space was soon realized, and the existing building was enlarged. This addition was completed in 1888 and was named Lincoln Grammar School. It was torn down in the 1920s.

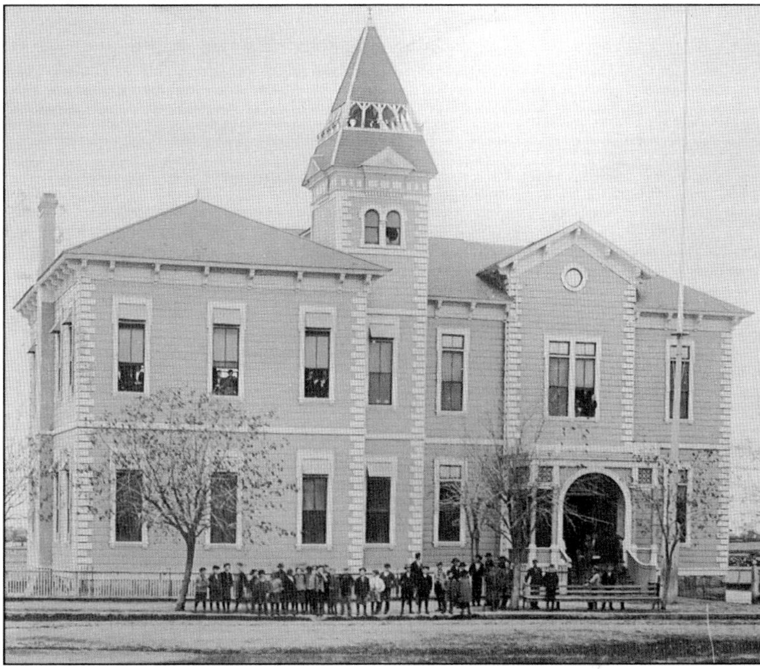

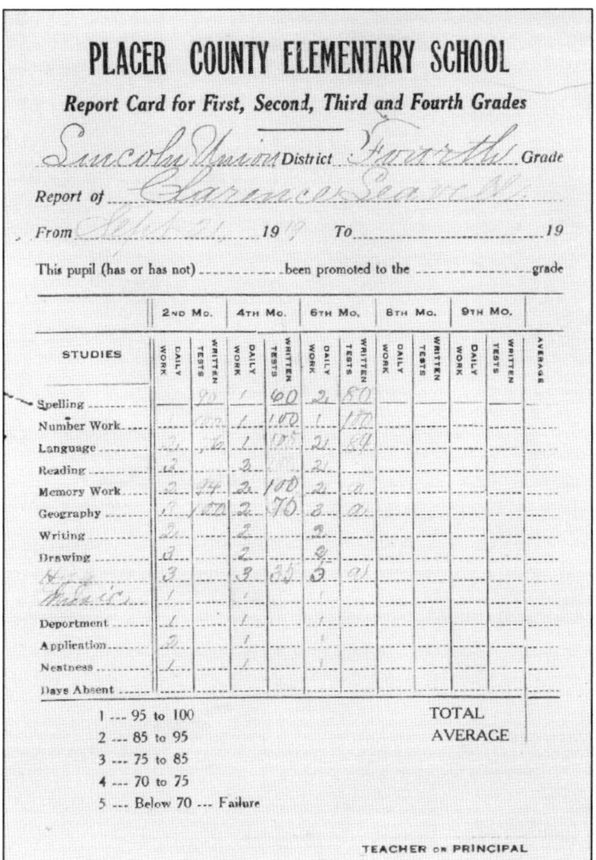

PLACER COUNTY ELEMENTARY SCHOOL

Report Card for First, Second, Third and Fourth Grades

Lincoln Union District Fourth Grade

Report of Clarence Leavell

From Sept 21 1919 To 19

This pupil (has or has not) .... been promoted to the .... grade

STUDIES	2nd Mo. Daily Work	2nd Mo. Written Tests	4th Mo. Daily Work	4th Mo. Written Tests	6th Mo. Daily Work	6th Mo. Written Tests	8th Mo. Daily Work	8th Mo. Written Tests	9th Mo. Daily Work	9th Mo. Written Tests	Average
Spelling	—	90	1	60	2	80					
Number Work	[illegible]	100	1	100	1	100					
Language	2	[illegible]	1	[illegible]	2	84					
Reading	2		2		2						
Memory Work	2	94	2	100	2	[illegible]					
Geography	3	100	2	70	3	[illegible]					
Writing	2		2		2						
Drawing	3		2		2						
Hyg.	3		3	35	3	[illegible]					
Music	1		1		1						
Deportment	1		1		1						
Application	2		1		1						
Neatness	1		1		1						
Days Absent											

1 --- 95 to 100
2 --- 85 to 95
3 --- 75 to 85
4 --- 70 to 75
5 --- Below 70 --- Failure

TOTAL AVERAGE

TEACHER OR PRINCIPAL

This 1919 report card from the Lincoln Grammar School shows the grades earned by fourth-grader Clarence (Tom) Leavell. Leavell was a fourth-generation descendant from the pioneer family of Richard Fuller. Clarence Leavell's mother, Etta Fuller, married Louis Leavell, who was also a pioneer descendant and a merchant in Lincoln.

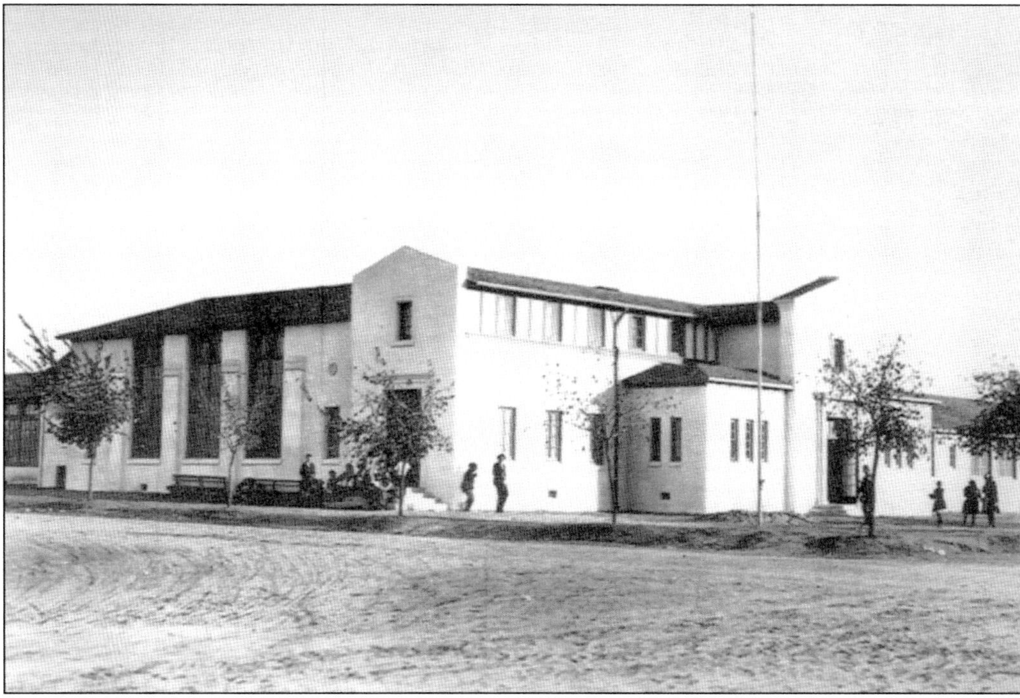

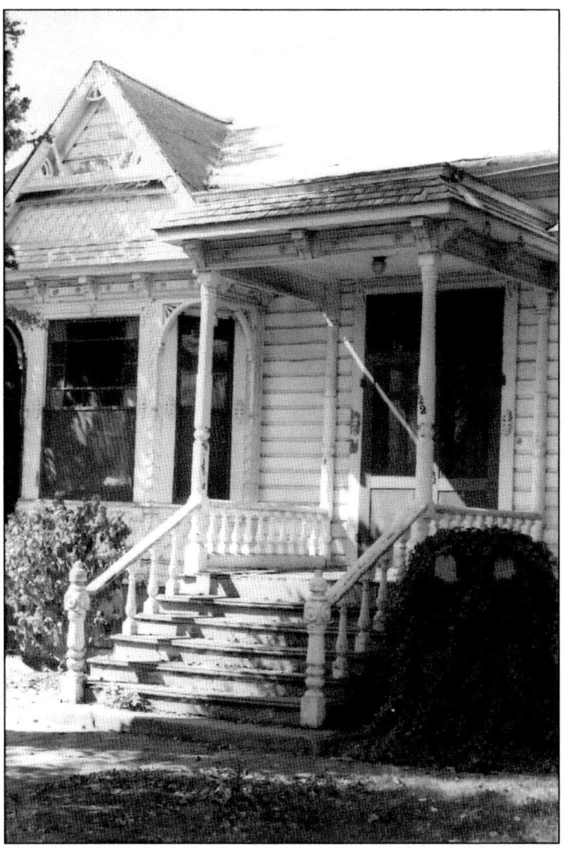

In 1919, the town began to discuss the idea that a new grammar school was needed, and in 1920, residents voted yes on a bond for $40,000. The first section of the Lincoln Union Grammar School was completed in 1921, and additional classrooms were added through the years. The school was later renamed Mary Beermann after the well-known citizen and trustee.

The first high school in Lincoln was temporarily in the Mariner home, located at 622 H Street between Sixth and Seventh Streets. Ten separate school districts were feeder schools for Lincoln Union High School when classes began. Nine trustees made up the school board that year, each one elected by the voters in one of the elementary school districts. The home is pictured here many years after it was used as a school.

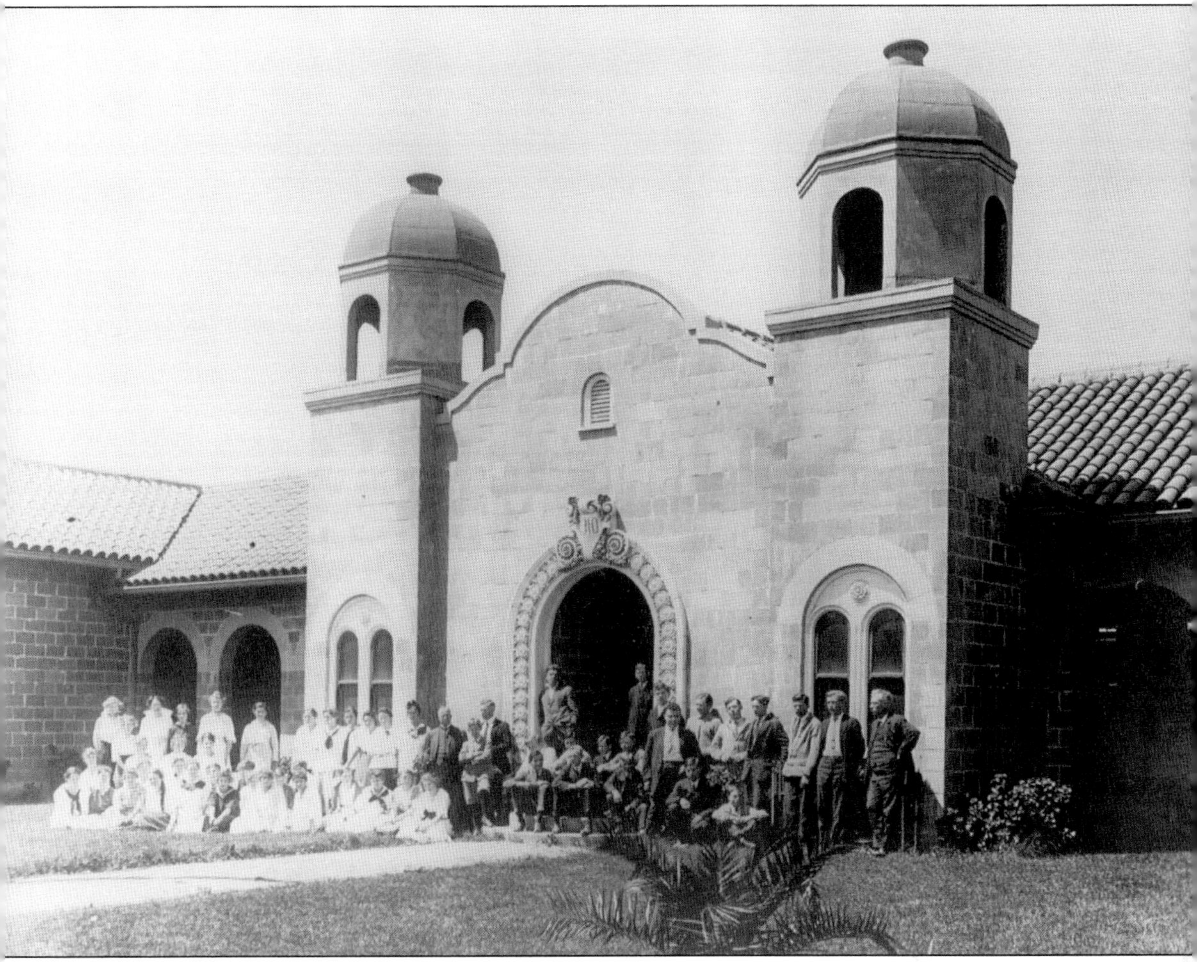

The 1910–1911 construction of the Lincoln Union High School building was accomplished thanks to a $20,000 bond issue; the bonds passed with an 82 percent "yes" vote. The beautiful, Mission-style high school building was constructed mainly of terra cotta materials manufactured at Gladding, McBean.

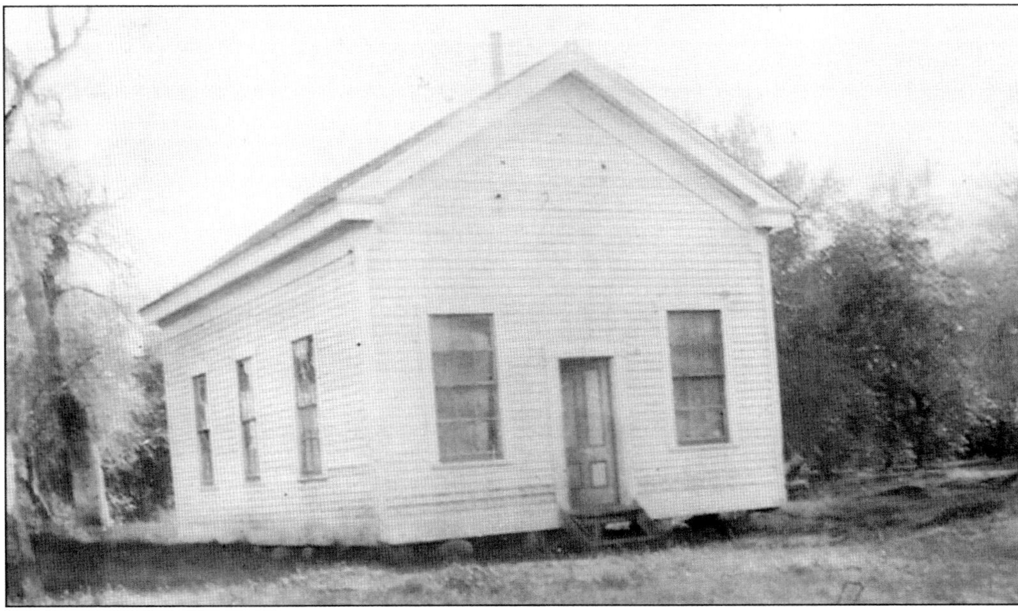

The Manzanita/Coon Creek School was established in 1857 and was located on the west side of Manzanita Cemetery. In 1862, Phillip H. Dippel deeded 12 acres of land to the Coon Creek School District for use as a permanent school site. The school was often referred to as Manzanita School because of its location near the Manzanita Cemetery. The trustees paid double the average salary of the time in order to hire the best teachers. The school closed in 1899 because it had too few students.

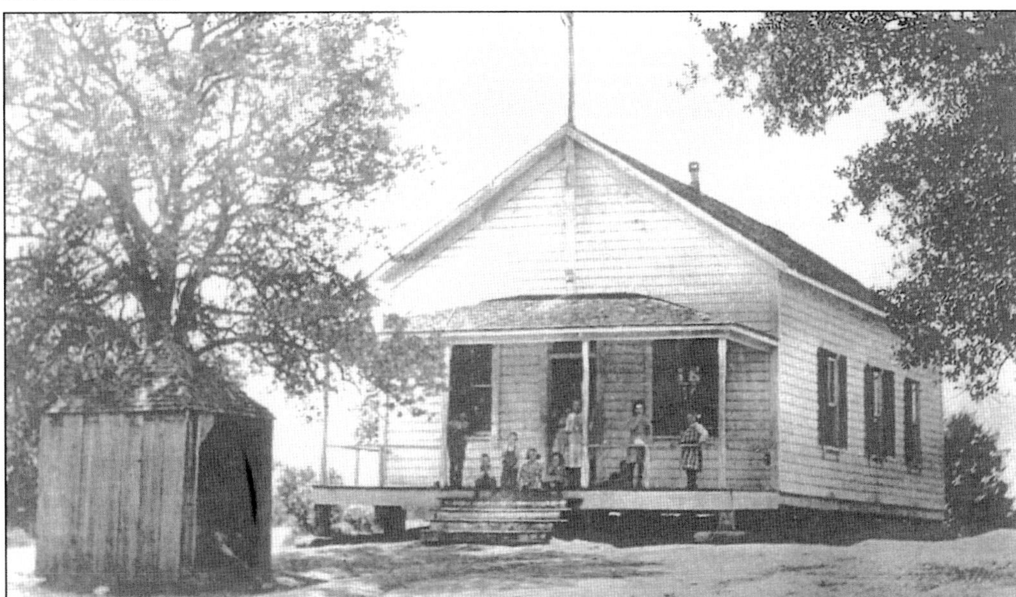

Mt. Pleasant School began in 1855 and existed on four different sites. The last site, at 3750 Mt. Pleasant Road, was chosen after the schoolhouse—which was previously across Mt. Pleasant Road to the east—burned down in 1890. The school had 34 students in attendance in 1856. Money received from the state and county that year totaled $190.50, or $5.60 per student. The school's first teacher was W.A. Henry. He was followed in 1859 by F. Dewing and in 1860 by C.W. Bradbury.

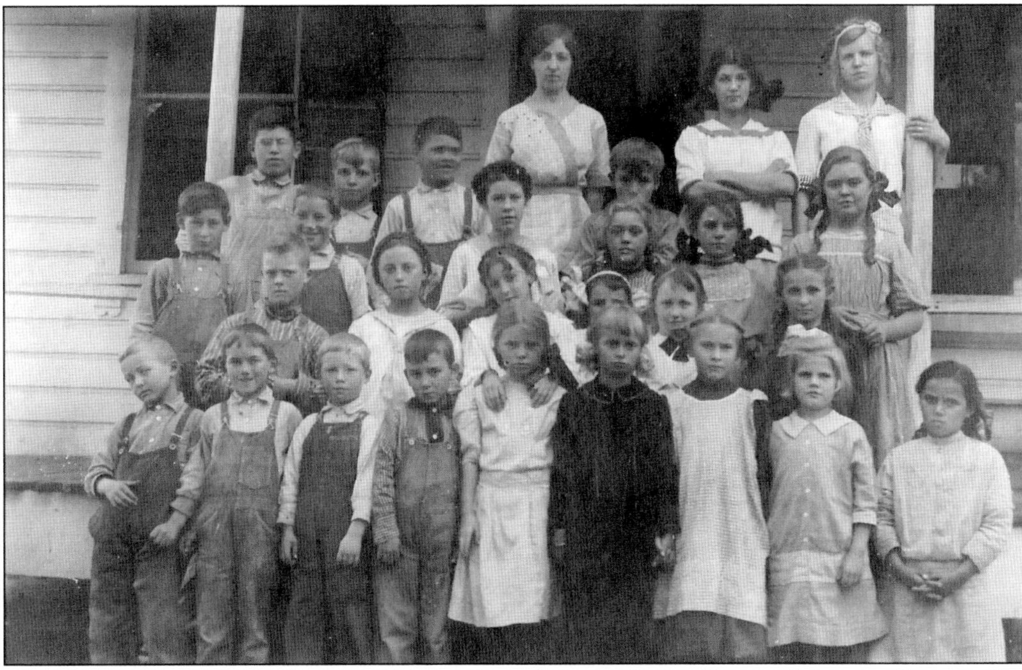

This is the Mt. Pleasant School class of 1913. From left to right are (first row) Austin Obenour, Ken Abbick, Jack Bursill, Joe Mendes, Hildegarde Cate, Phyllis Cullen, Dorothy Falconer, Grace Firch, and Virgil Arruda; (second row) Otto Obenour, Bernice Herold, Sherrill Holman, Marve Cullen, Jimilla Cullen, and Gladys Logan; (third row) James Falconer, William Bursill, Ercel Falconer, Mary Obenour, unidentified, and Doris Obenour; (fourth row) Eugene Mizzy, Fred Chase, Francis Arruda, and George Logan; (fifth row) substitute teacher Miss Allison, Eleanor Mizzy, and Fern Chase.

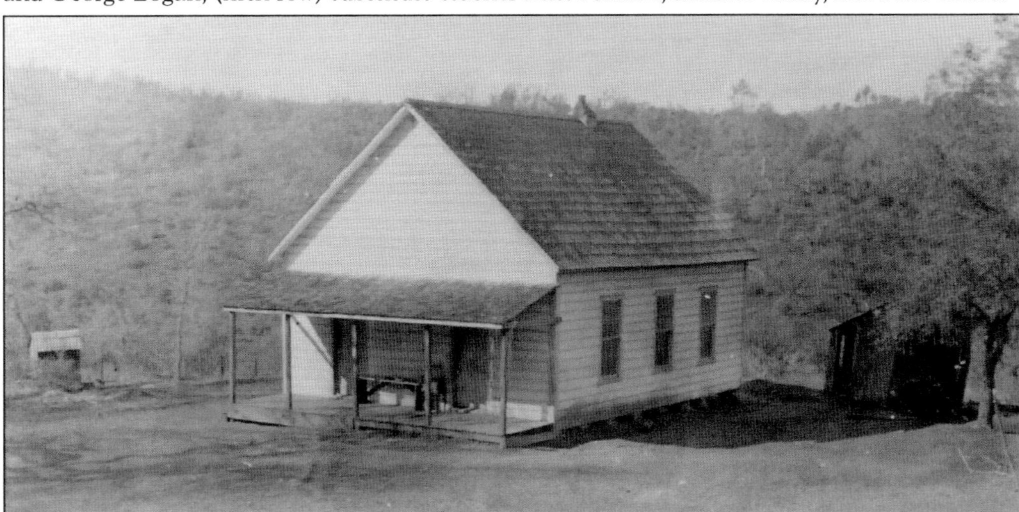

The New Hope School opened in 1884, a few hundred feet north of Coon Creek on the east side of what is now Garden Bar Road. Adela T. Keeler was the first teacher. The school served 13 families when it opened. In 1901, it had 14 students in its one room. Nellie Curtis was the teacher that year, and she remained for several years. In 1919, an election was held to consolidate the schools at New Hope, Mt. Pleasant, and Daneville with Lincoln. The proposal to unify passed in all three districts, and in the fall, students were bussed to Lincoln Union Grammar School.

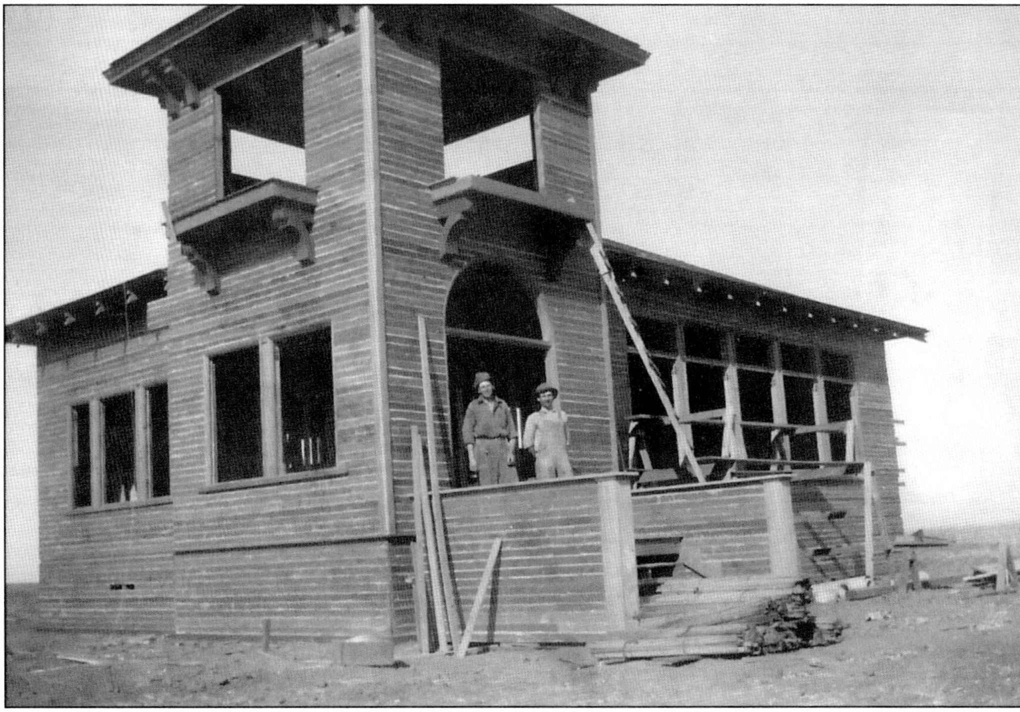

The Rivervale School stood on Moore Road close to the Sutter County line. The school's official opening date is unknown, but it was in operation for the 1916–1917 school term. Dave McCartney owned the land and suggested the entire community pool its resources for a school. Although some people (particularly rural families) were far less affluent, they often had great respect for education and took considerable personal interest in schools. The community came together, and the school was built in a single year. Arthur Allison was the trustee and clerk of the school from 1916 to 1929. The first teacher was James F. Huffaker. Some of the students who attended Rivervale School include Rosemond Worsfold, Myrtle Poston, Ernest Poston, Robert Lockhart, Elmer Worsfold, Jean Poston, Myrtle Frati, Robert Jerstad, Amoly Frati, Dorothy Poston, Lois Dillard, and Marjorie Poston.

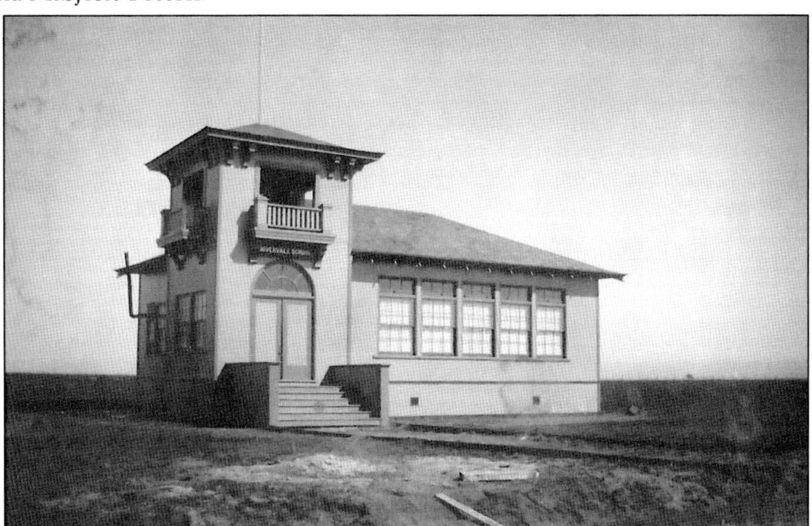

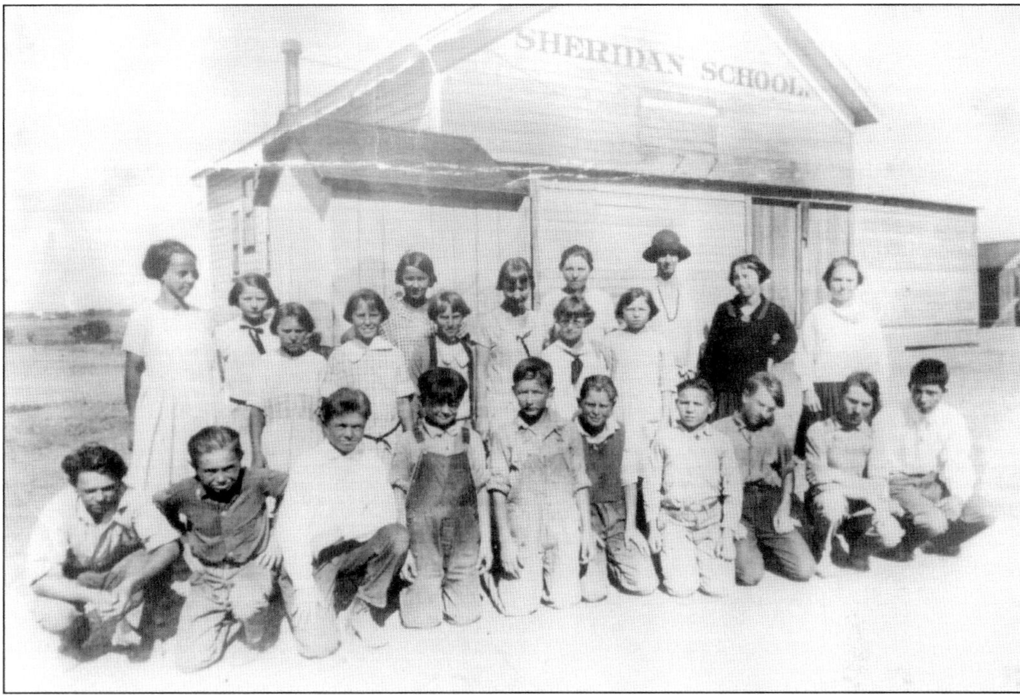

The Sheridan School has a long history. C.E. Rogers, who owned two large buildings in Sheridan named Roger's Shed and Union Shed, originally started it as a private school in town. He hired M.E. Reynolds as the teacher, boarded her, and paid her $60 a month for two months out of his own pocket. Roger's Shed was often used as a ballroom, and he provided that space for the school. It quickly became the Sheridan School, a public school for all children in town.

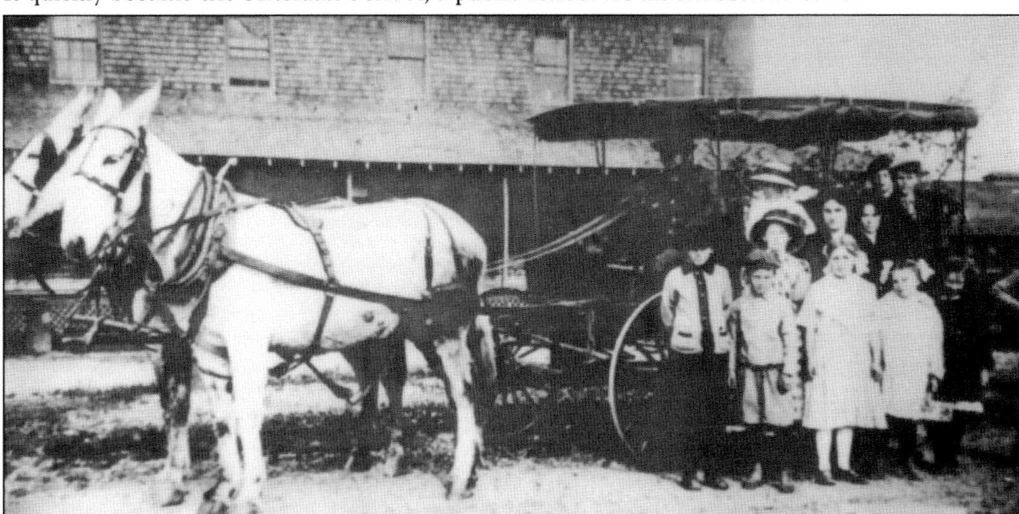

This is a Sheridan School bus in the early 1900s. Roger's Shed burned in 1868, and there seems to be no record of where school was held until a wooden two-room schoolhouse was constructed in 1877. In 1882, the building was 30 feet by 60 feet and could seat up to 60 pupils. Lauanna Carns was the teacher of 50 pupils at that time. The Sheridan School, which is a grammar school, has been in continual operation in Sheridan, and high school students attend class in Lincoln Union High School.

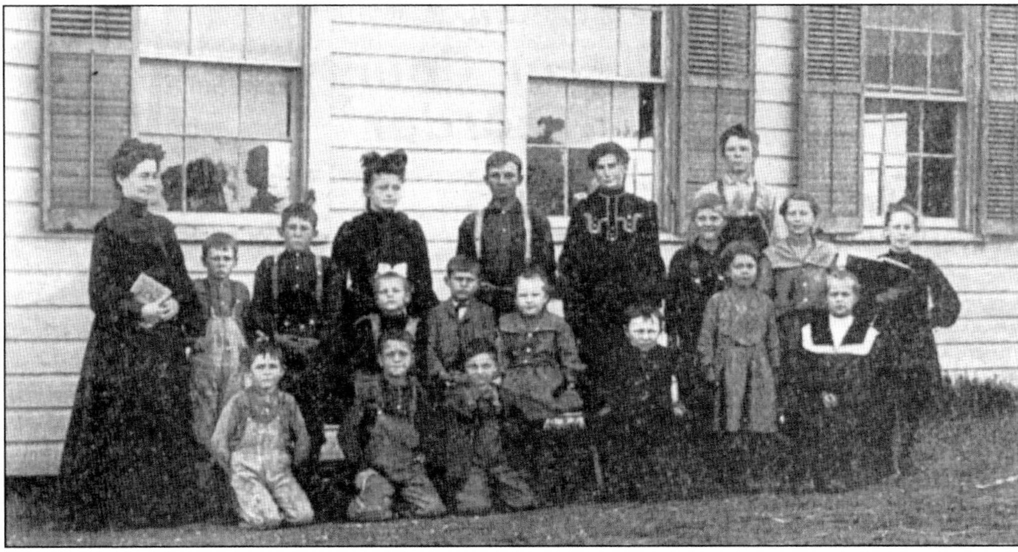

This Valley View School picture is believed to have been taken sometime between 1901 and 1905. The teacher at left is Helen Geren, and the only students identified in the photograph (although their locations are unknown) are Clarence Haslett, George Haslett, Everett Haslett, and Daisy Clark.

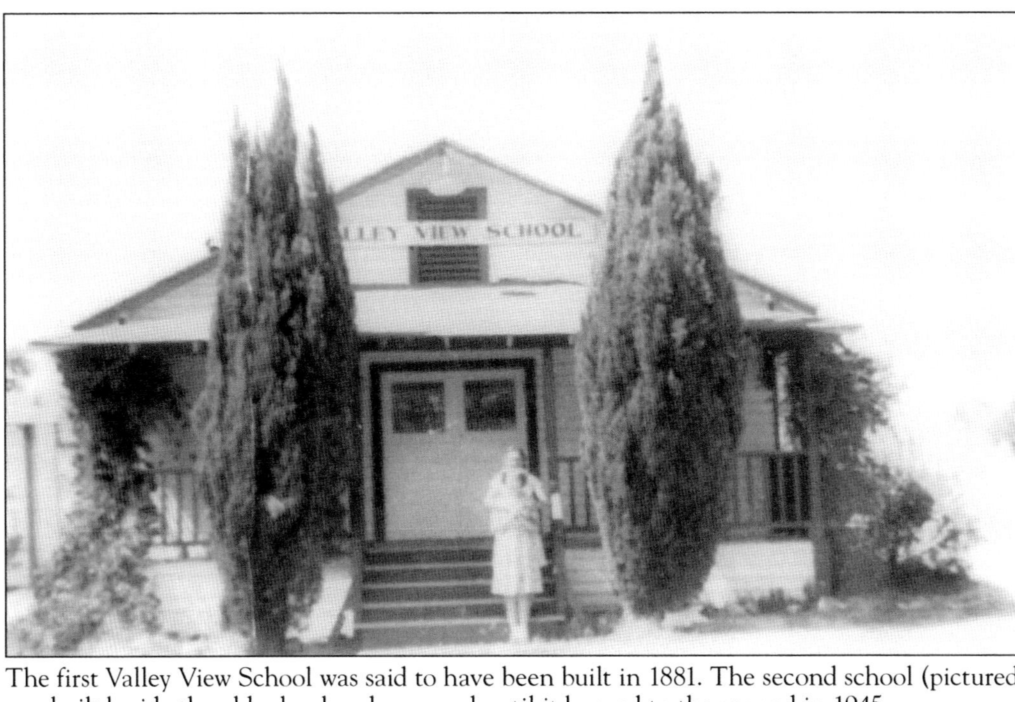

The first Valley View School was said to have been built in 1881. The second school (pictured) was built beside the old school and was used until it burned to the ground in 1945.

The Old Brick Church, built in Lincoln on Sixth Street between K and L Streets, was the area's first church building of any permanence. On April 23, 1866, Henry Rood (Charles Wilson's brother-in-law) sold one and a half lots to the Congregational church for $1. A church was built, but it is not clear who built it. Within a few years, the church was sold because the declining population made it impossible to keep it in operation. It was eventually torn down to extend the Lincoln Union High School property.

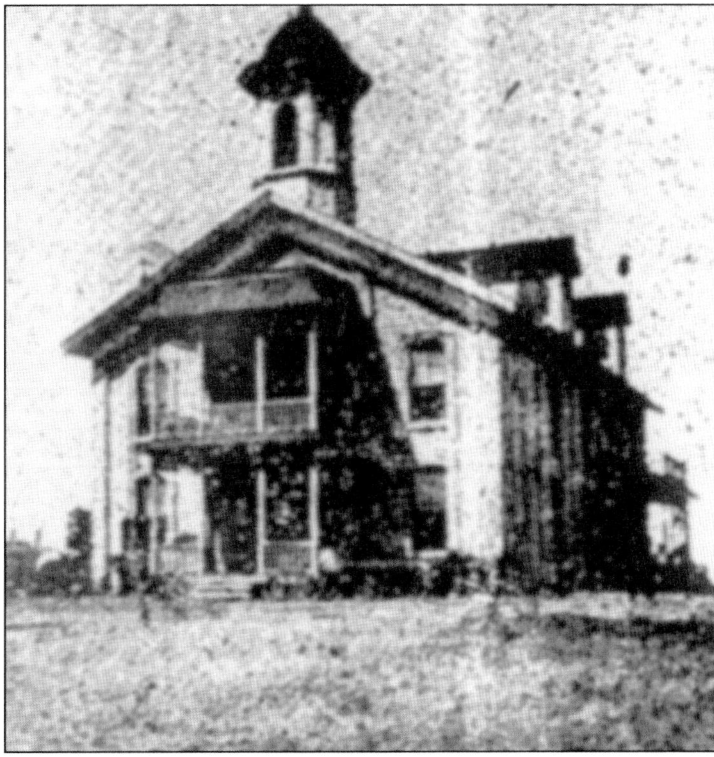

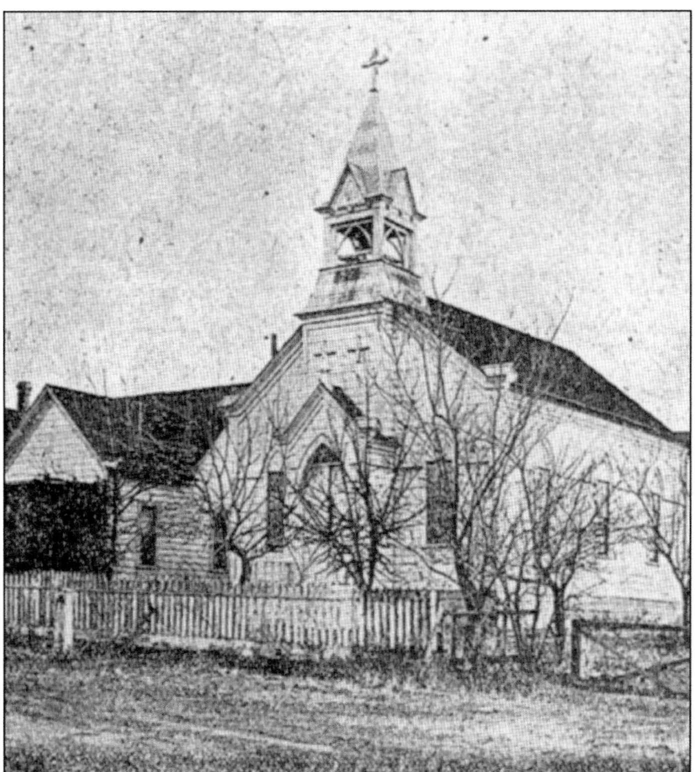

The *Lincoln News Messenger* reported that St. Joseph's Catholic Church was organized in 1863 by Father John Leahey. It does not appear that a substantial church building was constructed until many years later. The *Auburn Herald* reported on May 7, 1881, that a new Catholic church had been erected in town, and the structure was a very creditable improvement. It was located on the south side of First and F Streets and was dedicated on Sunday, May 9, 1881.

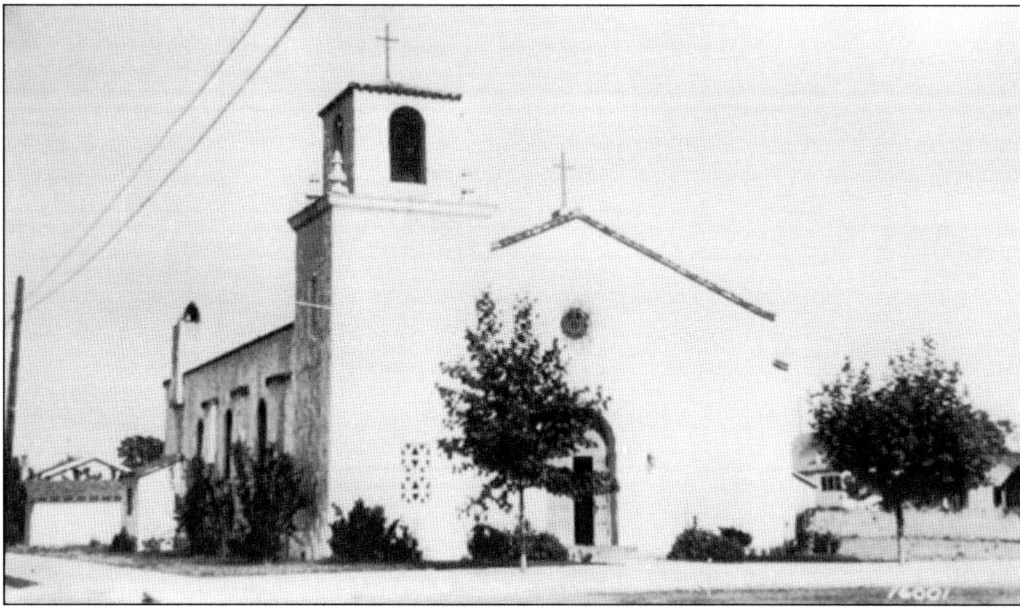

In 1926, St. Joseph's Catholic Church moved into a new building on the southeast corner of Sixth and D Streets under the direction of Father Donnelly. H.A. Petticord was the contractor, and $12,000 was the contract price. Dean and Dean of Sacramento were the architects, and the fireproof partition tile and tile roof came from Gladding, McBean. The church was dedicated on Sunday, May 23, 1926, and its final cost was $20,000.

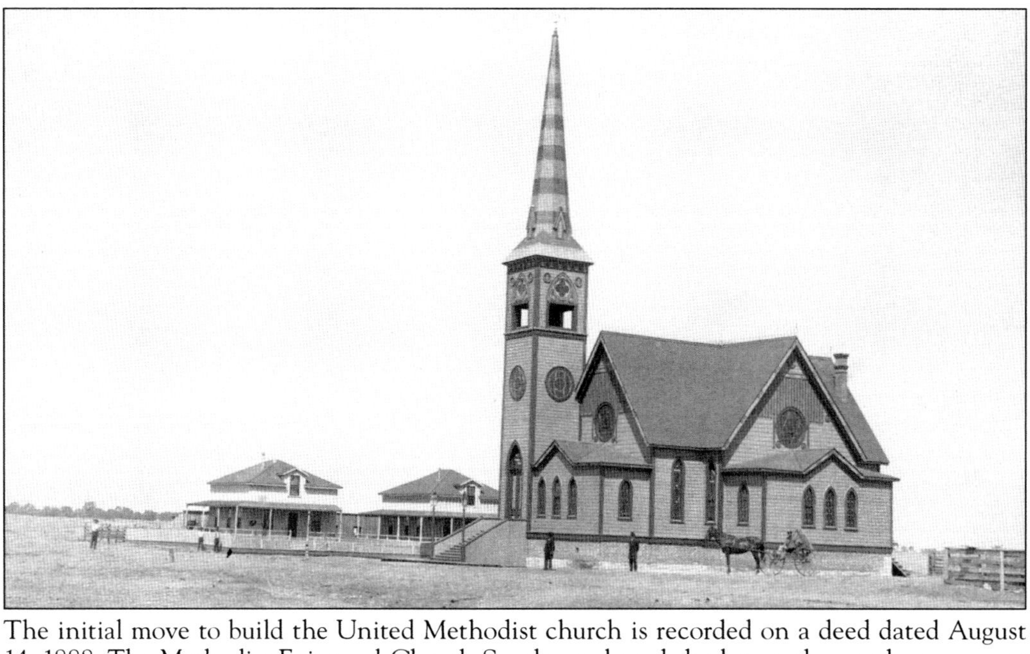

The initial move to build the United Methodist church is recorded on a deed dated August 14, 1888. The Methodist Episcopal Church South purchased the lot on the northwest corner of Fourth and E Streets for $200. The trustees who signed the deed were Rhonda Ann Flint, Jennie S. Aldrich, Betsey B. Hinman, Justus M. Hinman, and Charles E. Allen. This purchase may have been initiated by a splinter group, because the "official" organizing of the church took place in February 1889.

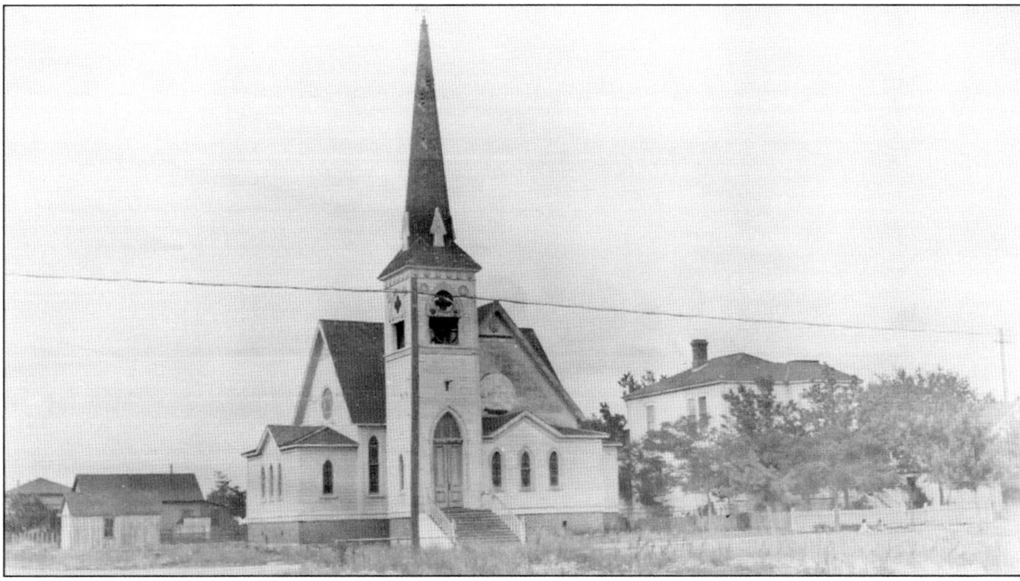

The "official" trustees for the United Methodist church were Charles Beermann, John T. Howard, Verne E. Burdick, B. William Dipple, and Peter Ahart. John Howard had been serving as pastor. In September 1891, Rev. H.M. McKnight, from Woodland, was appointed pastor and in October, 200 people welcomed him at a reception in Ahart's Hall (later named Emmada Building). In June 1890, the church broke ground for the building on lots donated by Elisha Heryford on the northeast corner of Sixth and I Streets.

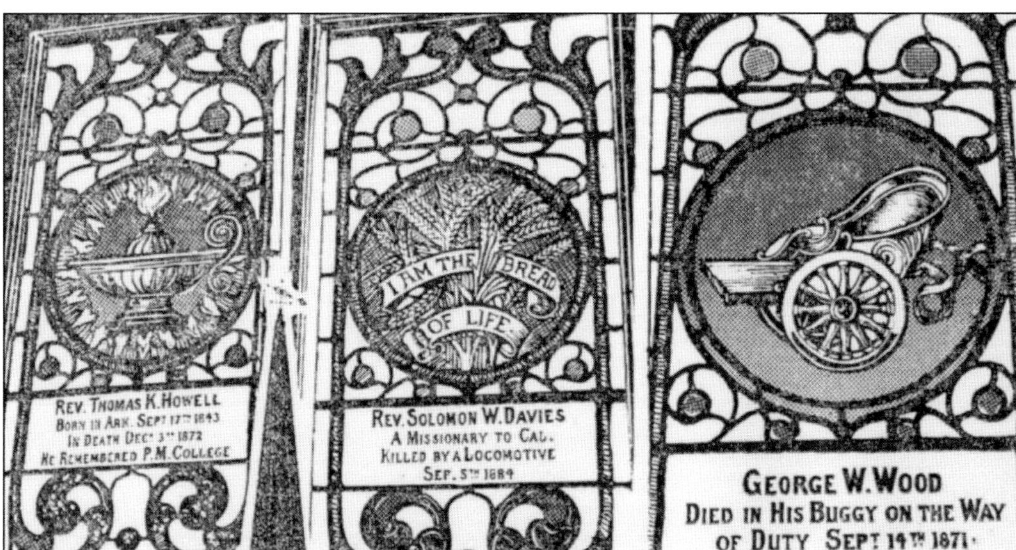

The United Methodist church was dedicated on June 1, 1891, and has been in continuous use since then. After the original steeple burned in a fire, it was replaced with a shorter one. This photograph shows three of the church's many stained-glass windows with curious captions.

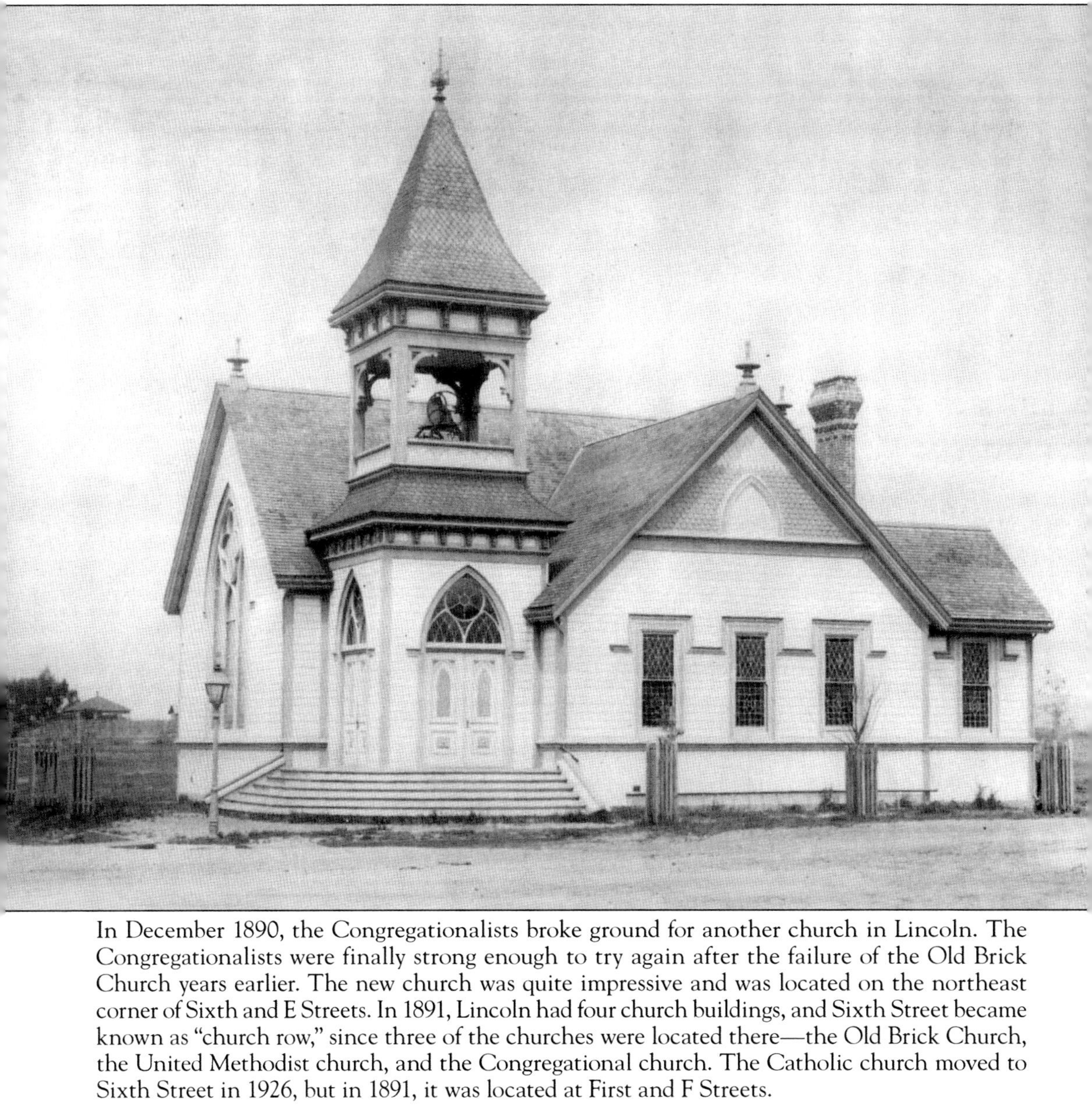

In December 1890, the Congregationalists broke ground for another church in Lincoln. The Congregationalists were finally strong enough to try again after the failure of the Old Brick Church years earlier. The new church was quite impressive and was located on the northeast corner of Sixth and E Streets. In 1891, Lincoln had four church buildings, and Sixth Street became known as "church row," since three of the churches were located there—the Old Brick Church, the United Methodist church, and the Congregational church. The Catholic church moved to Sixth Street in 1926, but in 1891, it was located at First and F Streets.

Seven

COMMUNITY EVENTS

With no electronic means of bringing entertainment into their homes, community members found amusement and pleasure mainly through getting together. Clubs, lodges, societies, dances, picnics, horse racing, hunting parties, church affairs, sporting events, and holiday celebrations took place frequently and were well attended. Participation and interaction were the key features of entertainment in the 19th century in California.

During Lincoln's first years of existence, numerous dances were held in local hotels, in several of the large warehouses in town, in nearby Sheridan, and at various community schoolhouses (especially to raise funds for school improvements). The town's volunteer fire department was famous for the Firemen's Ball, a popular formal dance.

Other celebrations with activities other than dancing included horse racing, rodeos, political rallies, community picnics, church meetings, the country's centennial celebrations in 1876, and state and county fairs. Lincoln's annual Fourth of July celebrations—with parades at Towle's Grove, north of town—drew visitors from out of town, and Gladding, McBean's annual picnics were popular affairs. Mt. Pleasant picnics, which began in 1878, promised fun and games all day and dances and bonfires at night; these were also very popular.

Organized hunting parties pursued deer, raccoons, ducks, geese, quail, and doves. Gun clubs held shooting contests, including turkey shoots during the holidays. The gun club also held an annual dove stew—a highly anticipated and well attended event.

Local lodges included Gold Hill Lodge No. 32 (Masonic) and the Virginia Division No. 41 (Sons of Temperance). These two lodges cooperated to build the area's first lodge hall in Gold Hill in 1853. In 1863, the Masons moved to Lincoln and cooperated with International Order of Odd Fellows (IOOF) Valley Lodge No. 107 to construct a lodge building on Fifth Street near F Street. The Knights of Pythias, Oak Leaf Lodge No. 86, organized in Lincoln in 1883. The Native Sons of the Golden West, Silver Star Parlor No. 63, was chartered on May 1885. There were also various other clubs and societies.

Other entertainment included theatrical presentations at the Old Brick Church, traveling shows and performances at the True Blue Hall (popularly called the Lincoln Opera House), occasional circuses, and many performances and exhibitions at the 12 schoolhouses in Western Placer.

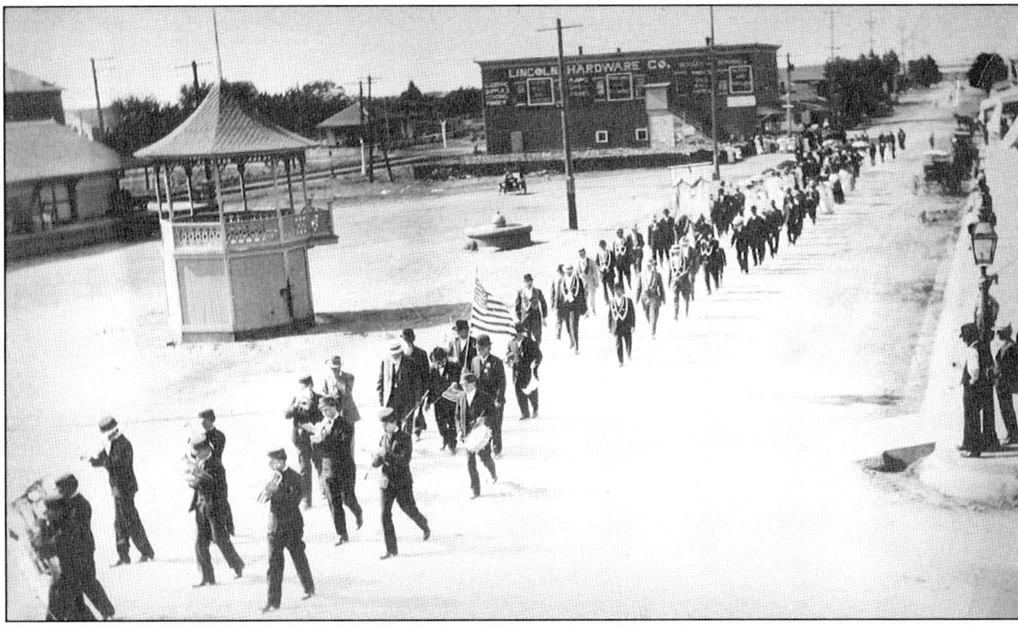

Celebrations in town included parades that marched down G Street, the main road through Lincoln. A fire hose cart was stored under the bandstand at left for quick use in case of a fire. The True Blue Hall building, which burned in 1919, advertises Ingram-Mason Hardware, which was in business from 1909 to 1913. The round water trough near the bandstand is now located behind the Lincoln Public Library.

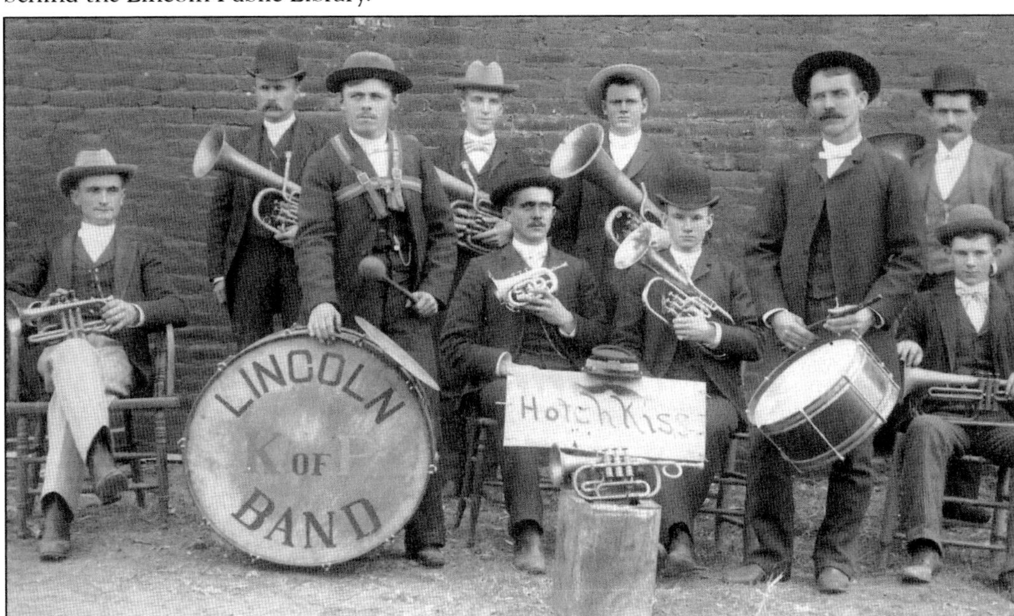

One of the bands that marched in local parades and special events consisted of Knights of Pythias members. The KoP lodge in Lincoln formed in 1883. The band members in this 1890 photograph are, from left to right, (seated) Grant Allen, Frank Sanders, Will Hickey, and Bragg Barry; (standing) Tomas Coffey, James Husse, William D. Ingram, Laben Gray, Albert Luce, and James Allen.

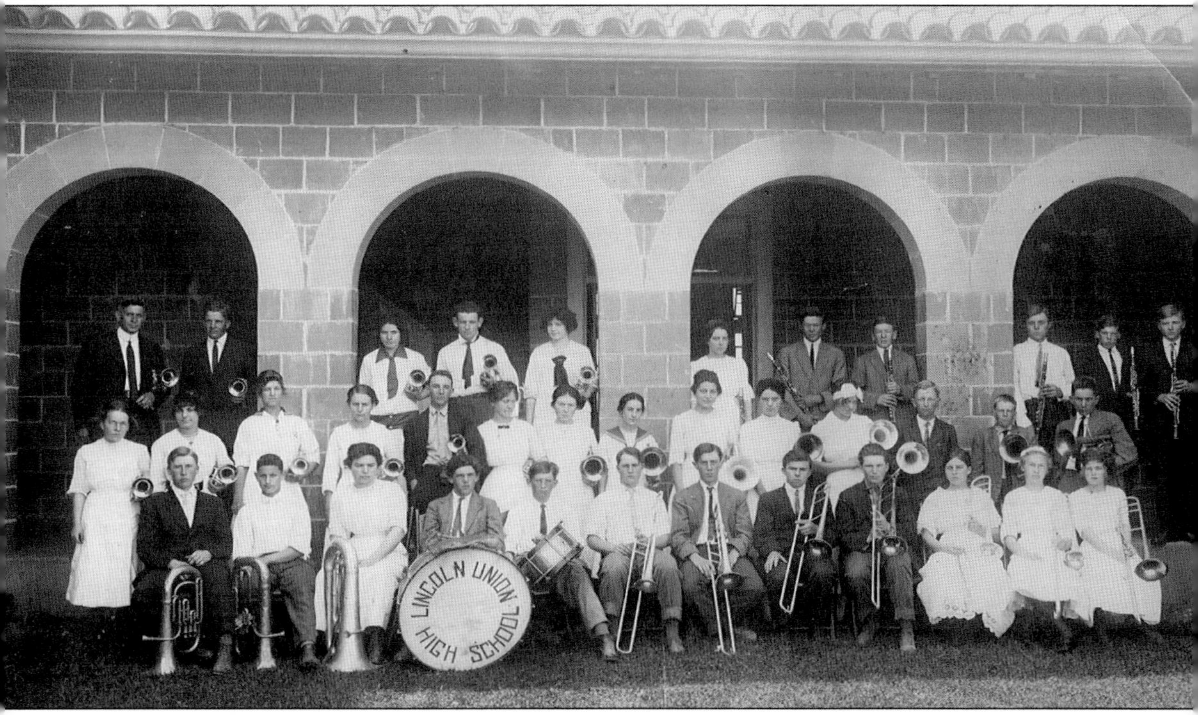

Under the leadership of Mr. Lane, the Lincoln Union High School band reigned supreme in 1912. The 50-piece band performed at shows, concerts, parades, the World's Fair in San Francisco, bond rallies, and athletic contests. A drum-and-bugle corps, various instrumental ensembles, and special music groups also formed from this relatively small assembly of musicians.

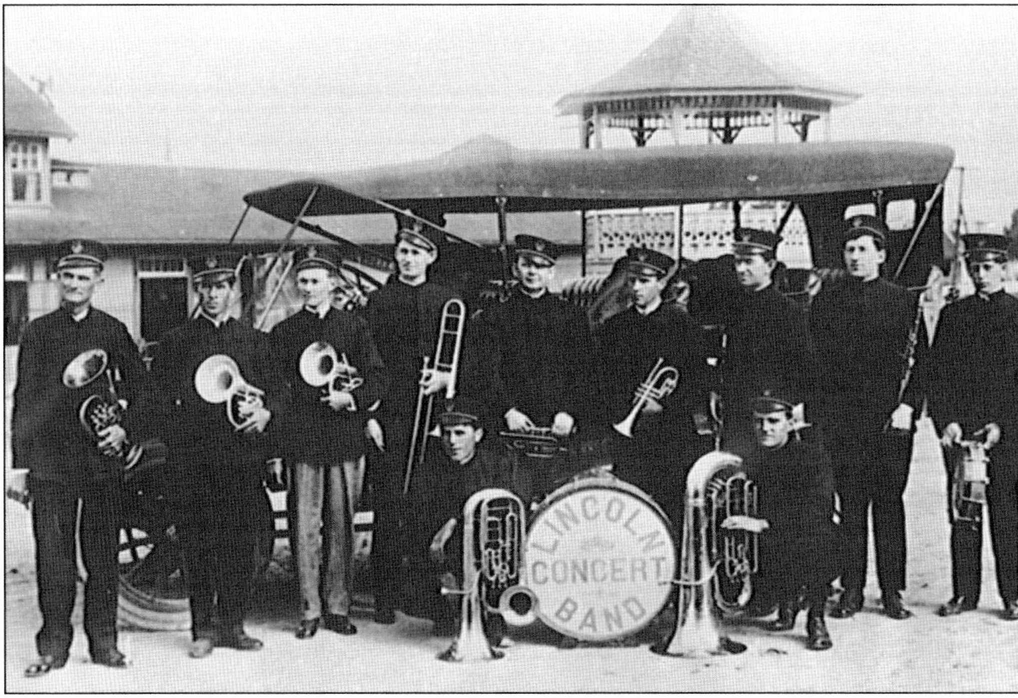

The town had other bands in addition to the high school band, including the Lincoln Concert Band (above), the Clay City Band (below), the Lincoln Town Band, the Lincoln Military Band, and the Knights of Pythias Band. Listening to music or being part of a musical group was obviously important to the citizens of Lincoln judging from the number of groups and bands that existed in the city's early years. The groups played at dances, marched in parades, and gave concerts in all the available halls. They also entertained local citizens at the large bandstand at the intersection of Fifth and G Streets.

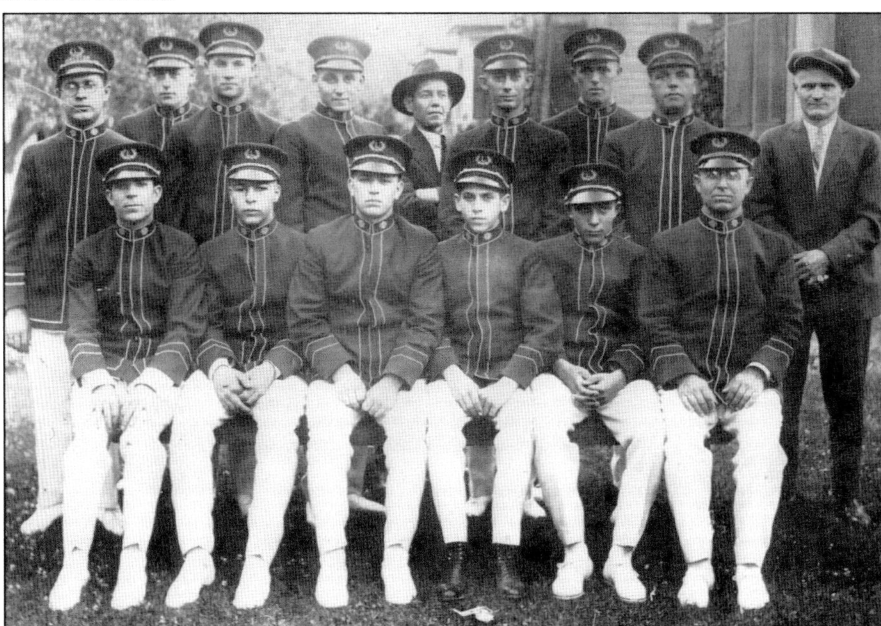

The Firemen's Ball was very popular, and this dance card is from one held on March 17, 1917. Twenty-six dances were listed inside the card, with space for gentlemen's names. The card was held by young women, and if a man wanted to dance with her, she would pencil his name next to a dance. The back of the card listed the floor managers and floor director along with charter and current members of the volunteer fire department.

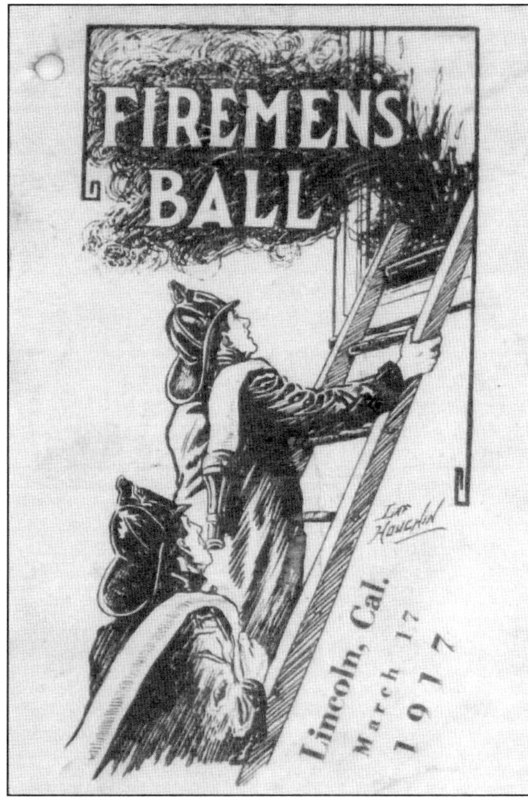

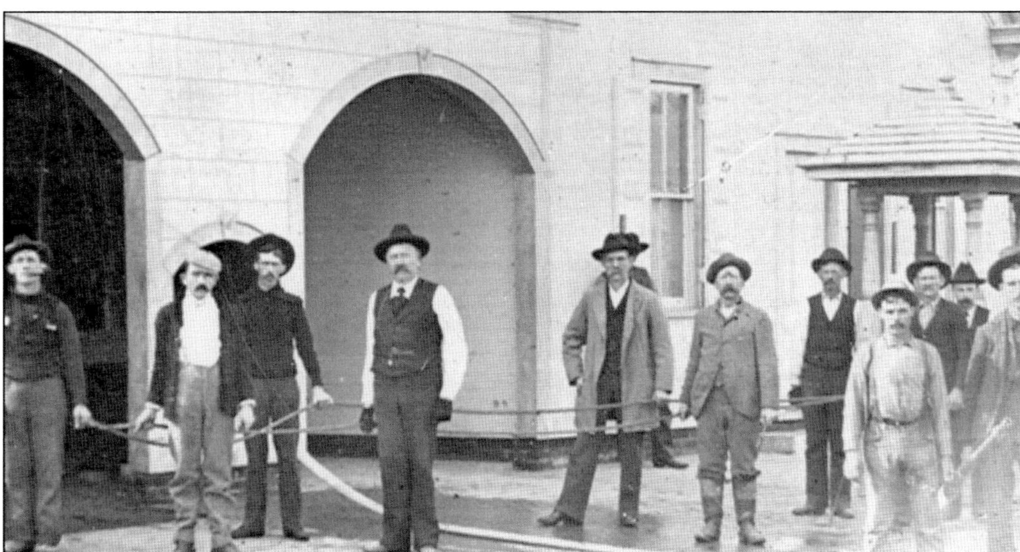

Firehouse No. 1, home of Lincoln's volunteer fire department, was located on Fifth Street in the present-day location of the Veteran's Hall. The department formed in the 1890s, and most able-bodied men were members. Pictured here are, in no particular order, Harry S. Williamson, Benjamin Logan, Charles Kennedy (who ran a saloon in the Hotel Burdge), John Haenny, George Ahart, Judge Allen, Lloyd Brown, William Sparks, and Martin Michael (in boots), who owned Martin Michael's Meat Market from 1883 to 1903.

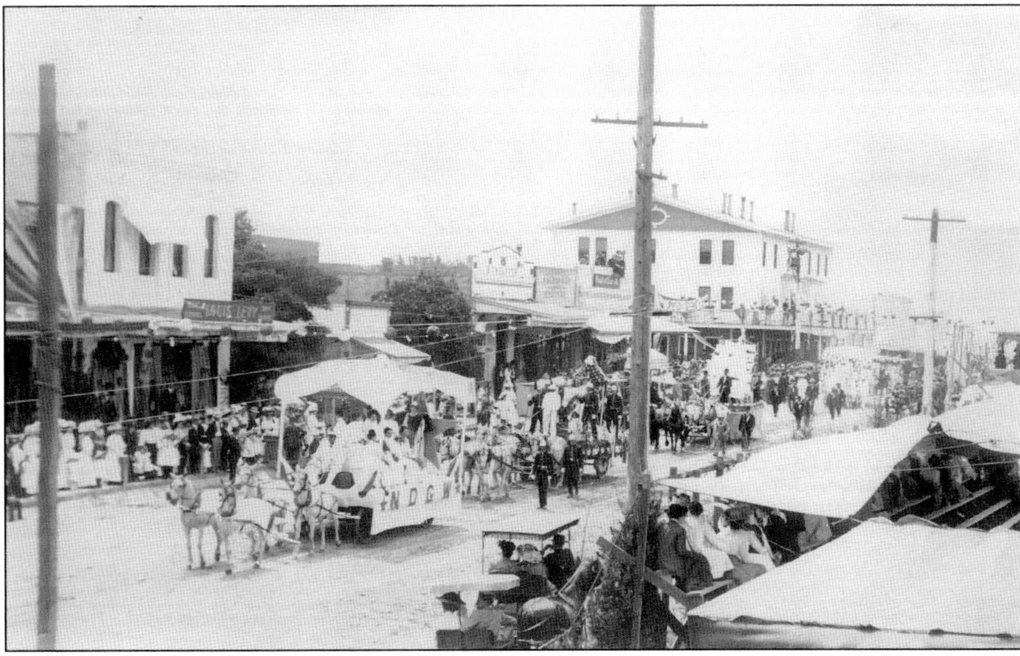

Most of the residents of Western Placer eagerly awaited large community events. This 1909 parade was held in celebration of the 50th anniversary of the founding of Lincoln and featured several floats (shown traveling down G Street). The first float honors the Native Daughters of the Golden West, followed by the Knights of Pythias float. Spectators line the walkways, pack the grandstand, and are also standing on the balcony on the second story of the Hotel Burdge.

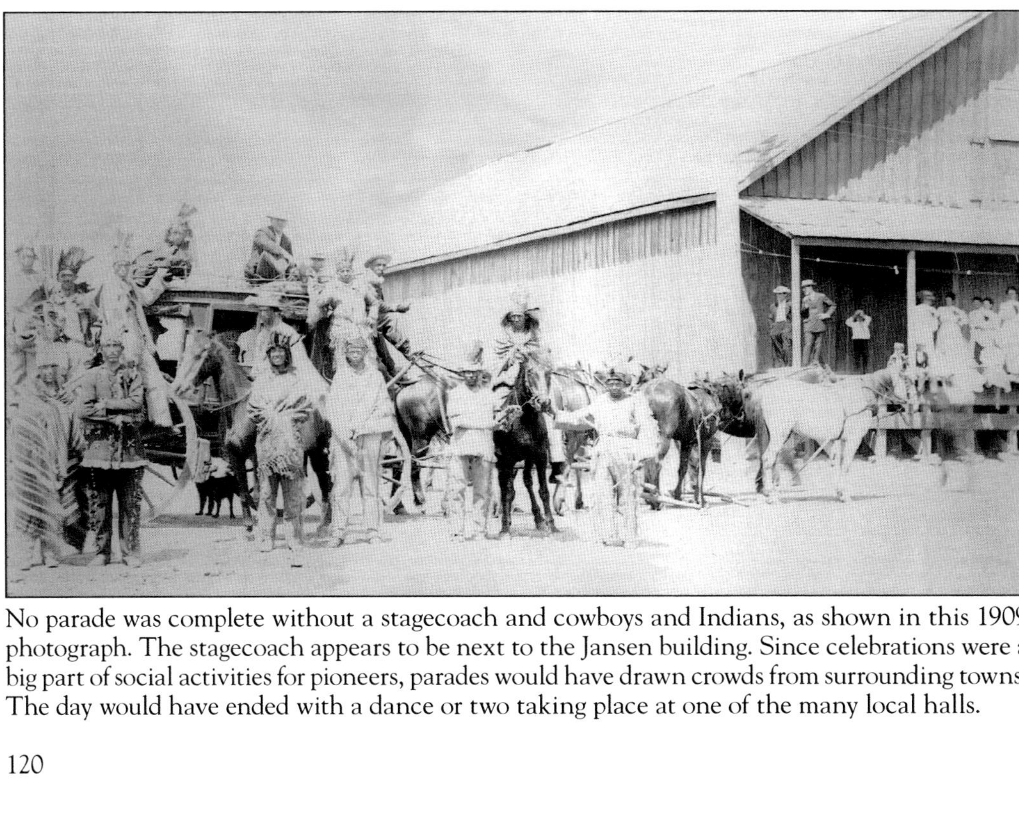

No parade was complete without a stagecoach and cowboys and Indians, as shown in this 1909 photograph. The stagecoach appears to be next to the Jansen building. Since celebrations were a big part of social activities for pioneers, parades would have drawn crowds from surrounding towns. The day would have ended with a dance or two taking place at one of the many local halls.

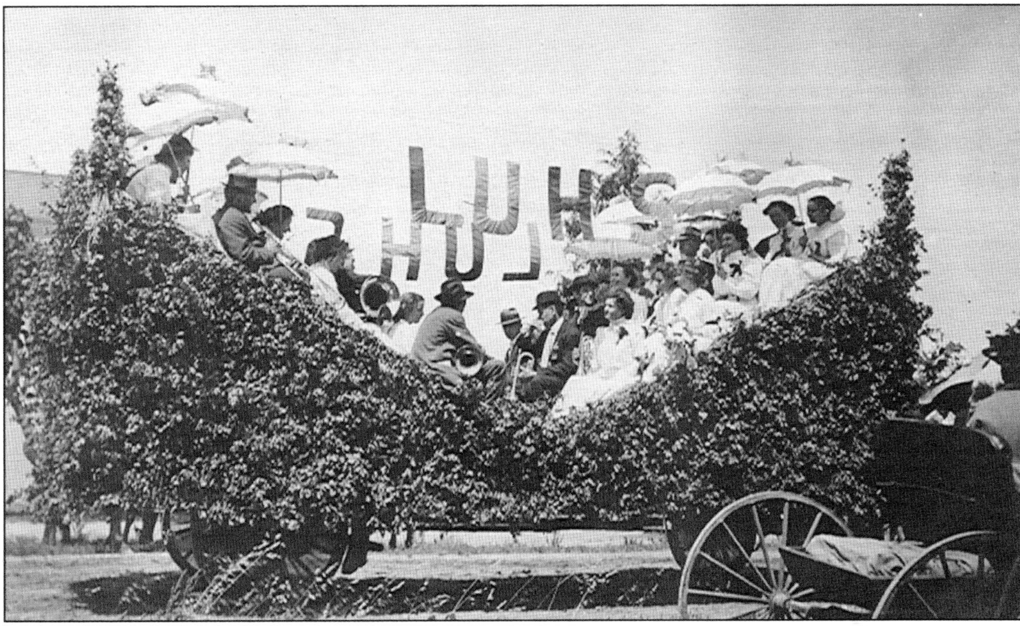

Lincoln High School band members sit on raised tiers on a decorated float in 1909 as they wait to participate in Lincoln's 50th anniversary parade. The young men are wearing hats, and the young women are holding parasols to block the sun. Since many students are holding instruments, the float probably stopped at strategic points during the parade so students could entertain spectators.

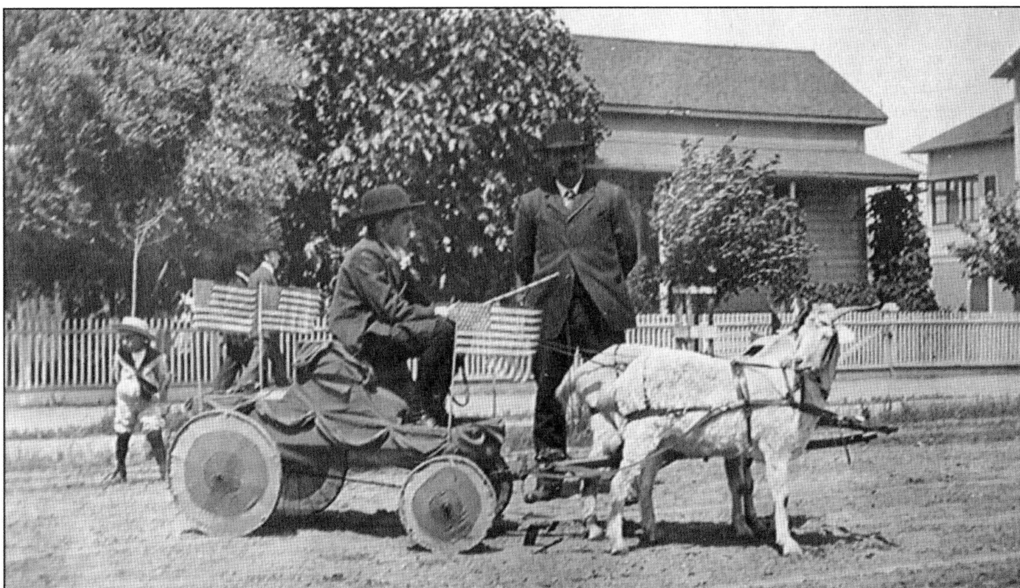

Young and old alike enjoyed dressing up and participating in the festivities. Children especially loved decorating carts and attaching their favorite pets—like ponies, dogs, or goats—so they could be in a parade. Event days were eagerly anticipated and filled with floats, bands, picnics, dancing, and sometimes fireworks.

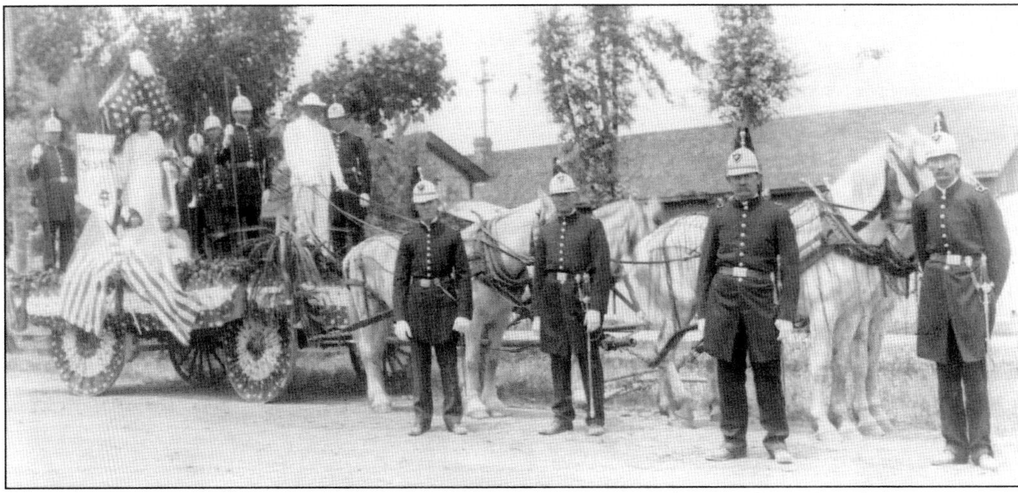

The Knights of Pythias are standing by their float in preparation for marching in the Lincoln 50th anniversary parade. The order was founded in the United States in 1864 and was the first fraternal organization chartered by an act of Congress.

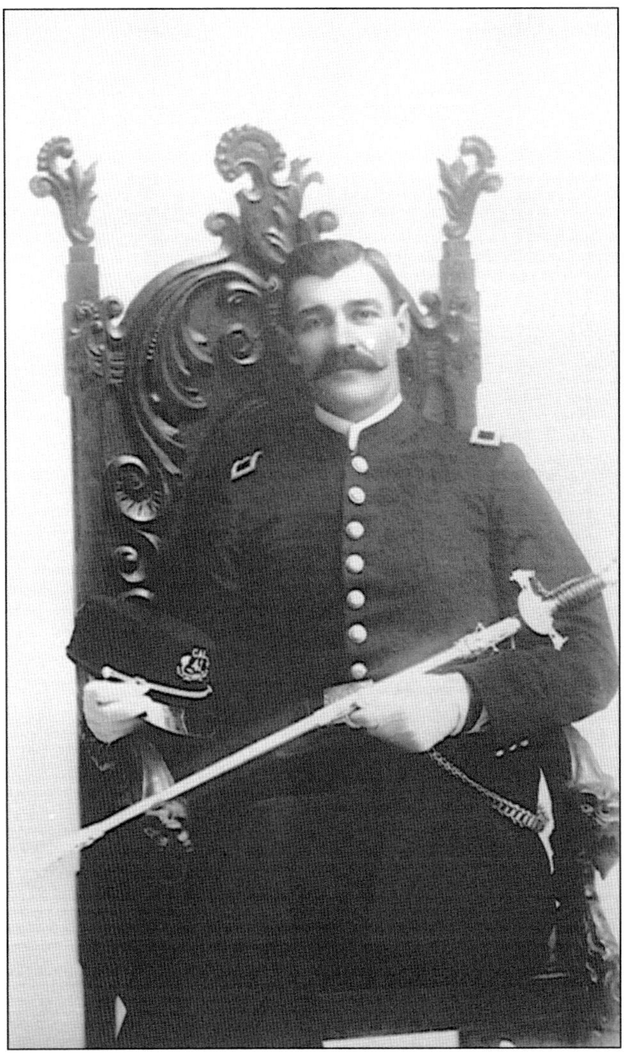

J.D. Saunders, a first cousin of pioneer John DeLos Logan, is dressed in his Knights of Pythias uniform and is holding his ceremonial sword. Saunders was a member of the Lincoln chapter.

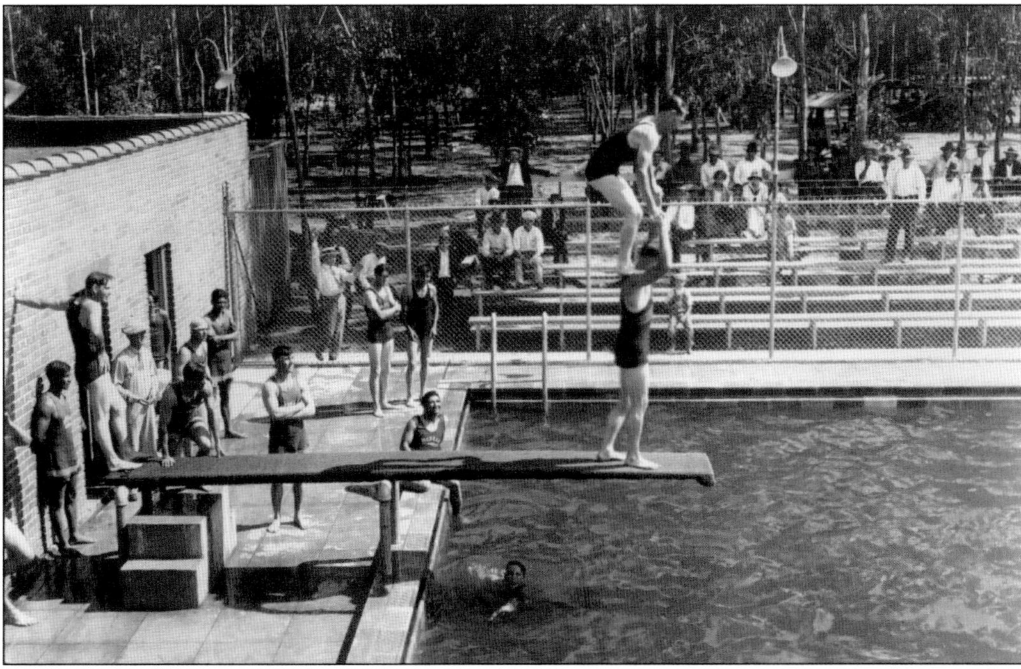

On May 23, 1925, Agnes Perkins McBean presented the people of Lincoln with the McBean Memorial Pool in memory of her husband Peter McGill McBean. Peter McBean was one of the three founding partners who established Gladding, McBean & Company in 1875. She made the gift to Lincoln on the occasion of the 50th anniversary of Gladding, McBean. The people of Lincoln wanted to show their gratitude to Agnes McBean by holding a massive celebration. The above photograph shows two divers—one on the shoulders of the other—taking part in a diving competition. Bleachers were set up on the south side of the pool for spectators. As seen below, at various times during the day it was standing room only as everyone enjoyed watching activities in the newly dedicated pool.

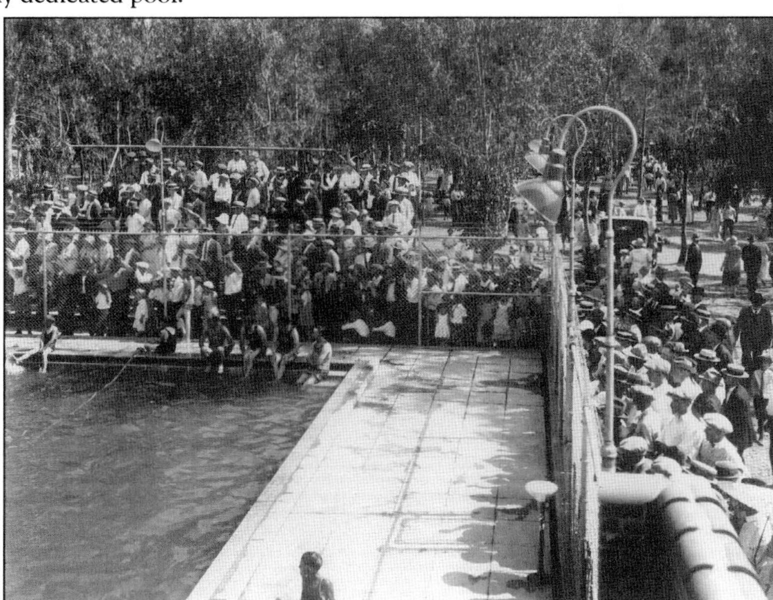

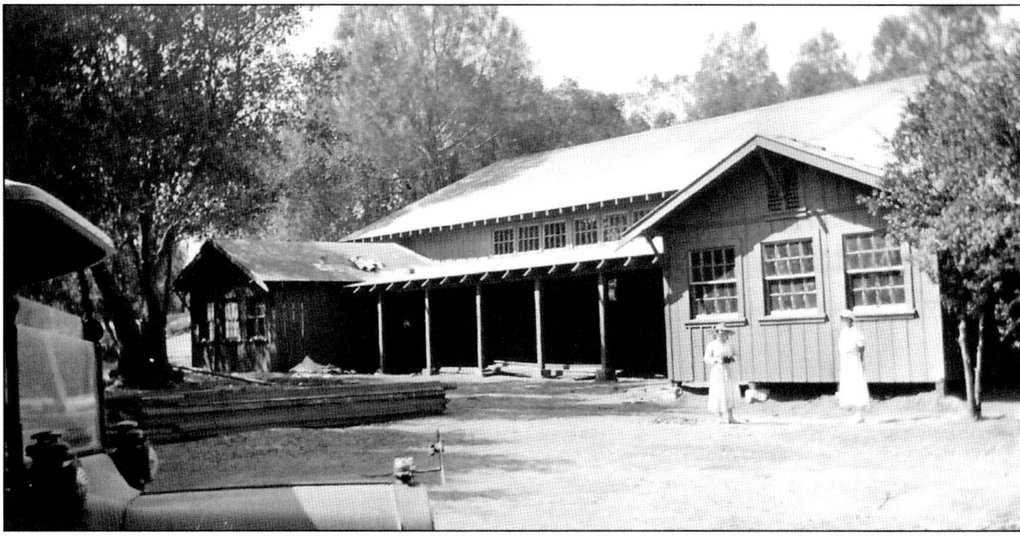

Dances were held quite often starting with the founding of Lincoln. Some of the area's early dance locations included Paul Cox's Colonial House, the Cordillion Hotel, the Independence Saloon and Dance Hall in Newtown (Mt. Pleasant), at Virginia(town) hotels, and at Roger's Shed in the Sheridan area. This photograph shows the new Mt. Pleasant Hall shortly before it was completed in October 1917; some 2,000 people attended the opening. Pioneer Hiram Cartwright, who donated the land for the original Mt. Pleasant Hall, which stood from 1892 to 1910, died in Lincoln the same year the new hall was completed.

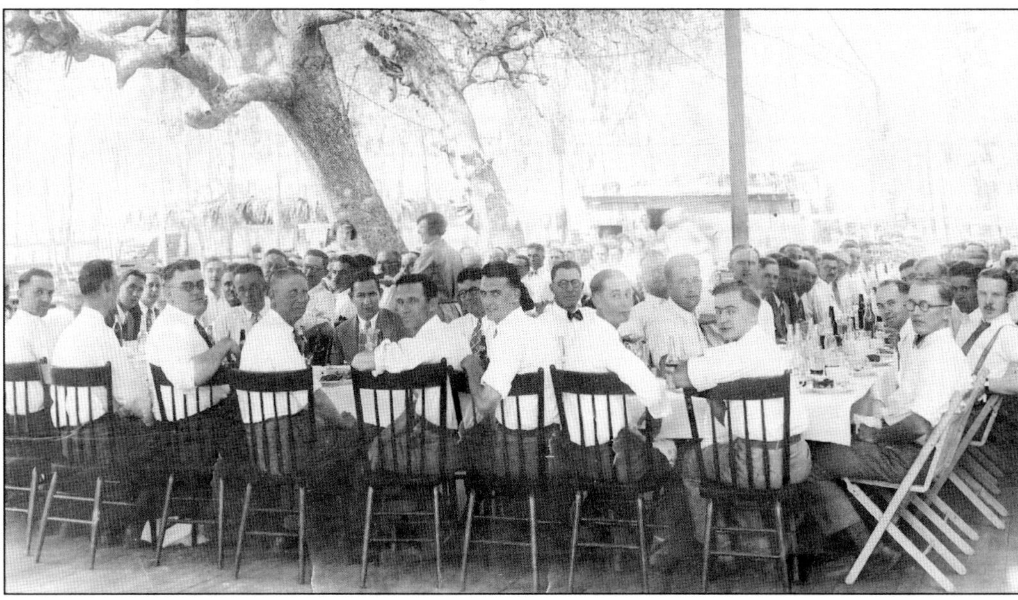

This June 1924 photograph shows Gladding, McBean's third annual picnic. The picnic was held at McBean Memorial Park and included a baseball game and other events. It was advertised all over northern California, and the company made preparations to accommodate at least 5,000 people. The picnic was organized and funded by employees who enlarged the dancing platform, making it the largest one north of San Francisco. Music was provided by the Hotel Senator Orchestra. People came from San Francisco, Sacramento, Oakland, Marysville, Oroville, Gridley, and Lincoln's surrounding areas.

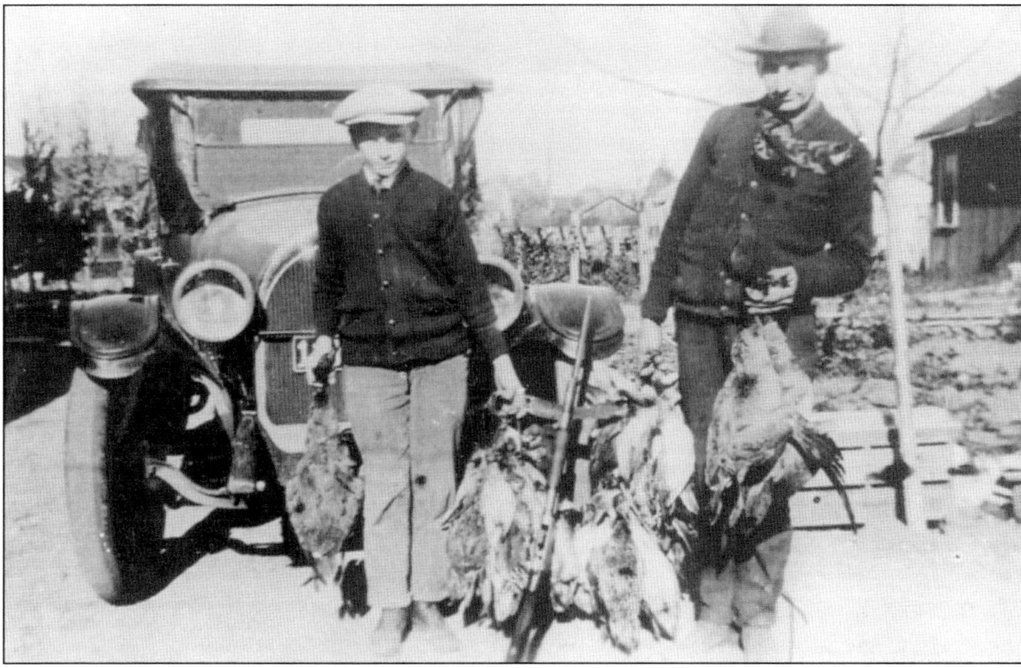

Jute Tofft and his son Robert are pictured in December 1923 after a successful goose shoot. Game prized by local hunters included deer, ducks, quail, geese, and doves. Not only did the local wildlife end up on dinner tables, but local gun clubs often hosted dinners to serve the recently acquired bounty.

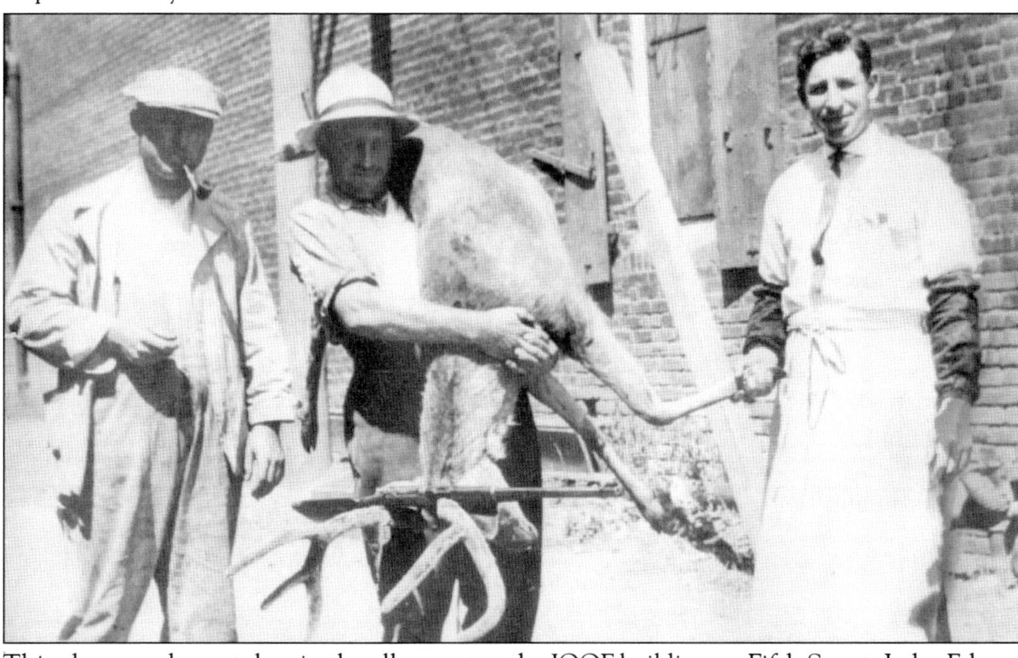

This photograph was taken in the alley next to the IOOF building on Fifth Street. Judge Edward Grey is on the left, Elmer Beermann is standing in the middle holding the deer, and Fred Lazzari is on the right. Note the rifle resting on the deer's antlers. The Procissi families are descendants of Fred Lazzari.

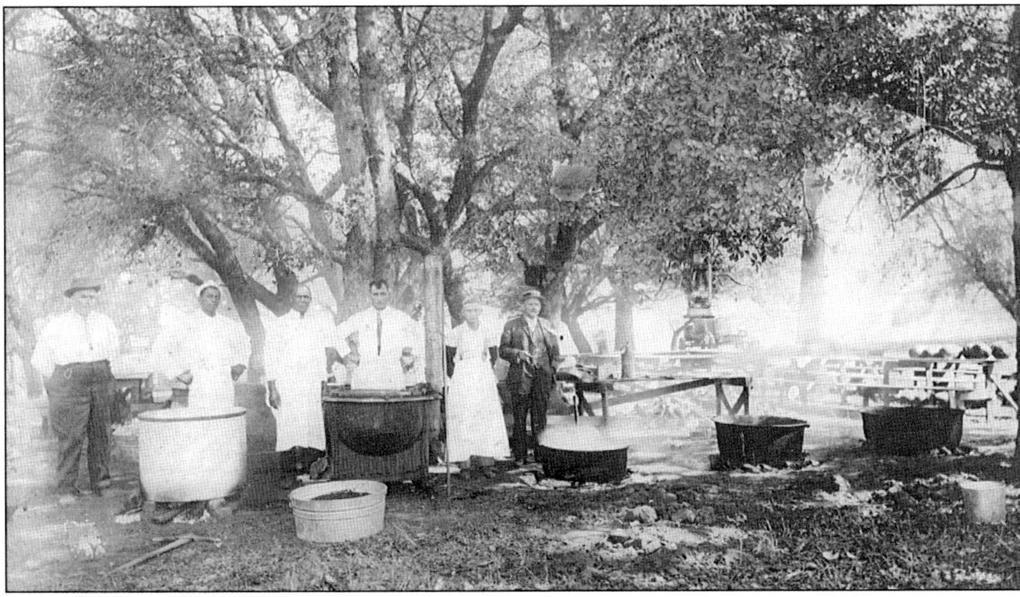

This photograph shows Lincoln Gun Club members getting ready for one of their stews. Large pots of water were used to cook the birds, then other important ingredients and condiments were added to create a tasty stew. These stews were well attended by members and guests, and no one went away hungry. Based on the number of people attending the stews, it would have taken a great many doves or other birds to feed everyone.

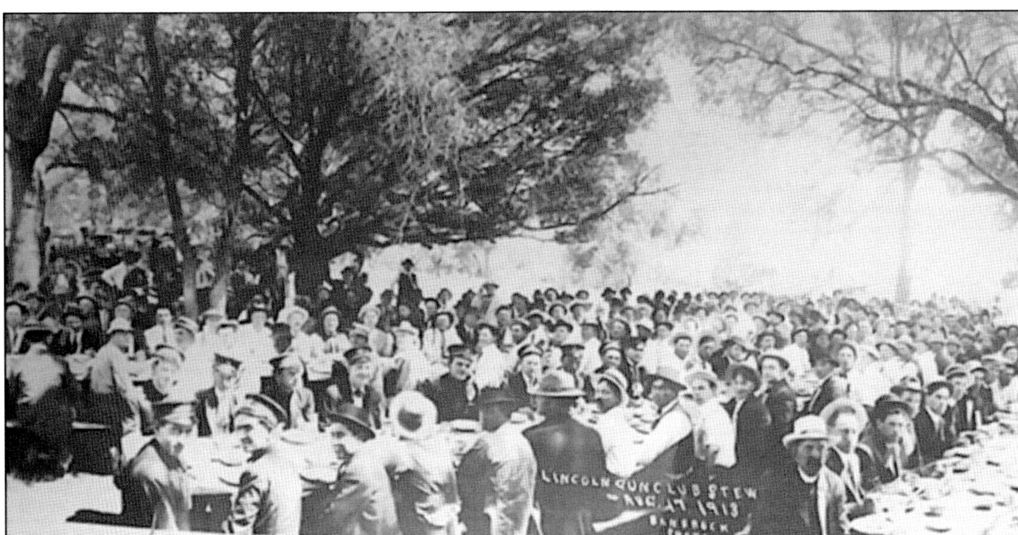

These members of the Lincoln Gun Club and their family and friends are enjoying a stew in August 1913. Game was provided by members the day before in order for it to be properly prepared. Side dishes would have included bread, beans, potatoes, and plenty of liquid refreshments. A band provided music, and the gun club held shooting contests.

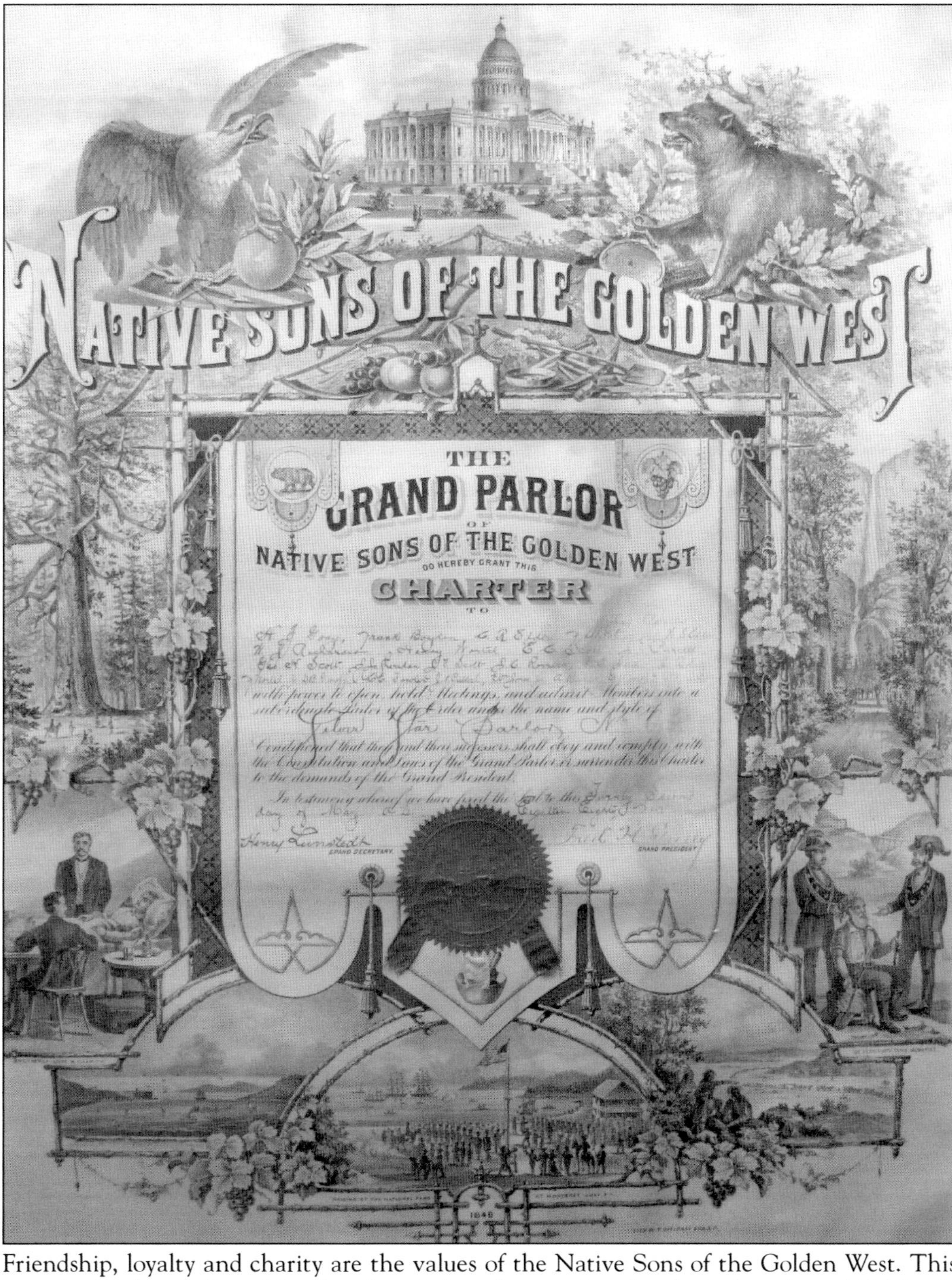

Friendship, loyalty and charity are the values of the Native Sons of the Golden West. This organization has dedicated itself to the mission of preserving the physical vestiges of California history. Starting in San Francisco in 1875, the organization now has 75 "parlors," or chapters, statewide and nearly 9,000 history-minded members. The Silver Star Parlor No. 63 was established in Lincoln on May 22, 1885. Twenty-three names are written on this original document, including Boyden, Fowler, Purcell, Richardson, and Wortell. This parlor is still active and is credited with establishing many memorial plaques in and around Lincoln.